Praise for *Overcoming E*
Community College

"*Overcoming Educational Racism in the Community College* shows us the complex challenges and ripe opportunities we face in ensuring that all students, especially underserved, underrepresented and minority students, across this nation achieve a postsecondary education. Community colleges are often a critical gateway to success for these students who must compete in today's global economy. At Helios Education Foundation, we believe that every student, regardless of zip code, deserves a high quality education, and that belief is central to everything we do. I challenge all of us, as leaders in education, to work collaboratively, remove the barriers and build and reform our education systems with a focus on equity and postsecondary education success for all."

—Paul J. Luna, President and CEO, Helios Education Foundation

"Persistent equity gaps threaten the future of our society, and there is only one institution in America that has the potential to close them. *Overcoming Educational Racism in the Community College* draws upon the perspectives of our best researchers and leaders to remind us of the urgency of the problems and to identify promising practices that can make a difference."

—Dr. George Boggs, President & CEO Emeritus, American Association of Community Colleges

"*Overcoming Educational Racism in the Community College* is a vital resource for all Native American educators entrusted with the crucial task of improving minority retention rates at our community colleges."

—Governor Bill Anoatubby, Chickasaw Nation, Oklahoma

"I am deeply moved and impressed with the depth of knowledge provided on African American, Asian American/Pacific Islanders, Native Americans/American Indians, Hispanic Americans, and Caucasian American students and the effects of poverty on their educational journey and success. I will be recommending *Overcoming Educational Racism in the Community College* as part of our reading materials for our current leadership development institute for faculty and staff."

—Ervin V. Griffin, Sr., President/CEO, Halifax Community College, North Carolina (2016 AACC Advancing Diversity Award Winner)

"America's community colleges are well positioned to act, with urgency, to address the issues of racism that are inhibiting the academic progress and success of far too many students. *Overcoming Educational Racism in the Community College* uses evidence to point the way toward changes colleges can make—and must make—to end the structural inequities that keep students of color from completing their educational journeys ready to achieve their full potential. Dr. Long's essential book shows colleges how to plan with equity in mind and act with equity in mind."

—Dr. Karen Stout, President, Achieving the Dream

"What an incredible collection of research, best practices and leaders on the most important topic of our nation - how to address inequity caused by educational racism. Community colleges are uniquely positioned to provide the opportunity for consciousness and job skills for those most underserved. As was the aim of the Obama administration, improving the graduation rates from community colleges—where the majority of first-generation, African American, Latino, Native American and working class students attend – is the only way to educate our Nation and be, once again, the most educated country."

—José A. Rico, Former Executive Director, White House Initiative on Educational Excellence for Hispanics

"Community colleges are one of the great economic engines of America and this groundbreaking new book by Dr. Long highlights the importance of community colleges as they operate with rapidly changing demographics, funding headwinds and requirements for increased social impact. Educational equity requires inclusion for all Americans and this textbook traverses all the racial and ethnic mosaic of what makes America great including a rational portrayal of the Asian and Pacific Islanders American diaspora and the AANAPISI campuses who support them."

—Neil Horikoshi, President and Executive Director, Asian and Pacific Islander American Scholarship Fund

OVERCOMING EDUCATIONAL RACISM IN THE COMMUNITY COLLEGE

INNOVATIVE
IDEAS for
Community
Colleges

Series Editors: Angela Long and Susan Slesinger

OVERCOMING EDUCATIONAL RACISM IN THE COMMUNITY COLLEGE

Creating Pathways to Success for Minority and Impoverished Student Populations

Edited by Angela Long

Foreword by Walter G. Bumphus

1996-2016 20TH ANNIVERSARY

Sty/us
PUBLISHING, LLC.

STERLING, VIRGINIA

Published by Stylus Publishing, LLC.
22883 Quicksilver Drive
Sterling, Virginia 20166-2102

Library of Congress Cataloging-in-Publication Data
Names: Long, Angela (Angela C.)
Title: Overcoming educational racism in the community college :
creating pathways to success for minority and
impoverished student populations /
edited by Angela Long ; foreword by Walter G. Bumphus.
Description: Sterling, Virginia : Stylus Publishing, 2016. |
Includes bibliographical references and index.
Identifiers: LCCN 2016014462 (print) |
LCCN 2016015186 (ebook) |
ISBN 9781620363478 (cloth : alk. paper) |
ISBN 9781620363485 (pbk. : alk.   paper) |
ISBN 9781620363492 (library networkable e-edition) |
ISBN 9781620363508 (consumer e-edition)
Subjects: LCSH: Children with social
disabilities--Education (Higher). | Minorities--Education (Higher). |
Poor--Education (Higher). | Educational equalization. |
Community colleges.
Classification: LCC LC4065 .O94 2016 (print) |
LCC LC4065 (ebook) |
DDC 378.0086/94--dc23
LC record available at https://lccn.loc.gov/2016014462

13-digit ISBN: 978-1-62036-347-8 (cloth)
13-digit ISBN: 978-1-62036-348-5 (paper)
13-digit ISBN: 978-1-62036-349-2 (library networkable e-edition)
13-digit ISBN: 978-1-62036-350-8 (consumer e-edition)

Printed in the United States of America

All first editions printed on acid-free paper
that meets the American National Standards Institute
Z39-48 Standard.

Bulk Purchases

Quantity discounts are available for use in workshops and for
staff development.
Call 1-800-232-0223

First Edition, 2016

Educational Racism

This term, used throughout this book, is defined as a cultural bias manifested either overtly or covertly by a system of education and/or educators that benefits or punishes/inhibits its students based on their culture, race, ethnicity, ideologies, and/or socioeconomic status.

CONTENTS

Our nation's approach to the issue of race is the most fundamental—often emotionally searing—test of our national character and our democratic values.

One need only scan the headlines in daily news reports or listen to the increasingly virulent rhetoric of U.S. politicians to find evidence of our collective and continuing angst. In recent years, there has also been a disturbing increase in the number of race-related incidents on college campuses, putting higher education squarely in the crosshairs of the debate.

However, as educators, we must look past the sensationalized symptoms of racism on campuses and analyze the root causes of escalating racial discord and imbalance. As representatives of the most diverse sector of higher education, community colleges bear a special responsibility to champion the values of inclusiveness and equity.

In taking on the task of looking at the community college learning experience through the lens of the minority student, the editor and contributors of *Overcoming Educational Racism in the Community College: Creating Pathways to Success for Minority and Impoverished Student Populations* have set a high bar indeed. Taking their cue from a key finding of the American Association of Community Colleges' *Report from the 21st-Century Commission on the Future of Community Colleges* (2012), they have wisely focused on a single, persistent, and troubling question: Why do students of color end their community college experience twice as often as do middle- to upper-income White students?

Despite the tension such analysis evokes, we must, as editor Angela Long asserts, put this issue "under the spotlight for a full and frank discussion" (p. xiii, this volume).

To frame that dialogue, the book's publisher has engaged 20 chapter authors whose experiences and insights powerfully inform the issues of inclusiveness and minority student success. As Long states, "This book is about problem-solving with specific regard to students of color and those who are impoverished attending community colleges," offering "core" solutions to "promote an egalitarian" (p. xiii, this volume) learning experience.

For organizational simplicity, the chapters are presented according to five key student demographics reflective of U.S. Census descriptors: African

American/Black, Native American/American Indian, Hispanic/Latino American, Asian American and Pacific Islander, and Caucasian American students in poverty. However, to gain the optimum benefit from the unique compilation this book presents, the reader would be well advised to examine the full breadth of insights and proven solutions conveyed across the spectrum of chapters. Common elements and experience-grounded strategies resonate throughout.

Adding depth to the firsthand experiences of content provided by college leaders—the educational equivalent of boots on the ground—is historical research tracing the uneven and sometimes punitive evolution of U.S. immigration policy. Equally arresting is a wealth of data documenting the nation's seemingly inexorable shift toward a majority-minority nation in the coming decades. It is a cultural and demographic shift that will have profound political and societal consequences—especially for community colleges, which serve the highest proportion of low-income and minority students.

In this book, Long also poses what some may consider a provocative question: Are minority students at community colleges disadvantaged by *educational racism,* defined in part as a "a systemic network of rules, expectations, and cultural norms based on a model of education that caters to a middle- and upper-class White mind-set in America" (p. 238, this volume)? She posits that some educators, perhaps unintentionally and often unconsciously, express biases toward students because of inherent differences in the ways those students define success, communicate, or hold ideals relating to upward mobility as compared to the White, middle-class majority.

Whether one agrees with Long's characterization or not, subsequent analysis by this book's contributors repeatedly affirms that too many minority and low-income students enter community colleges with feelings of being different, not fitting in, and being unprepared for the college learning experience. Gateway Community Technical College president Edward Hughes puts it succinctly: "Unfortunately, many of today's students carry with them self-concepts created and reinforced by a lifetime of misleading public and private messages" (p. 203, this volume). He continues, "They arrive feeling that they may not belong, are not smart enough, and have few tangible resources or skills with which to succeed" (p. 205, this volume). It is the challenge of helping such students find their voice and realize their potential that cuts to the heart of the community college mission.

The analogy is often made by educators, including myself, characterizing community colleges as the Ellis Island of higher education. That historic port of entry brought wave on wave of immigrants to our country in search of opportunity and greater personal freedom. But while community colleges have historically prided themselves on being the welcoming entry point to higher learning and a change agent for millions, we must now acknowledge that access is not enough. For without the means and a pathway to succeed, access is an empty promise.

Miami Dade College president Eduardo Padrón knows about change, having come to the United States to escape Cuba's Castro regime in the 1960s. A community college student himself who now leads one of the most diverse and exemplary colleges in the United States, he sums up the wrenching dilemma we face, as educators and as a nation: "But this is not a challenge of keeping up with change; quite the contrary, the issue of balance rests on what we value. And if we don't value the inalienable opportunity to learn . . . then all the change in the world risks being worthless and without direction" (chapter 6).

Padrón cites Nobel laureate Joseph Stiglitz, who puts the challenge we face starkly: "Inequality of opportunity is indefensible."

Walter G. Bumphus
President
American Association of Community Colleges

PREFACE

In the course of human affairs, people encounter problems of all shapes and sizes. Certain individual problems are well-defined; others are ill-defined. Generations of learned academicians have studied both sides of the spectrum in their search for efficacious problem-solving methodologies. Many of those learned academicians concluded that well-defined problems are best solved by using a set of recursive operations and algorithms that rely on indisputable diagrams. The work of those learned academicians has taught us two things concerning problem-solving: (a) that most of the problems encountered by people are caused by other people and (b) that once in a while, academicians fall into the category of "other people" when they devise complex theories on problem-solving that cannot be understood by the people needing to solve problems.

This book is about problem-solving with specific regard to students of color and those who are impoverished attending community colleges. It differs from most other books that deal with problem-solving on racial issues inasmuch as this book provides actual solutions—in such a way that a cookbook provides tried and true recipes that work—to a single problem that is both well-defined and ill-defined. The single problem addressed in this book commonly manifests itself at nearly all of this nation's 1,132 community colleges. That single problem pertains to educational disparities that exist between White students and students of color and puts this issue at hand under the spotlight for a full and frank discussion.

Another key difference between this book and other problem-solving books on race and ethnicity is the carefully compiled work of 20 of our nation's top education experts into one document. There is an old adage that asserts two minds are better than one (especially so when creating solutions to perplexing problems). And logic dictates that when 20 of the best and brightest people work together instead of two, that condition is even better yet. Furthermore, when those 20 people happen to be gifted above all others in their knowledge of how to solve student retention issues in regard to racial minorities and the underserved, the correct descriptive word is "illuminating." Thus, it is fair to say that this book is not only unique from others but also a great resource for community college presidents and all their administrators and faculty who daily serve minority student populations at community colleges.

In order to analyze and solve the problems associated with the educational disparities of student minorities attending community colleges, it becomes imperative to identify those with whom we serve by analyzing the historical roots of our nation's changing citizenry.

Historical Review of Our Nation's Changing Demographic

As a people, we have become both racially and ethnically diverse within a relatively short time. Beginning in the early 1890s and continuing to 1905, wave after wave of immigrants came to America from Europe's northern and western regions—Germany, Poland, England, Ireland, Scotland, Holland, and the Scandinavian nations. They flooded onto Ellis Island in hopes of achieving the American Dream. Then, between 1905 and 1915, millions more left their native countries in eastern and southern European nations (e.g., Italy, Hungary, Czechoslovakia, Greece, France), coming to America in numbers ranging from 6,000 to 10,000 people each and every day. And from 1916 to 1921, yet another surge of immigrants arrived at Ellis Island from their homelands of Russia, Armenia, Syria, and Turkey. It is noteworthy that roughly 40% of all current U.S. citizens alive today can trace their ancestral heritage back to Ellis Island's busiest years, that is, 1905 to 1920.

But as America's population dramatically burgeoned during that span of 30 years, the federal political leadership concurrently experienced public criticism for its failure to moderate America's excessively high rate of population growth. Members of both houses of Congress heeded the public's outcry and enacted the Immigrant Quota Act of 1921—a law that capped the number of annual visas the government could issue at 350,000. Three years later, both the U.S. Senate and the U.S. House of Representatives passed the Immigration Act of 1924. This piece of federal legislation prohibited any person of Asian birth (e.g., the peoples of China, Japan, and all nations in Southern Asia) from obtaining an American visa. As a consequence, between 1925 and 1955 only 2.3 million immigrants gained entry into America, almost all being White Europeans.

Unquestionably, the Immigrant Quota Act of 1921 and the Immigration Act of 1924 were conceived with the political objective of achieving a high degree of racial homogeneity throughout the 48 states. The following is the demographic summary of racial data as listed in the U.S. Census Bureau's 1950 Decennial Report:

Total U.S. Population	=	**150,325,798**
Number of "Whites"	=	134,942,028
Number of "Blacks"	=	15,043,286
Number of "American Indian/Eskimo"	=	343,410
Number of "Asian/Pacific Islander"	=	321,033
Number of "Other"	=	48,604

Source. U.S. Census, 2002.

Because of immigration reform legislation enacted during the 1920s, nine out of every 10 Americans were racially White when General Dwight D. Eisenhower was elected president in 1953. Yet the Census Bureau's 1950 Decennial Report leaves us wondering about this question: Did the people of Hispanic ancestry self-report themselves as "Whites," or did they instead mark the box titled "Other" when filling out their survey questionnaires? (The 1950 General Assembly of the United Nations voted in that same year to replace the term *race* with *ethnicity* for the purpose of identifying people on the basis of common nationality and/or shared cultural traditions, rather than physical traits and attributes.)

For the 10% of Americans who did not report themselves to be racially White, it can be argued that many hardships were felt during this same time. For example, the Native Americans/American Indians had been forced off their homeland less than 100 years prior, promoting feelings of isolation and abandonment that exists to this day. And for the Black American, many roots of bitterness and hurt were evident as years of slavery, oppression, and misplacement as a people uncovered deep sorrow. Even so, despite the many adversities and controversies of our past, we have emerged as a nation to represent a people of all races, backgrounds, and political beliefs in search of common ground.

An Unprecedented Rise in Minority Populations

A 1998 study published in *Scientific American* revealed that 5,000 different ethnic groups are living now throughout the world (Doyle, 1998). Even so, the U.S. census only officially recognizes six major ethnic and racial categories: White American, Native American and Alaska Native, Asian American, Black or African American, Native Hawaiian and Other Pacific Islander, and people of two or more races. ("Some other race" is also used in the census and other surveys but is not official.) The U.S. Census Bureau also classifies Americans as "Hispanic or Latino" and "Not Hispanic or Latino," which identifies Hispanic and Latino Americans as a racially diverse ethnicity that composes the largest minority group in the nation. White Americans are the racial majority, with a 77.7% share of the U.S. population, and according to the 2014 U.S. Census, Hispanic and Latino Americans amount to 17.1% of the population, making up the largest minority. African Americans are the second largest racial minority, amounting to 13.2% of the population, with a third significant minority of Asian Americans comprising 13.4 million in 2008, or 4.4% of the U.S. population (U.S. Census, 2014).

The changing demographics of the United States stemming from shifting birthrates of minority student populations, high immigration rates, and changes in family dynamics have massively altered the country's racial makeup. At least four times more Hispanics resided in the United States in the year 2015 (excluding millions of undocumented immigrants) than the total number of Black Americans listed in the U.S. Census Bureau's 1950 Decennial Report. One of the societal impacts of this phenomenal growth rate was set forth in another research paper released by the U.S. Census Bureau in 2015 and titled "Projections of the Size and Composition of the Total U.S. Population, Native and Foreign Born": "By the year 2020, approximately 50.2% of all children aged seventeen years and younger who reside in the fifty states will be part of a minority race or ethnic group" (U.S. Census, 2015).

The U.S. Census Bureau's researchers who issued this projection went on to say that any "policy decisions" made by government officials (i.e., presidential amnesty or comprehensive immigration reform) could significantly alter their 2020 prediction.

Further census data reveal that an unprecedented shift in the nation's racial makeup is occurring in 14 states and is reshaping U.S. schools, workplaces, and the electorate. Due to immigration, a combination of more deaths and fewer births among Whites, and an explosion of minority births, the United States is poised to become a majority-minority country no later than 2020 (Frey, 2013). Such a shift will require immediate attention to changes in national educational policy, future job outlooks, and the role of the community college in providing an open-access education for all with a common focus.

Within this discussion, it is important to note that Americans commonly believe that more Hispanics are illegally flooding across America's southern border than all other racial and ethnic populations combined. But that impression is not reality. Beginning in 2010, the numbers of immigrants from the Far East, Southwest Asia, and India have annually exceeded the number of Hispanic immigrants. According to data published by the Pew Research Center (2013), more than half of all Asian immigrants earned a bachelor's degree prior to immigrating to the United States; and many of them had secured employment in the United States before they left their native countries. As of 2013, Asian Americans numbered 19.3 million (2.9% annual growth rate) versus nearly 56 million Hispanics (2.1% annual growth rate). Whereas the causative force behind the 2.1% annual growth rate of the Hispanic population in this country is their birthing children on U.S. soil, it is immigration that has been fueling the annual 2.9% growth rate of the Asian American population. The bottom line of all of these statistics is simply this:

> *In 1950 America's population numbered 150,325,798, with 90% of that number being racially White. It is projected that by 2050, America's population will have tripled, with less than half of its residents being racially White.* (Pew Research Center, 2013)

In view of these demographic and statistical figures, one thing becomes clear: We have become a nation of *hyphenated Americans.*[1] Supposedly, our system of education has been revamped and restructured to accommodate the needs of a more diverse student population. Yet it is clear that there is a continuance of disparities in academic achievement rates among students of various racial backgrounds and ethnic makeups, especially when considering the retention of minority student populations attending community colleges in America.

The Many Problems Facing Community Colleges

Population growth estimates issued by both governmental agencies and privately funded research groups reckon the United States' population to fall within the range of 440 million to 460 million legal residents by 2050, depending on policy decisions made by government officials (e.g., amnesty by means of a presidential pardon or congressional immigration reform legislation). Of the projected 130 million or so people added to America's current population (320 million in 2015), approximately 80% of that increase will consist of non-Whites. And if tensions continue to mount in the Middle East, we should not be surprised if millions of people from that area of the world—perhaps 10 million or more—seek political asylum in the United States. One thing is certain: Within a few decades, America's White majority will be toppled from its traditional throne of power.

But long before grade schools, high schools, community colleges, and universities are confronted with problems associated with an overflowing abundance of students of color, there are numerous present-day problems that need to be solved. The following are a few of those problems:

- About 4 out of every 10 high school seniors cannot draw inferences from written materials.
- About 8 out of every 10 high school seniors cannot write a persuasive essay.
- Approximately 70% of community college freshmen take a remedial class in mathematics.
- Out of the 32 nations that participated in the 2014 Program for International Assessment, America's tested students placed in the bottom half in both reading (20th) and science (23rd).
- As many as 40% of African American and Hispanic students who hold high school diplomas are functionally illiterate.
- The average college freshman has a seventh-grade reading skill level and an eighth-grade math skill level.
- Nearly half of each year's community college cohort voluntarily terminates their college experience within 12 months of matriculating.
- Roughly one out of every three students of color who enroll at community colleges become dropouts within a few months after having been matriculated.

How can community college instructors be expected to teach college-level courses when their students have eighth-grade skill levels? And why are the persistence and attainment rates of minority students who attend community colleges significantly lower than those of their White counterparts? This discussion and much more will be covered in depth in this book.

What Makes This Book Unique

There is an old axiom that applies to the nature of this publication: "It is better to be a master in one skill than a jack of all trades." Because this adage is truthful, the aim of this book is to identify the various causative factors that motivate students of color to prematurely abandon their college experiences and to make recommendations for solving that particular problem. As for all of the other kinds of problems mentioned previously: with one exception, each is deserving of a book of its own.

This book is unique in that the enrollment and persistence patterns of five key student demographics registered in America's community college system will be analyzed in depth for the first time: African American/Black, Native American/American Indian, Hispanic/Latino American, Asian American and Pacific Islander, and Caucasian American students in poverty. It is important to note that many publications have been authored on Black and Hispanic student demographics. A strong push has been given to promote national initiatives such as My Brother's Keeper and Educational Excellence for Hispanics. And irrespective of the U.S. Department of Education's concerted efforts to help these select students succeed, retention rates for both Black and Hispanic students remain disturbingly low, as you will read in parts one and two of this book.

Beyond these two student groups, no other publication has sought to take into account three other highly overlooked populations enrolled in our nation's community colleges, namely, Asian American and Pacific Islander students, Native American/American Indian students, and Caucasian students in poverty. Common misconceptions are perpetuated regarding the achievement rates of Asian students (i.e., that they are all 4.00 high achievers, proficient in STEM fields, and persistent beyond any other student demographic). However, as you will read in part four of this book, Asian and Pacific Islander students attending community colleges have a 40% dropout rate nationally. Another student group that is given little reference and support is Native American students (accounting for 1% of all credited community college students), who have been largely marginalized and forgotten within the community college system. And as you will read in part three of this book, Native American students face insurmountable obstacles, including high poverty rates, inadequate resources, unemployment, transportation issues, and lack of government funding assistance.

And perhaps of least consideration are Caucasian students in poverty. In general, Caucasian students are viewed as advantaged individuals living in a "White Privilege" society. Yet most educators are unaware that 44% of all Caucasian students attending community colleges are living daily in poverty. As you will read in part five of this book, poverty is the single greatest barrier to student success facing higher education. The author of chapter 13 puts it succinctly, "By acknowledging the presence of poor White students, our nation may better address the financial barriers of all students while more accurately portraying the faces of poverty" (p. 198, this volume). Whereas political leaders are incredulous when they first learn that large numbers of Asian students struggle in college studies, they are much less surprised by statistics that show poor White students are equally likely to drop out of college as Hispanic students.

This groundbreaking publication is the first of its kind in that the contributing writers involved have gathered from across the United States to combine best practice ideas on the topic of race and ethnicity in a never-before-published format. And beyond their expertise on the topics of race and ethnicity, the contributors to this book also are at the cutting-edge of educational reforms within the domain of postsecondary education. The advice set forth in this book commands the attention of all 1,132 community college presidents, their administrative staffs, and their campus faculty.

Angela Long, EdD, Editor

Notes

1. The term *hyphenated Americans* became popularized during the late nineteenth to early twentieth centuries to disparage Americans who were of foreign birth or origin. During the second wave of immigration, the term became universally recognized as a way to encourage assimilation and discourage those who identified as anything other than American. In modern times, the term has perpetuated debate. One faction of Americans perceive the phrase as demeaning, divisive and derogatory; while others are quick to adjudge the usage of the word as being uniquely American, highlighting the strength of diversity in its collective citizenry.

References

Doyle, R. (1998). Ethnic groups in the world. *Scientific American, 279*(3). Retrieved from http://www.scientificamerican.com/magazine/sa/1998/09-01/

Frey, W. (2013). *Shift to a majority-minority population in the U.S. happening faster than expected.* Brookings Institution. Retrieved from http://www.brookings.edu/blogs/up-front/posts/2013/06/19-us-majority-minority-population-census-frey

Pew Research Center (2013). *The rise of Asian Americans.* Washington, DC: Social and Demographic Trends. Retrieved from http://www.pewsocialtrends.org/2012/06/19/the-rise-of-asian-americans/

U.S. Census Bureau. (2002, September). Measuring America: The decennial censuses from 1790 to 2000. *1950 census of population.* Retrieved from http://www.census.gov/prod/www/decennial.html

U.S. Census Bureau. (2014, March 15). *2014 national population projections.* Retrieved from http://www.census.gov/population/projections/data/national/2014.html

U.S. Census Bureau. (2015, March 3). New Census Bureau report analyzes U.S. population projections. Retrieved from http://www.census.gov/newsroom/press-releases/2015/cb15-tps16.html

INTRODUCTION

Angela Long

America is another name for opportunity. Our whole history appears like a last effort of divine providence on behalf of the human race.

—Ralph Waldo Emerson

On July 2, 1776, the members of the Continental Congress voted in favor of a now famous document that contains these three words:

> We hold these truths to be self-evident, that all men are created equal, that they are endowed by their Creator with *certain unalienable rights*, that among these are Life, Liberty, and the Pursuit of Happiness. (Preamble to the Declaration of Independence; emphasis added)

Eighty-seven years later, President Abraham Lincoln used these words in a dedication ceremony held at a Civil War battlefield located near Gettysburg, Pennsylvania. Lincoln seemed to have understood the phrase "endowed by their Creator with certain unalienable rights" as a clear statement that the men who founded the thirteen states of the American nation adamantly believed that a democratic republic is *not* empowered in any way to enact laws which privilege some groups over others and that every human being is naturally entitled at birth to "Life, Liberty, and the Pursuit of Happiness" without government interference. But as every adult American who is alive today knows, the Civil Rights Act of 1965 would not exist if all government leaders had embraced what both Lincoln and this nation's founders deemed as "certain inalienable rights."

Now, more than 240 years since the writing of the Preamble to the Declaration of Independence, the 324,438,950 residents living in our nation today who represent a myriad of diverse backgrounds and ethnicities continue to be both inspired and challenged by the phrase that "all men are created equal, that they are endowed by their Creator" to pursue "Life, Liberty, and the Pursuit of Happiness." For some of these select groups in the United States, the pursuit to find happiness and the "American Dream" has become an unattainable goal due to a lack of education, lack of access, societal division, and limited resources. In order to understand our educational mission as a nation, we must reflect on our nation's history as a people and, perhaps of greatest importance, exercise foresight to envision our nation's future progression.

The Birthing Pangs of Educational "Equality"

In order to understand the premise of this book, it becomes necessary to first underscore the foundations leading to educational equality in the United States. Following the American Civil War, the political leaders in Washington, DC, sought to rectify the social and legal inequities that White people had imposed on Black people. On July 9, 1868, the Fourteenth Amendment to the U.S. Constitution was ratified by the state legislatures. The goal of this amendment was to ensure that "All persons born in the United States . . . excluding Indians not taxed" were given the "full and equal benefit of all laws."

Twenty-four years later, a Black man named Henry Plessey brought a legal suit against the state of Louisiana for allowing a railroad company to violate his Fourteenth Amendment equality rights (*Plessy v. Ferguson,* 1896). Plessey's complaint was this: A railroad conductor instructed Plessey to forfeit his window seat located at the front of a train passenger car to a White gentleman that wanted it and to relocate himself to a seat at the back of the train. After having lost his battle in the lower courts, Plessey appealed to the U.S. Supreme Court. By a vote of 8 to 1, the Supreme Court justices ruled against Plessey. The justice who penned the Court's majority opinion summarized the Court's rationale in this brief statement:

> The object of the [Fourteenth] amendment was undoubtedly to enforce the equality of the two races before the law, but in the nature of things it could not have been intended to abolish distinctions based on color, or to endorse social, as distinguished from political, equality. If one race be inferior to the other socially, the Constitution of the United States cannot put them upon the same plane.

The U.S. Supreme Court interpreted the language used in the Fourteenth Amendment to the U.S. Constitution as saying that Henry Plessey and his Black brethren have the same legal rights as White people in all respects except for "social" matters. In language less "legalese," the U.S. Supreme Court told Henry Plessey to keep a seat warm for Rosa Parks at the back of the bus! Thus, the Native American people—the "Indians not taxed," who were exempted from the right to vote for congressmen by the Fourteenth Amendment—had to vacate their traditional seat and move to the caboose, so to speak.

The famous case of *Brown v. The Board of Education of Topeka* (1955) is commonly perceived as being the Supreme Court decision that overturned Plessey's "equal but separate" ruling. But a case decided five years earlier, *McLaurin v. Oklahoma State Regents* (1950), was the *terminus a quo* (point of origin) of significant change in public education for students of color.

George McLaurin applied for admission into a doctoral program at the University of Oklahoma. The strength of his résumé persuaded college administrators to approve his application. But the approval decision was conditioned on McLaurin, a Black man, agreeing to sit apart from White students when eating at the university's cafeteria, as well as sitting apart from White students when attending classes. McLaurin filed suit against the University of Oklahoma's Board of Regents, claiming that the conditions imposed on him for continuing enrollment were negatively affecting his ability to both study and learn. After the case had wound its way through lower courts, the justices of the U.S. Supreme Court who heard McLaurin's appeal concluded that the conditions imposed by the University of Oklahoma had indeed adversely affected the plaintiff's ability to learn and ruled in George McLaurin's favor. In the eyes of this writer, the McLaurin case touched on a critically important factor in student retention—yet a covert problem seldom discussed—that the reader will review in greater depth in the concluding chapter of this book: educational racism.

America's Shift Toward a Hyphenated Citizenry

When Martin Luther King Jr. and his associates marched in Selma, the term *minority race* was commonly understood to be people of African heritage. No mention was made during the several civil rights marches held during the 1960s of the hundreds of thousands of Native Americans who lived in dire poverty on reservations far removed from the public's eye. And during this same era, the U.S. Census Bureau counted people who were born in Spanish-speaking nations as "Whites."

In the twentieth century, the United States has been transformed into a multicultural nation with multiethnic perspectives. Briefly stated, societal characterizations have categorized Americans into factions of hyphenated citizenry for the purpose of conjoining both ethnic and American identities: African-Americans/Black-Americans, Native-Americans, White-Americans, Asian-Americans, Hispanic-Americans and so forth. Because educators mold the national perspectives of America's citizenry, our public schools and community colleges will face increasing pressures to modify their traditional teaching methodologies in order to accommodate multicultural students with diversified perspectives. Yet, it is clear that there is a continuance of disparities in academic achievement rates among students of various racial backgrounds and ethnic makeups, especially when considering the retention of minority student populations attending community colleges in America.

Community Colleges at the Racial Crossroads

The 1947 Truman Commission on Higher Education was instrumental in popularizing the community college concept—a distinctively different American invention—throughout all rural and urban parts of the United States. Tens of millions of post–World War II baby boomers started their postsecondary educations at community colleges, having been matriculated into one of the following fundamental types of schooling: (a) technical and vocational education; (b) general education in the liberal arts and sciences; (c) continuing adult and community education; and (d) remedial/developmental education. But did the Truman Commission's concept of the community college's public mission actually come to fruition as expected? Consider these words penned by a subsequent body of educators, popularly known as the 21st-Century Commission on the Future of Community Colleges, that convened 65 years thereafter in search of a factual answer to this particular question:

> This Commission believes that the unique and powerful contribution of community colleges lies in preserving access while also emphasizing student success, enhancing quality, and closing attainment gaps associated with income, race and ethnicity. To abandon the open door would be to betray the historic mission of these institutions. Access without support for student success is an empty promise. If the door is to remain open, virtually everything else must change. (American Association of Community Colleges [AACC], 2012)

The numerous men and women who drew this opinion—a committee comprising nationally prominent educators—were sponsored by the AACC, the Bill and Melinda Gates Foundation, the Kresge Foundation, ACT, and the Educational Testing Center. They jointly concluded that educational training programs in America are becoming increasingly noncompetitive in comparison to those in other industrialized nations.

Certainly the commission's usage of the phrase "virtually everything else must change" sends an ominous forewarning to community college administrators and their respective faculty. In regard to student retention, here is a small sampling of their findings:

The community college landscape is littered with lost credits that do not add up to student success. Fewer than half (46%) of students who enter community colleges with the goal of earning a degree or certificate have attained that goal, transferred to a baccalaureate institution, or are still enrolled six years later. The rates, unfortunately, are lower for Hispanic, Black, Native American, and low-income students. Nearly half of all community college students entering in the fall term drop out before the second fall term begins. (AACC, p. 9)

Completion rates for students of color in some groups—often those students facing the greatest challenges—are disappointing in the extreme. (AACC, p. 14)

The following key ideas are presented within these two excerpted texts: (a) community college students often take courses that bear no fruit for their vocational aspirations, (b) nearly half of all community college freshman drop out of college within 12 months following enrollment, and (c) *the retention rates for students of color are far worse, being described by the committee members as "disappointing in the extreme."*

Approximately 12.8 million people were registered as students in America's 1,132 community colleges during the 2013–14 academic year (AACC, 2014). Sadly, nearly *half* of that year's freshman cohort chose not to register for classes during the subsequent 2014–15 academic year. This statistic also applies to the 2013–14 cohort, as well as the 2012–13 cohort, and to numerous other freshmen cohorts dating back to the early 1990s. What caused millions of students to become college dropouts? Numerous researchers have sought to pinpoint the causative factors of this phenomenon. This much we know for certain: Every one of those "dropouts" thought a college education would enhance their lifestyle when they first registered for college classes, and a problem of some kind changed their minds.

In the AACC's (2010) report titled *Reclaiming the American Dream: Community Colleges and the Nation's Future*, several problems were identified as common among the bulk of America's public two-year institutions of higher learning, including the following: (a) students are arriving at college unprepared for college-level work; (b) degree and certificate completion rates are too low; and (c) attainment gaps across groups of students are unacceptably wide. In order to effectively remedy each of these three problems, the 21st-Century Commission on the Future of Community Colleges recommended that three conceptual notions be adopted by the AACC's membership as *terminus a quo*:

1. Community colleges must *redesign* the educational experiences of their respective student populations;
2. Community colleges must *reinvent* their institutional roles; and
3. Community colleges must *reset* their entire educational system. (p. x)

Pause for a moment to consider the scope and import of the commission's first recommendation, that community colleges "must redesign the educational experiences of their respective student populations." Does the term *educational experiences* used here refer to course curricula, or to student activities, or to both? And how ought we to understand the term *respective student populations* as it relates to demographics centered on race and ethnicity? If nearly half of all freshmen attending community colleges do not register at their respective institutions for a second year of studies, then what statistical evidence caused the members of the AACC's 21st-Century Commission on the Future of Community Colleges to conclude that "retention rates for students of color . . . [are] disappointing in the extreme"?

Ever since Joliet College in Illinois—America's first community college—opened its doors in 1901, a minimum of 130 million men and women have been matriculated in both rural and urban community colleges. For most of that 114-year span, community colleges served their respective student bodies in differing roles. But something has altered the community college environment so dramatically in recent years that the 21st-Century Commission on the Future of Community Colleges felt compelled to issue this harsh warning to the AACC's membership: If community college presidents and their administrative staffs fail to substantially change the traditional institutional roles of their respective community colleges in the very near term, the viability of these unique postsecondary institutions will further wither. In other words, time is of the essence—and minor modifications will not suffice!

Solving Tough Problems Requires Remarkable Problem-Solvers

A "problem" is merely a matter that is difficult to arrange. The people most skilled at problem-solving are skilled at rearranging the component parts of a problem back into their proper order. In essence, problem-solving involves three fundamental stages of decision-making. The first stage is to recognize a problem within the scope of its pure reality (i.e., the problem is factually real and not imagined). The second stage, which is more difficult to accomplish, requires the problem-solver to conduct an etiological search for the root cause of the problem. And the third stage, the most difficult feat to accomplish of the three, entails the development of a strategic plan that is capable of permanently resolving the problem.

But every now and then, America encounters a national problem so enormous in its geographical scope, so complex in its intertwined details, and so profound in its potentially damaging consequences that only the very best of the country's most elite corpus of problem-solvers has any likelihood of solving it. For example, the nationally prominent educators on the 21st-Century Commission on the Future of Community Colleges identified this knotty problem: The educational training programs in other industrialized nations are excelling in comparison to America's system of community colleges. As noted earlier, this committee published its findings in *Reclaiming the American Dream: Community Colleges and the Nation's Future* (AACC, 2012). So startling were the committee's findings that they called on community colleges to completely redesign their educational experiences, reinvent their institutional roles, and reset their entire educational system (excepting their open-door policy). But where are the strategic plans that serve as models for the accomplishment of these three recommendations?

Needless to say, both the scope and number of the problems identified by the committee far exceed the printing constraints of a single book. Instead of taking a random "whiff of buckshot" approach in the hope of resolving just a few of the many identified problems, this book has focused on a single sentence found on page 14 of the committee's report: "Completion rates for students of color in some groups—often those students facing the greatest challenges—are disappointing in the extreme."

As previously mentioned, the 20 educators who contributed to the making of this book are seen by their peers as being among the most knowledgeable and insightful problem-solvers on questions involving race and ethnicity not only in the United States but also in the Western Hemisphere. Simply put, America's top educators recommended the 20 people who made this book possible as "the best of the best." I am both honored and humbled to have my thoughts added alongside theirs.

Never before has a book been published involving 20 education experts on matters of race and ethnicity who have collectively gathered to share their top insights on Asian American and Pacific Islander, African American, Native American, Latino, and Caucasian students in poverty. The 20 authors in this book are not only experts on the topics of race and ethnicity but also at the cutting edge of educational reforms within higher education.

Early in our nation's history, key leaders discovered this truth: Change comes either by crisis or by planning. Political leaders sometimes foster perceived crises for the purpose of effecting political change. The leaders of commerce and industry develop strategic management plans that are designed to avert harmful crises. And all generations of educators discovered from their own personal experiences that even though no young person ever plans to fail, far too many young people are failing to plan, and in so doing, failing to identify their own personal means for success leading to "Life, Liberty, and the Pursuit of Happiness." Hence, this book presents the strategic plans recommended by America's top community college leaders, educators, and researchers as to how this troublesome disparity in degree attainment can be averted, especially in light of our nation's changing demographic, with the aim of pursuing an equal-access education for all.

References

American Association of Community Colleges. (2012). *Reclaiming the American Dream: Community colleges and the nation's future.* A report from the 21st-Century Commission on the Future of Community Colleges. Retrieved from http://files .eric.ed.gov/fulltext/ED535906.pdf

American Association of Community Colleges. (2014). *Empowering community colleges to build the nation's future: An implementation guide.* Companion to *Reclaiming the American Dream: Community colleges and the nation's future.* Retrieved from http://www.mtsac.edu/president/cabinet-notes/Empowering-CommunityColleges_final.pdf

Brown v. Board of Education, 347 U.S. 483 (1954).

Plessy v. Ferguson, 63 U.S. 537 (1896).

McLaurin v. Oklahoma State Regents, 339 U.S. 637 (1950).

PART ONE

AFRICAN AMERICAN/BLACK STUDENT POPULATIONS

I

VOICE OF THE NATIONAL RESEARCHER

African American Student Populations in Community Colleges

Glennda M. Bivens and J. Luke Wood

> *If a nation expects to be ignorant and free, in a state of civilization, it expects what never was and will never be.*
> —Thomas Jefferson

Since 1901, community colleges have served as the principal pathway into postsecondary education for those who have been the most marginalized in society. Early community colleges (pre-1920) provided postsecondary access to college for low-income students who were not of the desired "pedigree" for attendance at four-year universities (Nevarez & Wood, 2010) and those for whom nearby postsecondary institutions were hundreds of miles away (Cohen & Brawer, 2009). However, it was not until the equal opportunity era of the 1960s through 1980s that expansive enrollment growth in racial/ethnic diversity became evident, particularly among students of color. Enrollments of students of color bolstered expansive growth in both the total enrollment and total number of community colleges (Nevarez & Wood, 2010). Chief among the many student groups seeking enhanced economic and social mobility through community colleges are Black students. However, access to postsecondary education is not always associated with actual success (e.g., persistence, achievement, attainment, transfer) in college, as community colleges have long struggled to facilitate positive student outcomes for their students of color.

In this light, Black students represent one of the most key demographic subgroups served by community colleges. Simply put, Black students are the greatest challenge and opportunity for postsecondary institutions. Black students are among those most underserved by community colleges. These institutions overwhelmingly fail to provide necessary supports and environments that foster success among these students. However, Black students also account for those students who are the most likely to benefit themselves, their families, their communities, and society (as a whole) from college, provided enhanced success in serving their needs. Moreover, when colleges effectively structure themselves (via programs, policies, practices) to serve the needs of this historically underserved community, they better serve other student groups as well (Lewis & Middleton, 2003). Bearing this perspective in mind, this chapter will address three primary foci. First, the authors will share pertinent demographic information and current trends on Black students in community colleges. Second, they will highlight national data that overview success outcomes and resultant economic implications of these outcomes for society. Third, the authors will explicate research findings and resultant recommendations for practitioners on how to better serve Black students in community colleges. In addressing these three foci, this chapter will be attentive to the gendered realities of Black students. In doing so, the authors will portray the background and status of these students by focusing on uniqueness between Black women and Black men.

Demographic Data and Trends

In this section, we provide context to this chapter's focus on Black students by discussing the types of community colleges they attend and general student characteristics.

Institutional Characteristics

As of 2012, there were over 12.8 million students enrolled in community colleges; of these attendees, 44.2% were racial and ethnic minorities. Black students represented a third (33.4%) of these students of color (16% of the total population) (National Postsecondary Student Aid Study [NPSAS], 2012l). As noted, community colleges are the principal pathway for students of color into postsecondary education. This fact is also evident for Black students, as 41.0% of Black men and 37.6% of Black women are enrolled in community colleges. In contrast, no other sector of higher education serves such a large percentage of these students (see Table 1.1) (NPSAS, 2012h). This is a noticeable point, given that the vast majority of published scholarship on Black students focuses on their experiences in public four-year colleges and universities, which account for less than a quarter (22%–23%) of their total postsecondary

TABLE 1.1
Percentage Distribution of Undergraduate Black Students, by Institutional Type, 2012

	Public Four-Year (%)	Private Nonprofit Four-Year (%)	Community College (%)	Private For-Profit (%)	Others or More Than One School (%)
Black Men	23.1	10.1	41.0	18.6	7.3
Black Women	22.1	9.5	37.6	21.7	9.2

Source. NPSAS, 2012h.

enrollment (Wood & Hilton, 2012). Many Black students are concentrated in city (urban) community colleges. In fact, approximately 51% of Black college students are enrolled in urban colleges. That being said, there is also a sizable portion of these students, about 27% to 30%, who attend suburban institutions. This leaves roughly 19% to 21% of Black students who attend colleges in rural/town areas (NPSAS, 2012i).

Following national demographic concentrations of Black populations, Black community college students are collated in specific regions of the United States. The percentage breakdown by region is as follows: 3.2%, New England; 13.4%, Mideast; 17.4%, Great Lakes; 6.0%, Plains; 37.1%, Southeast; 12.5%, Southwest; 0.4%, Rocky Mountains; and 10.0%, Far West (NPSAS, 2012m). Clearly, these data indicate that Black students are highly concentrated in southeastern community colleges in states such as Alabama (5.8%), Georgia (8.1%), and North Carolina (7.5%). Of course, large populations of these students also attend school in California (8.8%), Illinois (6.7%), and Texas (8.4%) (NPSAS, 2012o). Given these concentrations, it is not surprising that a noticeable percentage of Black community college students attend institutions that meet the federal government's enrollment threshold for colleges classified as predominantly Black institutions (PBIs). One criterion for a PBI is that the institution enrolls at least 40% Black students. Based on this guideline, 24% of Black students attend institutions that could potentially be classified as PBIs (NPSAS, 2012j). Possibly more interesting is the percentage of Black students enrolled in community colleges that could be classified as Hispanic-serving institutions (HSIs). For HSIs, the government has established a population threshold of at least 25% students of Hispanic/Latino descent. In all, 18.1% of Black students attend institutions that meet these specific HSI criteria (NPSAS, 2012k). This fact further reifies the notion that large contingents of Black students are educated in environments with high percentages of students of color.

Student Demographics

Based on federal TRIO standards, *low-income students* are defined as those who have a total income of $25,000 or less. Using this classification standard, a strikingly high percentage of Black men (at 58.5%) and Black women (at 65.3%) in community colleges are low income (NPSAS, 2012p). Given that finances and financial challenges are often attributed as primary rationales for student departure, this is a salient consideration (Flowers, 2006; Freeman & Huggans, 2009; Mason, 1998). Low-income students are often faced with additive challenges to college success (e.g., paying for classes, books, school supplies, and other school related costs) while attempting to navigate external cost commitments (e.g., rent, gas, electric, familial needs). These factors can complicate students' success in college. As a result, a large percentage of Black students must work. For instance, 63.8% of Black women work while attending community college. Of these women who work, nearly half (49.1%) work full-time. In contrast, a slightly lower (but still noticeable) percentage of Black men (59.8%) also work while attending school. For Black men, working while attending college can be complicated by the nature of work they are able to obtain (NPSAS, 2012e). Specifically, Wood and Nevarez (2012) found that Black men reported being concentrated in jobs that were temporary/transitional in nature, had late-night hours, and were physically demanding. They concluded that the actual employment opportunities available for Black men challenged their ability to succeed in work and in college. Moreover, recent data indicate that 20% to 21% of Black men and women work multiple jobs while attending school. Multiple jobs concentrate students' efforts on navigating the cultures and expectations of several jobsites and school simultaneously, making success in either domain (work or school) more difficult.

Other external commitments also influence the experiences of Black students in community colleges. For example, while only 28.3% of Black men attending these institutions had dependents (those reliant on them for support) (NPSAS, 2012c), the primary reason these men attributed to leaving the community college was family responsibilities (Wood, 2012). However, a significantly higher percentage of Black women had such commitments. Specifically, 55.6% of Black women enrolled in community colleges have dependents (NPSAS, 2012c). Most of these women have more than one dependent, with 66.7% having at least two dependents and 33.1% having three or more dependents (NPSAS, 2012d). Given the high percentage of external work and familial commitments held by Black students, it is not surprising that the majority of these students do not attend community college full-time. For instance, 55.1% of Black women and 50.9% of Black men are enrolled in community colleges part-time (NPSAS, 2012f). This is an integral consideration, given that part-time status is typically employed in success models for Black students because it can have a deleterious effect on student success.

A popular misconception of community college students in general is that they are similar to their counterparts in four-year institutions (Wood, 2013). One key area of difference is age. While four-year students typically transition from high school to college and are therefore between 18 and 24 years old, the same pattern is not necessarily evident among community college students. For example, approximately 50% of Black men and 60% of Black women attending community college are at least 25 years of age or older. Of the total Black enrollment in community colleges, 7.2% and 15.6%, respectively, of Black men and women are between the ages of 25 and 29. A greater percentage, 18.1% and 23.2%, is between 30 and 39 years of age. Still yet, 14.3% of Black men and 20.0% of Black women are at least 40 years of age or older (NPSAS, 2012a). Partially, these age differences explain the high percentage of Black students who have dependents, work full-time, and attend school part-time. These data also indicate that the nontraditional student is the "traditional" student in the community college.

One obvious rationale for the age patterns of Black students is delayed enrollment. In fact, 53.6% of Black men and 50.7% of Black women who attend community colleges delayed their entry to postsecondary education after high school. The average Black male student who does not enter college immediately after high school waits 5.6 years before doing so. Similarly, the average enrollment delay for Black women was 5.5 years (NPSAS, 2012b). This could explain why 43.8% of Black men and 49.4% of Black women have taken a remedial course (NPSAS, 2012g). The gap between high school preparation and college enrollment can make once-known concepts harder to remember. For example, students may have taken algebra, geometry, and precalculus during secondary school when they were 16 to 18 years old. However, after nearly six years of delay, at 24, they are then assessed on their ability to perform at college-level mathematics. Obviously, delayed enrollment can then be detrimental to students' progress in credit course work.

It should also be noted that many Black students do not simply take one remedial course. Often, they are enrolled in multiple remedial courses within and across disciplines. For example, in the 2011–2012 academic year, 30.4% of Black women who reported that they had been enrolled in remedial English took two or more remedial courses. In math remediation, this pattern was even more acute: 36.4% of Black female remedial math takers will take at least two courses or more in remedial math (NPSAS, 2012n). Logically, enrollment in multiple remedial courses can have a negative effect on students' confidence in their academic abilities, a critical component in student persistence. Finally, a large percentage (71.1%) of students in the community college are also first-generation college-goers. In comparison to their peers, a slightly higher percentage of Black men and women are also first-generation college students, at 74.0% and 79.2%, respectively. Moreover, a sizable percentage of students are also both first-generation collegians and the first in their family to attend college. In fact, 53% of Black men and 55.3% of Black women indicated that they are the first in their family to attend college (NPSAS, 2012e). As such, these students may be less aware of formal and informal practices, structures, and cultural norms in postsecondary education.

Success Outcomes and Economic Implications

While the previous section has provided contextual information on institutional characteristics and student demographics, this section will explore success outcomes for Black students. This section will then conclude by explicating some of the economic implications of attrition for community college students.

Student Success Outcomes

Unfortunately, many students who enter into the community college do not complete their studies; in fact, 38.1% of Black men and 40.8% of Black women left school without a degree within six years. However, 10.6% of Black men and 10.2% of Black women obtained a certificate or degree in the same time frame, while 21.5% and 21.4% of these individuals transferred to a four-year college. A high percentage, 29.8% of Black men and 27.6% of Black women, were either still enrolled or had transferred to a community college. Stated more simply, only 32.1% of Black men and 31.6% of Black women experienced success (e.g., earned a certificate, degree, or transferred) within six years of their enrollment in the community college (Beginning Postsecondary Students Longitudinal Study [BPS], 2009d).

Disaggregation of success outcomes is integral to a fuller understanding of differential student experiences. Specifically, it is important to identify the rate at which Black students complete their associate degrees, given that these are the highest degrees offered in most community colleges. According to the National Center for Education Statistics (2014), there are significant differences in graduation rates for Black students at two-year institutions and public two-year institutions. Data for each type (e.g., two-year, two-year public) are presented separately for first-time, full-time students who graduated within 150% of normal time (three years). For two-year institutions, between 2005 and 2008, the percentage of first-time, full-time Black students who completed their academic programs increased from 22.6% to 27.7%; however, the 2004 and 2009 starting cohorts experienced a decrease in completing their respective academic programs. Additionally, there are significant degree completion differences according to gender. Between 2005 and 2008, the graduation rates of Black males increased from 18.6% to 22.8%; however, it is important to note that the percentage of Black male students that began in the 2004 and 2009 cohorts experienced a decrease in the number of conferred degrees and credentials. Conversely, Black female students who began their academic careers between 2004 and 2009 experienced a more steady degree completion rate. The percentage of Black female students with conferred degrees increased from 25.2% in 2004 to 31.0% in 2008. Similar to their Black male peers, the 2009 cohort of Black female students experienced a decrease in degree conferment, with 29.4% of Black women completing their respective programs of study (see Table 1.2).

While examining the degree completion rates for Black students at two-year institutions reflects positive trends, data can be further disaggregated to reflect the percentage of Black students with conferred degrees at two-year public institutions. Of the Black students that started at public two-year institutions between 2004 and 2009, the percentage of students with conferred degrees within 150% of normal time hovered around 11.3% and 12%. Black males completed their degrees of study at a higher rate than their Black female peers. Although there are slight variations in the percentage of Black students that completed their respective degrees of study, the completion rate is dismal (see Table 1.2).

While community colleges offer an array of degree programs, it is important to consider that Black students have higher representation in certain fields. For example, between 2004 and 2012, liberal arts and sciences/general studies and humanities were the most commonly conferred associate degrees among Black men and women. Although there was variation in the frequency of conferred associate degrees for Black males and females, liberal arts and sciences, general studies and humanities, business, computer and information sciences, and health-related programs were the most common fields of study that Black students graduated from (see Table 1.3). The primary variation between genders is seen in engineering technologies and engineering-related fields as well as computer and information sciences, in which men are more likely to be concentrated then women. In contrast, women are more likely to be concentrated in education, security and protective services, and homeland security, law enforcement, and firefighting. Beyond these differences in degree programs, likely the starkest differences

TABLE 1.2

Percentage of Black Students That Graduated With a Certificate or Associate Degree Within 150% of Normal Time

All Two-Year Institutions	Black Students (%)	Black Males (%)	Black Females (%)
2004 Starting Cohort	22.9	19.1	25.2
2005 Starting Cohort	22.6	18.6	25.2
2006 Starting Cohort	24.5	20.5	27.1
2007 Starting Cohort	25.3	20.4	28.4
2008 Starting Cohort	27.7	22.8	31.0
2009 Starting Cohort	26.4	22.1	29.4
Two-Year Public Institutions			
2004 Starting Cohort	11.5	11.5	11.5
2005 Starting Cohort	12.1	12.0	12.1
2006 Starting Cohort	12.0	12.2	11.8
2007 Starting Cohort	11.9	12.0	11.8
2008 Starting Cohort	11.8	12.0	11.7
2009 Starting Cohort	11.3	11.4	11.2

Source. U.S. Department of Education, 2012.

evidenced by this data are the sheer numerical differences in graduates by gender. For example, in 2011–2012, of the 141,886 degree earners, only 32.5% were Black men. In contrast, 67.5% were Black women. While the population of Black degree earners has increased, from 86,402 in 2004–2005 to 141,886 in 2011–2012 (a 64.22% increase), the disparities in gender outcomes remained constant (see Table 1.3).

Economic Ramifications for Student Success

As noted earlier, only one-third of Black students earned a certificate or degree or transferred within six years. The inability of community colleges to foster success for these students can have negative effects on students' life chances and opportunities. Data from the BPS provide insight into short-term effects of premature departure. This data source tracked students when they began college in 2003 over six years, to 2009. According to these data, the average Black student who dropped out of a community college earned approximately $26,408 per year. This is lower than the average wages of their White peers at $30,723. For those who earn a degree and are no longer pursuing further levels of education, the average wage earned increased slightly. For Black students, the average wage of certificate or degree earners was $28,619. In comparison, their White peers earned $36,802. Thus, the average wage increase for an earned certificate/degree for Black students was $2,211 in comparison to $6,079 for White students (BPS, 2009c). It is important to recognize that these data account for short-term wage benefits and that long-term wage trends for those who complete college in comparison to those who do not can be exponential. Thus, despite wage gaps between White and Black graduates, there remains a net financial benefit for college attendance, a benefit that grows over time.

While not completing college can have a negative effect on earning potential, student costs for attending college (regardless of success) must also be considered. Data from the BPS (2009b) study indicated that the average cost of attendance per year for Black students was $6,692. Every year a student continues in college without completing his or her degree goals increases the costs for college and has financial consequences for his or her life. Moreover, one of the most integral advantages of earning a certificate or degree is employment. For Black students who left college and did not return, only 62.9% were employed six years later. Another 23.3% were employed and looking for additional work, and 13.8% were not employed or looking for employment opportunities. In contrast, for those who earned a certificate or degree, 82.4% were employed (nearly 20 percentage points higher than for dropouts). Of the remaining graduates, 8.0% were unemployed but looking for work, and 9.7% were both unemployed and not actively looking for employment opportunities (BPS, 2009i). Clearly, these data indicate that (in addition to income benefits for college success) graduates are significantly more likely to be employed.

Community colleges are generally considered a less expensive alternative to four-year institutions. As such, fewer students in community colleges take loans to pay for school than do their four-year counterparts. Fortunately, 86.8% of Black men and 83.9% of Black women in the BPS cohort did not take any loans to pay for community college in their first year of college. Moreover, 98% of Black men and 93% of Black women took only federal loans (as opposed to higher interest private loans) (BPS, 2009j). However, while only 15% of Black students in community colleges used loans to help pay for school, those that did experienced debt accumulation. Debt accumulation is felt for all students, regardless of whether they completed college. The average Black female who began community college in 2003, took student loans, and dropped out had $3,767 in cumulative loan debt six years later. For Black men who dropped out, loan debt amounts were even higher at $4,242 (BPS, 2009a). For students who dropped out and had loan debt, the effect of this debt on their lives, goals, and ambitions was evident. For example, 60.6%

TABLE 1.3
Associate Degrees Conferred by Gender: Top Five Fields of Study by Year

	2004–2005		2005–2006		2006–2007		2007–2008	
	Black Males	Black Females	Black Males	Black Females	Black Males	Black Females	Black Males	Black Females
All Fields, Total	27,151	59,251	27,619	62,165	28,273	63,256	30,016	65,686
1st	Liberal arts and sciences, general studies and humanities	Liberal arts and sciences, general studies and humanities	Liberal arts and sciences, general studies and humanities	Liberal arts and sciences, general studies and humanities	Liberal arts and sciences, general studies and humanities	Liberal arts and sciences, general studies and humanities	Liberal arts and sciences, general studies and humanities	Liberal arts and sciences, general studies and humanities
2nd	Business	Health professions and related programs	Business	Health professions and related programs	Business	Health professions and related programs	Business	Health professions and related programs
3rd	Computer and information sciences	Business	Computer and information sciences	Business	Engineering technologies and engineering-related fields	Business	Computer and information sciences	Business
4th	Engineering technologies and engineering-related fields	Computer and information sciences	Engineering technologies and engineering-related fields	Security and protective services	Computer and information sciences	Security and protective services	Health professions and related programs	Security and protective services
5th	Health professions and related programs	Security and protective services	Health professions and related programs	Education	Health professions and related programs	Education	Engineering technologies and engineering-related fields	Education

Source. Digest of Education Statistics, 2013a, 2013b.

of Black men and 54.9% of Black women who dropped out noted that loan debt influenced their employment plans (BPS, 2009e). Moreover, 31.6% of Black students noted that they had to work more hours because of student loan debt (BPS 2009f) while 43.5% of Black students had to take a job outside their field because of student loan debt (BPS 2009g). Possibly more concerning is that 39.1% of Black students had to take a less-desirable job because of student loan debt (BPS, 2009h). Based on these data, the ubiquitous ramification of community college attrition on student's lives becomes evident.

Research and Implications

While the previous sections have sought to articulate demographic characteristics of Black collegians and their outcomes in community college, this section briefly explicates prior research. Herein, several lines of inquiry (e.g., campus practices, sense of belonging, campus racial climate, and validation) relevant to Black

TABLE 1.3 (Continued)

	2008–2009		2009–2010		2010–2011		2011–2012	
	Black Males	*Black Females*	*Black Males*	*Black Females*	*Black Males*	*Black Females*	*Black Males*	*Black Females*
All Fields, Total	31,994	69,493	36,136	77,769	41,596	87,107	46,124	95,762
1st	Liberal arts and sciences, general studies and humanities	Liberal arts and sciences, general studies and humanities	Liberal arts and sciences, general studies and humanities	Liberal arts and sciences, general studies and humanities	Liberal arts and sciences, general studies and humanities	Liberal arts and sciences, general studies and humanities	Liberal arts and sciences, general studies and humanities	Liberal arts and sciences, general studies and humanities
2nd	Business	Health professions and related programs	Business	Health professions and related programs	Business	Health professions and related programs	Business	Health professions and related programs
3rd	Computer and information sciences	Business	Computer and information sciences	Education	Computer and information sciences	Business	Computer and information sciences	Education
4th	Health professions and related programs	Security and protective services	Engineering technologies and engineering-related fields	Business	Health professions and related programs	Homeland security, law enforcement, and firefighting	Health professions and related programs	Business
5th	Engineering technologies and engineering-related fields	Education	Health professions and related programs	Homeland security, law enforcement, and firefighting	Engineering technologies and engineering-related fields	Education	Engineering technologies and engineering-related fields	Homeland security, law enforcement, and firefighting

Source. Digest of Education Statistics, 2013a, 2013b.

students and implications for practice are discussed. Fortunately, much of the recent research on Black students in community colleges has been conducted from an institutional responsibility vantage point. This perspective suggests that the onus for student success rests primarily on the institutions that serve them, as opposed to on the students themselves. This approach is perceived as empowering community colleges to focus on success factors within their locus of causality (Wood & Palmer, 2015).

For example, Glenn (2003–2004) examined factors that were associated with high graduation rates for Black men in community colleges. As opposed to focusing his analysis on student-specific considerations (e.g., age, high school performance, parents' education), Glenn focused on institutional-level factors associated with success for these students. Findings from institutional-level comparisons of colleges in the highest quartile and lowest quartile for graduation rates indicated several practices in place at high-quartile institutions that were less likely to be implemented at lower-quartile colleges. These practices included freshman-only advising, orientation for credit, staff development programs for retention enhancement, required tutoring programs, individual counseling, required meetings with advisers, attendance monitoring, and retention strategies for minority groups only. Wood and Ireland (2014) also focused on institutional factors influencing student success. However, in their study, the outcome of interest was faculty-student engagement. Using data from the Community College Survey of Student Engagement (CCSSE), they found that the strongest determinants of faculty-student engagement were participation in learning communities, reading remediation, study skills courses, and college orientation. Collectively, these studies demonstrate that institutions can implement interventions that can positively influence student success.

In addition to these practices, a significant portion of the literature on Black students in community colleges has focused on building climates of inclusion and belonging (e.g., Harris & Wood, 2013; Perrakis, 2008; Wood & Turner, 2011). Research posits that degree completion for Black collegians is due to sense of belonging (Hausmann, Schofield, & Woods, 2007). Specifically, Hausmann and colleagues' study on student persistence found that students who had interactions with faculty early in their postsecondary careers had higher levels of sense of belonging. They also found that the more peer support Black students had over time the higher their sense of belonging. As such, it is important that community college leaders and faculty engage Black students throughout the academic year and provide opportunities for them to engage with their peers. In addition, it is also essential that community colleges provide programming and support for adult students that foster learning.

An essential component of students' feelings of belonging and connectedness to colleges is associated with the campus racial climate. Campus racial climate is an important factor in the ways in which Black students navigate their educational experiences (Bush & Bush, 2010). Specifically, racial microaggressions (subtle racial insults) influence students psychologically and academically. Solórzano, Ceja, and Yosso (2000) found that Black students experienced microaggressions by way of being ignored by faculty, experiencing rejection from peers in regard to group assignments, and enduring verbal assaults. As such, it is imperative that community colleges provide support for Black students and students from underrepresented groups when they encounter such attacks. Specifically, community college administrators should support professional development opportunities for faculty and staff to learn about racial microaggressions and the creation of safe spaces that foster climates of inclusion and belonging.

One crucial theoretical perspective for understanding Black student success in community colleges is validation. Validation theory refers to the

  intentional, proactive affirmation of students by in-and-out of class agents
  (i.e. faculty, student, and academic affairs staff, family members, peers) in

order to: 1) validate students as creators of knowledge as valuable members of the college learning community and 2) foster personal development and social adjustment. (Rendón & Muñoz, 2011, p. 12)

Rendón (1994) posited that validation theory is applicable to college students who are non-traditional, first-generation, low-income, and racially and ethnically diverse (i.e., Black students). She proffered that validation takes both academic and interpersonal forms. Academically, validation theory can be operationalized by affirming students' identities in class assignments (e.g., using personal narratives in assignments) and through cocurricular activities via student organizations (e.g., providing opportunities for students to validate one another in their social and academic endeavors). Specifically, community college professionals can develop opportunities for Black college students to demonstrate that they are learners with valid knowledge and perspectives. Validation can also be interpersonal. Forming personal, meaningful relationships with students can serve as a source of motivation and encouragement that can help Black students persist through graduation.

The interrelationship among effective campus practices, environments of inclusion, and validating agents is evident. Simply stated, campuses that build practices and cultures that support Black students will foster better outcomes for these students than campuses that do not. This chapter has sought to explicate a brief yet comprehensive overview of Black student demographics, outcomes, and research in the community college. Using the information presented in this chapter as context, the next chapter highlights the voices of community college leaders who have become nationally recognized for their work with Black students.

References

Bush, E. C., & Bush, L. (2010). Calling out the elephant: An examination of African American male achievement in community colleges. *Journal of African American Males in Education, 1*(1), 40–62.

Beginning Postsecondary Students Longitudinal Study. (2009a). *Average cumulative total student loan amount owed in 2009 by race/ethnicity (with multiple) and gender, for first institution sector (level and control) 2003–04 (public 2-year).* Washington, DC: National Center for Education Statistics.

Beginning Postsecondary Students Longitudinal Study. (2009b). *Average>0 price of attendance 2003–04 by race/ethnicity, for first institution sector (level and control) 2003–04 (public 2-year).* Washington, DC: National Center for Education Statistics.

Beginning Postsecondary Students Longitudinal Study. (2009c). *Average>0 respondent's annual income for job 2009 by community college student 6-year retention and attainment 2009 and race/ethnicity.* Washington, DC: National Center for Education Statistics.

Beginning Postsecondary Students Longitudinal Study. (2009d). *Community college student 6-year retention and attainment 2009 by race/ethnicity (with multiple) and gender.* Washington, DC: National Center for Education Statistics.

Beginning Postsecondary Students Longitudinal Study. (2009e). *Debt from loan influenced employment plans 2009 by race/ethnicity (with multiple) and gender, for first institution sector (level and control) 2003–04 (public 2-year).* Washington, DC: National Center for Education Statistics.

Beginning Postsecondary Students Longitudinal Study. (2009f). *Debt from loan influenced plans 2009: Had to work more hours by race/ethnicity (with multiple) and gender, for first institution sector (level and control) 2003–04 (public 2-year).* Washington, DC: National Center for Education Statistics.

Beginning Postsecondary Students Longitudinal Study. (2009g). *Debt from loan influenced plans 2009: Took job outside field by race/ethnicity (with multiple) and gender, for first institution sector (level and control) 2003–04 (public 2-year).* Washington, DC: National Center for Education Statistics.

Beginning Postsecondary Students Longitudinal Study. (2009h). *Debt from loan influenced plans 2009: Took less desirable job by race/ethnicity (with multiple) and gender, for first institution sector (level and control) 2003–04 (public 2-year).* Washington, DC: National Center for Education Statistics.

Beginning Postsecondary Students Longitudinal Study. (2009i). *Job 2009: Employment status (includes looking for employment) by community college student 6-year retention and attainment 2009, race/ethnicity.* Washington, DC: National Center for Education Statistics.

Beginning Postsecondary Students Longitudinal Study. (2009j). *Loan package by source of loan 2003–04 by race/ethnicity (with multiple) and gender, for first institution sector (level and control) 2003–04 (public 2-year).* Washington, DC: National Center for Education Statistics.

Cohen, A. M., & Brawer, F. B. (2009). *The American community college* (4th ed.). San Francisco, CA: Jossey-Bass.

Digest of Education Statistics. (2013a, July). U.S. Department of Education, National Center for Education Statistics, Integrated Postsecondary Education Data System (IPEDS). *Associate's degrees conferred to males by degree-granting institutions, by race/ethnicity and field of study: 2009–10 and 2010–11 [Table 321.40].* Washington, DC: Author.

Digest of Education Statistics. (2013b, July). U.S. Department of Education, National Center for Education Statistics, Integrated Postsecondary Education Data System (IPEDS). *Associate's degrees conferred to females by postsecondary institutions, by race/ethnicity and field of study: 2010–11 and 2011–12 [Table 321.50].* Washington, DC: Author.

Flowers, L. A. (2006). Effects of attending a 2-year institution on African American males' academic and social integration in the first year of college. *Teachers College Record, 108*(2), 267–286.

Freeman, T. L., & Huggans, M. A. (2009). Persistence of African-American male community college students in engineering. In H. T. Frierson, W. Pearson Jr., & J. H. Wyche (Eds.), *Black American males in higher education: Diminishing, proportions* (pp. 229–252). Bingley, UK: Emerald Group.

Glenn, F. S. (2003–2004). The retention of Black male students in Texas public community colleges. *Journal of College Student Retention, 5*(2), 115–133.

Hausmann, L. R. M., Schofield, J. W., & Woods, R. L. (2007). Sense of belonging as a predictor of intentions to persist among African American and White first-year college students. *Research in Higher Education, 48*(7), 803–839.

Harris, F., & Wood, J. L. (2013). Student success for men of color in community colleges: A review of published literature and research, 1998–2012. *Journal of Diversity in Higher Education, 6*(3), 174–185.

Lewis, C. W., & Middleton, V. (2003). African Americans in community colleges: A review of research. *Community College Journal of Research and Practice, 27*(9–10), 787–798.

Mason, H. P. (1998). A persistence model for African American male urban community college students. *Community College Journal of Research and Practice, 22*(8), 751–760.

Nevarez, C., & Wood, J. L. (2010). *Community college leadership and administration: Theory, practice, and chance.* New York, NY: Peter Lang.

National Postsecondary Student Aid Study. (2012a). *Age as of 12/31/2011 by race/ethnicity (with multiple) and gender, for NPSAS institution sector (4 with multiple) (public 2-year).* Washington, DC: National Center for Education Statistics.

National Postsecondary Student Aid Study. (2012b). *Average>0 delayed enrollment into PSE: Number of years by gender and race/ethnicity (with multiple), for NPSAS institution sector (4 with multiple) (public 2-year).* Washington, DC: National Center for Education Statistics.

National Postsecondary Student Aid Study. (2012c). *Dependents: Has any dependents by race/ethnicity (with multiple) and gender, for NPSAS institution sector (4 with multiple) (public 2-year).* Washington, DC: National Center for Education Statistics.

National Postsecondary Student Aid Study. (2012d). *Dependents: Has any dependents (number) by race/ethnicity (with multiple) and gender, for NPSAS institution sector (4 with multiple) (public 2-year).* Washington, DC: National Center for Education Statistics.

National Postsecondary Student Aid Study. (2012e). *Employment by full-time status by race/ethnicity (with multiple) and gender, for NPSAS institution sector (4 with multiple) (public 2-year).* Washington, DC: National Center for Education Statistics.

National Postsecondary Student Aid Study. (2012f). *Enrollment intensity by race/ethnicity (with multiple) and gender, for NPSAS institution sector (4 with multiple) (public 2-year).* Washington, DC: National Center for Education Statistics.

National Postsecondary Student Aid Study. (2012g). *Ever taken remedial courses by race/ethnicity (with multiple) and gender, for NPSAS institution sector (4 with multiple) (public 2-year).* Washington, DC: National Center for Education Statistics.

National Postsecondary Student Aid Study. (2012h). *NPSAS institution sector (4 with multiple) by race/ethnicity (with multiple) and gender.* Washington, DC: National Center for Education Statistics.

National Postsecondary Student Aid Study. (2012i). *NPSAS institution sector (4 with multiple) by race/ethnicity (with multiple) and gender by urbanicity.* Washington, DC: National Center for Education Statistics.

National Postsecondary Student Aid Study. (2012j). *Percent enrolled: Black by race/ethnicity (with multiple) and gender and race/ethnicity (with multiple), for NPSAS institution sector (4 with multiple) (public 2-year).* Washington, DC: National Center for Education Statistics.

National Postsecondary Student Aid Study. (2012k). *Percent enrolled: Hispanic by race/ethnicity (with multiple) and gender and race/ethnicity (with multiple), for NPSAS institution sector (4 with multiple) (public 2-year).* Washington, DC: National Center for Education Statistics.

National Postsecondary Student Aid Study. (2012l). *Race/ethnicity (with multiple) and gender by NPSAS institution sector (4 with multiple).* Washington, DC: National Center for Education Statistics.

National Postsecondary Student Aid Study. (2012m). *Region of attendance by race/ethnicity (with multiple), for NPSAS institution sector (4 with multiple) (public 2-year).* Washington, DC: National Center for Education Statistics.

National Postsecondary Student Aid Study. (2012n). *Remedial courses: Number taken in reading in 2011–12 by race/ethnicity (with multiple) and gender, for NPSAS institution sector (4 with multiple) (public 2-year).* Washington, DC: National Center for Education Statistics.

National Postsecondary Student Aid Study. (2012o). *State of legal residence by race/ethnicity (with multiple), for NPSAS institution sector (4 with multiple) (public 2-year).* Washington, DC: National Center for Education Statistics.

National Postsecondary Student Aid Study. (2012p). *TRIO program eligibility criteria by race/ethnicity (with multiple) and gender, for NPSAS institution sector (4 with multiple) (public 2-year).* Washington, DC: National Center for Education Statistics.

Perrakis, A. I. (2008). Factor promoting academic success among African American and White male community college students. *New Directions for Community Colleges, 142,* 15–23.

Rendón, L. L. (1994). Validating culturally diverse students: Toward a new model of student learning and student development. *Innovative Higher Education, 19*(1), 33–51.

Rendón, L. L., & Muñoz, S. M. (2011). Revisiting validation theory: Theoretical foundations, applications, and extensions. *Enrollment Management Journal: Validation Theory* [Special Issue], *5*(2), 12–33.

Solórzano, D., Ceja, M., & Yosso, T. (2000). Critical race theory, racial microaggressions, and campus racial climate: The experiences of African American college students. *Journal of Negro Education, 69*(1/2), 60–73.

U.S. Department of Education. (2012). National Center for Education Statistics, Integrated Postsecondary Education Data System (IPEDS). (2014, January). *Graduation rates of first-time, full-time degree/certificate-seeking students at 2-year postsecondary institutions who completed a credential within 150 percent of normal time, by race/ethnicity, sex, and control of institution: Selected cohort entry years, 2000 through 2009 [Table 326.20].* Washington, DC: Author.

Wood, J. L. (2012). Leaving the two-year college: Predictors of Black male collegian departure. *Journal of Black Studies, 43*(3), 303–326.

Wood, J. L. (2013). The same . . . but different: Examining background characteristics among Black males in public two year colleges. *Journal of Negro Education,*
82(1), 47–61.

Wood, J. L., & Hilton, A. A. (2012). A meta-synthesis of literature on Black males
in the community college: An overview on nearly forty years of policy recommendations. In A. A. Hilton, J. L. Wood, & C. W. Lewis (Eds.), *Black males in*
postsecondary education: Examining their experiences in diverse institutional contexts,
pp. 5–27. Charlotte, NC: Information Age.

Wood, J. L., & Ireland, M-Y. S. (2014). Supporting Black male community college
success: Determinants of faculty-student engagement. *Community College Journal*
of Research and Practice, 38(2), 154–165.

Wood, J. L., & Nevarez, C. (2012). *Black males' perceptions of the work-college bal-*
ance: The impact of employment on academic success. Paper presented at the annual
meeting of the Council for the Study of Community Colleges, Orlando FL.

Wood, J. L., & Palmer, R. T. (2015). *Black male students in higher education: A guide*
to ensuring success. New York, NY: Routledge.

Wood, J. L. & Turner, C. S. V. (2011). Black males and the community college:
Student perspectives on faculty and academic success. *Community College Journal*
of Research and Practice, 35, 1–17.

2

VOICE OF THE NATIONAL LEADER

Retaining African American Students in the Community College

Jamillah Moore and Edward Bush

> *Education is the key to unlock the golden door of freedom.*
>
> —George Washington Carver

President Lyndon Johnson made the following statement the year he signed the 1964 Civil Rights Act:

> Education would help us demonstrate to the world that people of compassion and commitment could free their fellow citizens from the bonds of injustice, the prisons of poverty, and the chains of ignorance, help us open the doors of America's abundance and freedom's promise to every man whatever his race, region or religion. (Office of the White House Press Secretary, 1964, p. 2)

This legislation forced the dismantling of Jim Crow and helped to finally remove the shackles of bondage of a people President Abraham Lincoln had emancipated a century earlier.

Since the 1954 Supreme Court ruling in *Brown v. Board of Education* in which "separate but equal" was declared to be unconstitutional, there has always been a belief that education would be the great equalizer. According to the Forum for Education and Democracy (2011),

> the welfare of our nation rests heavily upon our system of public education. Throughout America's history, we have striven to provide all children with

equal access to a high-quality, free public education because we know that without it, our democratic way of life will be at peril.

The promise that every child has opportunity is the foundation of the American Dream, yet that promise is not a reality. In the United States, we cannot provide true equity to a high-quality education, and therefore, this dream cannot be realized. While we have made strides, we continue to fall short of the most basic democratic commitment, the ability to ensure that every student has equal access to a high-quality education. College completion data show that African American students are less likely to attain college degrees. The Education Trust did an analysis of four-year institutions (excluding for-profit institutions and historically Black colleges and universities) and found that nationally, African American students earn bachelor's degrees from four-year institutions at rates well below those of their White peers. Specifically, at public institutions, "only 43.3% of African American students graduate within six years, compared with 59.5% of whites, a 16.2 percentage gap" (Skinner, 2010, p. 1).

As a college chancellor and advocate with nearly 20 years of experience in higher education, my skills and background reflect a commitment to the philosophy and mission of equal access and opportunities. As a daughter to a mother who participated in the civil rights movement, I benefited from the fight and struggle for equity. Yet, when I arrived at college, it was not the welcome I had hoped for. Being one of perhaps two Black students in many of my courses, and the only Black student in several others, I spent the majority of my college education feeling very isolated. However, I was not deterred by this experience because I was the first in my family to earn a four-year college degree, so I made it my goal to finish.

What I was not prepared for, and what I have since come to realize, is that my experience was not that unique. Last year, I was invited to the California State University (CSU) chancellor's office to share my story and experience with the CSU trustees. As a new chancellor and alumna of the CSU system, I was asked to share my story of success. During my presentation to the trustees, I looked around the room, and as I have been in so many rooms I have walked into since I graduated from college, I was one of only two or three Black people there. At that presentation and many before it, I was asked to tell my story of success because, as a person of color at my level of leadership, I am as rare as a unicorn. I understand that my true role as a leader is to eradicate the "unicorn theory" and work to ensure equitable educational opportunities for all students, especially students of color.

My experiences and research indicate that in the twenty-first century, issues of race and access should be struggles of the past, but sadly, they are not. They continue to be challenges for African Americans. In order to have a better understanding of this reality and the ongoing challenges, we must start with a historical timeline. African Americans in the United States, from 1619 to 1865, were considered chattel (personal property rather than humans) and enslaved. From 1865 to 1964 we saw a post-slavery era with continued inequities. The civil rights movement and the struggle for equal rights are chronicled from 1965 to the present. The reality is that although the United States has been in the civil rights movement for 50 years—60 years after *Brown v. Board of Education*—the country has not been able to level the educational playing field and close the achievement gap.

Closing the achievement gap is the single largest challenge for education, and the timeline may shed some insight on this. The challenge is rooted in our history and a result of the ongoing inequities in higher education and the economy. In order for America to effectively participate in the global marketplace, we need an educated workforce to grow our economy. We must eradicate the achievement gap if America is going to continue to compete on the world stage and level the playing field. Community colleges open their doors to all students and, therefore, educate more people of color than any of the other higher education institutions. Community colleges are in the best position to help our nation address the ongoing inequities in achievement, moving one step closer to educational equity. In comparison to their Asian, White, and Chicano/Latino counterparts, African American students are performing at lower rates in most student outcome indicators, including graduation, persistence, grade point average, and transfer rates. The fact that African American students are underachieving and lag behind their counterparts in the community college system probably comes as no surprise to anyone who has even casually perused information regarding African Americans in postsecondary education. The underachievement of African American students in the community college system has profound societal implications. The educational underachievement affects the social positioning of African Americans in a larger societal context as degree attainment is directly attributed to one's increased income, increased social mobility, decreased likelihood of incarceration, and even increased life expectancy.

The social and economic impact of a community college education has gained recent attention in light of President Obama's American Graduation Initiative, which has a stated goal of doubling the number of Americans who hold postsecondary degrees by the year 2020. The president's initiative is an attempt by the White House to address the increasing need for highly skilled workers who are able to participate in the new global economy. The president in his plan speaks to the fact that the United States is currently ranked 12th in four-year degree attainment among 25-to-34-year-olds, while in 1990 the United States was ranked first. In order to have a citizenry that is prepared to compete in a global economy, President Obama has recognized and emphasized the role that the community colleges must play in meeting this challenge. The president describes the 1,132 community colleges in the United States as being the gateways to economic prosperity and educational opportunities, which provide students with the skills and training they need to be successful in the twenty-first century economy. With this in mind, President Obama called for an additional 5 million community college graduates by 2020.

While we agree with the president's assertions about the pivotal role community colleges play in the educational and economic outlook of this country, as community college insiders we are challenged since, for the most part, community colleges have been unable to produce the necessary student outcomes to meet this goal. In addition, given the lack of success community colleges have had in producing successful student outcomes for students of color, particularly African Americans, we know that meeting this goal becomes even more difficult. According to Harper and Wolley (2002), 31% of African American students, compared to 28% of White students, begin at community colleges. In California, where the authors of this chapter work, 75% of all African American students who are enrolled in a public postsecondary institutions are enrolled in a community college, and for African American males, it is 81%. Given these numbers, one can quickly realize that if we are going to see a significant increase in community college degree attainment as outlined in the president's initiative, this cannot be achieved without addressing the issue of how to increase the achievement rates of African American students. With this in mind, when we now juxtapose the success of African American students in community colleges with the social and economic impact of degree attainment that is outlined in the president's 2020 plan, we see that America cannot be in a position to be globally competitive unless community colleges find a solution to improve the success rates of African American students.

The national attention that has been placed on the nation's community colleges system can be viewed as a blessing or a curse, depending on your perspective. Community colleges are benefiting from additional resources from governmental agencies in the form of grants for workforce development, as well as funding from philanthropic organizations such as Lumina and the Bill & Melinda Gates Foundation, which have invested millions of dollars to improve the achievement rate among community college students. With this type of unprecedented interest also comes an unparalleled level of accountability. State legislatures from across the country are becoming increasingly interested in student outcomes, with some states adopting policies that link state funding allocation to student achievement. Over the last two decades, many states, including Florida, Ohio, Tennessee, and Washington, have adopted performance-based funding aimed at improving postsecondary performance. In a 2011 study by the Community College

Research Center (CCRC), *The Impacts of State Performance Funding Systems on Higher Education Institutions* (Dougherty & Reddy, 2011), it was found that performance-based funding increases institutional awareness of state priorities, data, planning, and student service policies. However, the report further indicated that inappropriate performance measures, instability in funding, length of time of performance funding programs, and institutional resistance, along with inequality of institutional capacity, were all factors in which performance funding did not increase institutional outcomes of retention, completion, or graduation of students. Therefore, we need to be mindful that lack of data showing that performance funding produces improved student outcomes should not be reason to dismiss it, and we need to continue to study and reexamine the policy.

The community college system must take full ownership for the underachievement of African American students within its institutions. As community college leaders, we have participated in many conversations across various college campuses regarding student equity and achievement. In each of these discussions, there is resistance on the part of faculty and administrators to accept the fact that the institution is the major contributor to the success of students in general, but African American students in particular. A blame-the-victim mentality is pervasive in these discussions, meaning that African American students themselves are perceived to be the reason they are not successful. Thoughts around the lack of social and academic preparation, parent support, economic status, negative peer influence, motivation, study habits, and the like are often cited as the reason why African American students are not achieving. While it is reasonable to believe that each of the aforementioned issues can play a role in the success of African American students, we also know that these issues are not limited to the African American student population. So the question then is, why are African American students so adversely affected by these dynamics? For example, community college leaders and scholars understand the significance of academic preparation in predicting student success. Data show that students who enter community college prepared to do college work as indicated on college placement instruments are much more likely to complete their degrees than students who have to enroll in development educational courses. However, we challenge colleges to analyze their data to control for academic preparation and examine whether a gap in achievement still exists. For example, in looking at data from our own institutions as well as data from several other colleges, we have found that when we look at the course success rate for students enrolled in freshmen composition, we see differential outcomes between African American students and their counterparts. Also, in comparing the completion and persistence rates of African American students in comparison to their White and Asian counterparts who also entered the institution at the college level, a gap in the achievement rates in these indicators still exists. The review of our data reveals that African American students who are college prepared outperformed their African American peers who were not college ready but did not succeed at the same rate as their Asian and White peers who entered the college with the same level of preparation. This type of examination has profound implications for those who work within the community colleges because it highlights the fact that something structural exists within the foundation of our colleges that is impeding the success of African American students.

Institutional structure as the leading contributing factor to African American student achievement has further been supported by studies analyzing the academic success rates of African American students enrolled in historically Black colleges and universities (HBCUs) in comparison to their counterparts at predominantly White postsecondary institutions (Nettles, 1988; Ross, 1998). Several studies (Allen, 1987; Allen & Jewell, 2002; Davis, 1994; D'Augelli & Hershberger, 1993; Ross, 1998) purport that African Americans in general, and African American males in particular, demonstrate greater success both academically and socially in HBCUs. Davis' (1994) study revealed that African American male students who attend Black colleges have a greater perception that they are supported by the institution and have a higher sense of connectedness to the college, exemplified by their interaction with faculty, campus climate, student involvement, and positive peer interaction. On the other hand, African American male students on predominantly White campuses perceive that the institutional environment is adversarial, citing greater feelings of unfair treatment, a devaluing of their academic capabilities, and increasing discriminatory or racist practices. As a result, the implications of these perceived institutional characteristics have affected the academic outcomes of both African American men and women attending both HBCUs and predominantly White institutions (Allen & Jewell, 2002; Holmes, Ebbers, Robinson, & Mugenda, 2001; Mallinckrodt, 1988). The institutional success of HBCUs has an important implication for the California community college system, given that the California community college students enter these institutions with lower college preparedness in comparison to students entering four-year institutions, and speaks to the possibility of the California community college system's developing systemic interventions that create an environment conducive to African American student achievement (Jalomo, 2000).

The body of literature that analyzes institutional characteristics and their relevance for enhancing the success of African American males has focused on institutional factors, such as student-to-faculty interaction, mentorship, counselor support, peer interaction, and engagement in student activities.

These institutional factors have emerged as viable predictors of student success (Cabrera, Nora, Terrenzini, Pascarella, & Hagedorn, 1999; Dawson-Threat, 1997; Endo & Harpel, 1982; Engstrom & Tinto, 2008; Harper & Wolley, 2002; Hood, 1990; LaVant, Anderson, and Tiggs, 1997; Pascarella & Patrick, 1977; Pascarella, Seifert, & Whitt, 2008; Ross, 1998; Spradley, 2001; Tinto, 1975; Tinto, 2006–2007; Tinto & Teaching, 2008). Moreover, studies have also suggested that the embedded practices of predominantly White institutions, whether conscious or unconscious, create an environment that is deleterious and in contrast to African American student ethos. What are the conscious and unconscious practices that permeate the community college system that must be addressed to create a conducive learning environment for African American students?

According to the American Association of Community Colleges (AACC; 2012), community colleges educate the majority of Hispanic students (56%) and a substantial percentage of students of color, including African Americans (49%), Asians and Pacific Islanders (44%) and Native Americans (42%). However, in the fall of 2012, only 18% of community college faculty were from underrepresented groups. In the authors' home state of California, where more than 50% of community college students are from underrepresented backgrounds, underrepresented faculty made up less than 30%. Davis (1994) and Dawson-Threat (1997) contend that there is a deficiency in the interaction between faculty and African American students. It is common for African American students to go through their entire community college experience without having a class taught by an African American instructor or having built a meaningful relationship with an instructor regardless of race. Kobrak (1992) concluded that one of the ways to address the disconnection between African American students and faculty members at predominantly White institutions is to increase the number of Black faculty members at these institutions. Kobrak wrote that "the most important step is clearly to educate and hire more Black faculty members as rapidly as possible" (p. 527), yet he recognized that there is no single panacea for addressing this issue.

The cultural disconnect that exists for African American students on our community college campuses affects not only their interaction with faculty but also their access to services such as student organizations and to campus facilities. Cabrera and colleagues (1999) reported that African Americans' perceptions and encounters with hostile campus climates substantially reduced their commitment to their particular institution. Nora and Cabrera (1996) posit that students of color were more likely to have perceptions of a discriminatory campus environment, believed that faculty and staff held racial bias, and were on average more likely to have negative in-class experiences than their White counterparts. Tinto (1975), Pascarella and Patrick (1977), Pascarella, Seifert, and Whitt (2008), Endo and Harpel (1982), and Astin (1999) point out that faculty interaction with students on both a formal and informal basis correlates with students' ability to persist through college. Astin (1999) concluded:

> Frequent interaction with faculty is more strongly related to satisfaction with the college than any other type of involvement or, indeed, any other student or institutional characteristic. Students who interact frequently with faculty members are more likely than any other students to express satisfaction with all aspects of their institutional experience including student friendships, variety of courses, intellectual environment, and even the administration of the institution. (p. 525)

Astin (1999) also emphasized the salient nature of student involvement in relation to other variables that were thought to be relevant in students' academic success in postsecondary institutions. Astin defined *student involvement* as the level of investment a particular student puts into the college measured by study time, amount of time on campus, participation in student organizations, and frequency of interaction with faculty members. He found that the greater the student connection the greater likelihood of higher student learning and individual growth. He further stated that all institutional policies and practices relating to nonacademic as well as academic matters can be evaluated in terms of the degree to which they increase or reduce student involvement.

As administrators in the community college system, we have seen the detrimental effects of this cultural disconnection between African American students and non–African American instructors. These effects manifest themselves in a variety of ways for many African American students. For example, one of the authors of this paper is responsible for overseeing student discipline. The subjectivity associated with student discipline, particularly as it relates to the perception of what is acceptable classroom behavior, provides a unique illustration of how this cultural disconnect plays out in the community college setting. Our experience has shown us the majority of discipline complaints from non–African American faculty are issues of cultural disconnection masked in the form of student behavioral issues. This is an issue for both African American males and females. We have found that some instructors hold conscious and unconscious bias and fear of African American students associated with the societal portrayal of this particular population. Complaints from faculty regarding students who are talking in class or are disengaged, intimidating, and loud are common for African American students and far exceed similar complaints about any other student population. We know that this experience plays out in a variety of ways, in various interactions between African American students and community college personnel. The notion of stereotype threat in the community college system is a real phenomenon that must be addressed, given what is known about the correlation between faculty-student interaction and student success.

At the colleges where the chapter authors work, we know that African American students are less likely than their counterparts to access such critical services as counseling, student government, enrichment workshops, tutoring, and instructional labs. We imagine that this paradigm also exists at other community colleges across the country. This lack of student engagement and participation is often viewed by those within our college as being oppositional, countercultural, disengaged, or generally disinterested in educational success. Ironically, when one of the authors examined that data at his college, he saw that African American students expressed higher educational aspirations in comparison to any other racial subgroup, meaning African American students were overwhelmingly more likely to indicate at the point of the admissions application that they want to achieve a long-term educational goal, such as transfer or associated degree completion. These data not only clearly indicate that African American students value education and desire to be successful but also vividly show that there is a huge gap in desire versus achievement. It is important for those of us within our colleges to understand that the educational ontology of African American students is not one of the devaluing of education or of disengagement. We posit that African American student disengagement, as evident in their under-usage of college services, is symptomatic of a larger disease, which is that African American students perceive the institution as being unsupportive, discriminatory, and not structured to operate in their best interest. These notions are rooted not only in the historical treatment of African Americans in this country but also in the students' own experiences in primary and secondary schools as well as the treatment they receive in a larger societal context. We find that personnel in community colleges do not "know" African American students. They do not know their history, cultural experiences, values, victories, or struggles, so they draw misplaced negative interpretations of the behaviors previously outlined because those of us inside the college are far too often symptom-focused. You cannot teach or serve those whom you do not know. The pervasive underachievement of African American students in the community college system reveals that we have much to learn. As educators, we have come to understand that in order to fully address the crisis of the achievement gap, we must acknowledge the systematic inconsistencies in access and opportunities for students of color in higher education. While this chapter touches on those challenges, there are some approaches and promising suggestions in the form of recommendations. We hope that the following recommendations will establish a pathway to reducing inequities in access and, one day, eradicate the achievement gap. Achieving true equity requires every community college to work together within the community it serves along with students, faculty, and staff to build awareness and put a system in place to address this crisis.

1. **Disaggregate the data:** Institutions need to use their data and engage and commit to making data-driven decisions.

2. **Provide faculty development on cultural competence:** Allows educators to be effective with students from different cultures, have an awareness of their own cultural identities and an appreciation of difference. We need to embrace our students' diverse cultural backgrounds and view them as assets on which to build college success. Encourage faculty members to include in their course work the significant contributions made by African Americans to humanity in all areas of academic disciplines.

3. **Make an authentic commitment to diversity and equity:** Improve diversity among faculty and staff on college campuses. Employ African American faculty, counselors, and staff and others who are interested in the success of African American students.

4. **Assign counselors and educational advisers:** Have counselors and advisers to specifically work with African American students utilizing a case management approach. Counselors and advisers will work with the same caseload of students from enrollment though completion.

5. **Host institution-wide courageous conversations:** Create opportunities for dialogue and venues for regular discussion of the issues and the challenges associated with race and student achievement. Have honest conversations around institutionalized racism, microaggressions, personal beliefs, and biases. Also find ways to capture student voices on their experiences as African American students.

6. **Consider alternative delivery of basic skills instruction:** Make sure that African American students are fully represented in any existing college programs, initiatives, or pilots that are intended to accelerate, support, or streamline students through the college's basic skills sequence. Learning communities, particularly programs that infuse cultural aspects into the curriculum, should be developed as a method of support for African American students who are enrolled or placed at the developmental educational level.

7. **Learn from best/promising practices and bring them to scale:** There are many programs within and outside our colleges that have

demonstrated success in producing positive outcomes for African American students; however, it is often difficult because of the resource-intensive nature of these programs to bring them to scale. Colleges should assess them to determine what aspects of them are effective and reallocate college resources to replicate these practices in order for a greater number of African American students can benefit.

8. **Engage African American students in the college**: Establish formal mentorship programs between faculty members and African American students. Develop an orientation program designed to target the needs and concerns of African American students. Create campus activities that engage African American students in the school culture. Institutionalize a peer program, pairing second- and third-year African American students with incoming first-time freshmen.

References

American Association of Community Colleges. (2012). *Reclaiming the American Dream: Community colleges and the nation's future.* A Report from the 21st-Century Commission on the Future of Community Colleges. Retrieved from http://files.eric.ed.gov/fulltext/ED535906.pdf

Allen, W., & Jewell, J. (2002). A backward glance forward: Past, present, and future perspectives on historically Black colleges and universities. *Review of Higher Education, 25*(3), 241–261.

Allen, W. R. (1987). College in black and white: Black students' experiences on black and white campuses. In A. S. Pruitt (Ed.), *In pursuit of equality in higher education, 30*(3), 247–269.

Astin, A. (1999). Student involvement: A developmental theory for higher education. *Journal of College Student Development, 40*(5), 518–529.

Cabrera, A. F., Nora, A., Terrenzini, P., Pascarella, E., & Hagedorn, L. (1999). Campus racial climate and the adjustment of students to college. *Journal of Higher Education, 70*(2), 134–160.

D'Augelli, A., & Hershberger, S. L. (1993). African American undergraduates on a predominantly White campus: Academic factors, social networks, and campus climate. *Journal of Negro Education, 62*(1), 67–81.

Davis, J. E. (1994). College in black and white: Campus environment and academic achievement of African American males. *Journal of Negro Education, 63*(4), 620–633.

Dawson-Threat, J. (1997). Enhancing in-class academic experiences for African American men. *Directions for Student Services, 80*, 31–41.

Dougherty, K. J., & Reddy, V. (2011). Implementation and impacts of performance funding in three states [Project description]. Retrieved from http://ccrc.tc.columbia.edu/Collection.asp?cid=74

Endo, J. J., & Harpel, R. L. (1982). The effect of student faculty interaction on students' educational outcomes. *Research in Higher Education, 16*(2), 115–138.

Engstrom, C., & Tinto, V. (2008, February). Access without support is not opportunity. *Change: The Magazine of Higher Learning, 40*(1), 46–50.

Forum for Education and Democracy. (2011). *Equity and access. Ohio.* Retrieved from http://www.forumforeducation.org/our-issues/equity-access

Harper, S. R., & Wolley, M. A. (2002). Becoming an "involving college" for African American undergraduate men: Strategies for increasing African American male participation in campus activities. *Association of College Unions International Bulletin, 70*(3), 16–24.

Holmes, S. L., Ebbers, L. H., Robinson, D. C., & Mugenda, A. E. (2001). Validating African American students at predominantly White institutions. *Journal of College Student Retention, 21*, 41–58.

Hood, D. W. (1990). Academic and non-cognitive factors affecting the retention of Black men at predominantly White university. Paper presented at the American Educational Research Association, Boston, MA.

Jalomo, R. (2000). Assessing minority student performance. *New Directions for Community Colleges, 28*(4), 7–18.

Kobrak, P. (1992). Black student retention in predominantly White regional universities: The politics of faculty involvement. *Journal of Negro Education, 61*(4), 509–526.

LaVant, B. D., Anderson, J. L., & Tiggs, J. W. (1997). Retaining African American men through mentoring initiatives. *New Directions for Student Services, 80*, 43–53.

Mallinckrodt, B. (1988, January). Student retention, social support, and dropout intention: Comparison of Black and White students. *Journal of College Student Development, 29*(1), 60–64.

Nettles, M. T. (1988). Contemporary barriers to Black student equality in higher education. In M. T. Nettles (Ed.), *Toward Black undergraduate student equality in American higher education.* New York, NY: Greenwood Press.

Nora, A., & Cabrera, A. (1996). The role of perceptions of prejudice and discrimination on the adjustment of minority students to college. *Journal of Higher Education, 67*(2), 119.

Office of the White House Press Secretary. (1964). *Remarks of the president.* University of California, Ervine. Retrieved from http://50th.uci.edu/wp-content/uploads/2015/01/Johnson-speech-June1964.pdf

Pascarella, E. T., & Patrick, T., (1977). Patterns of student-faculty informal interaction beyond the classroom and voluntary freshman attrition. *Journal of Higher Education, 48*(5), 540–552.

Pascarella, E. T., Seifert, T., & Whitt, E. (2008, Fall). Effective instruction and college student persistence: Some new evidence. *New Directions for Teaching and Learning, 2008*(115), 55–70.

Ross, M. (1998). *Success factors of young African-American males at a historically Black college.* Westport, CT: Bergin & Garvey.

Skinner, D. C. (2010, August 13). Education trust: Four keys to closing the higher education gap. *Black Enterprise Magazine*. Retrieved from http://www .blackenterprise.com/news/education-trust-4-keys-to-closing-the-higher-education-gap/

Spradley, P. (2001). Strategies for educating the adult Black male in college. *ERIC Digest*. Retrieved from http://eric.ed.gov/?id=ED464524

Tinto, V. (1975). Dropout from higher education: A theoretical synthesis of recent research. *Review of Educational Research, 45*, 89–125.

Tinto, V. (2006–2007). Research and practice of student retention: What next? *Journal of College Student Retention: Research, Theory & Practice, 8*(1), 1–19.

Tinto, V., & Teaching, C. (2008). *When access is not enough. Carnegie perspectives.* Carnegie Foundation for the Advancement of Teaching. (ERIC Document Reproduction Service No. ED502271). Retrieved from http://files.eric.ed.gov/ fulltext/ED502271.pdf

3

CUTTING-EDGE MODELS
FOR BEST PRACTICE

Hillsborough Community College, Tampa, Florida

Kenneth Atwater and Joan B. Holmes

Intelligence plus character—that is the goal of true education.
—Martin Luther King Jr.

According to Walter G. Bumphus, president and CEO of the American Association of Community Colleges (AACC), "America needs a highly educated population to strengthen our place in the world market, grow our economy, and engage in our democracy. But we cannot have an educated workforce and citizenry if our current reality persists." He further states, "Although this work is difficult, nothing could be more important. Community colleges are grounded in equity, and we cannot achieve equity until we identify *and actively address* inequity" (Center for Community College Student Engagement [CCCSE], 2014). Such a belief system is at the foundation and core of Hillsborough Community College's (HCC) mission as a national leader in retaining students of color in higher education.

HCC, a two-year public institution with five campuses in Hillsborough County, Tampa, is one of 28 community colleges in the state of Florida. Currently, HCC ranks fifth in the nation in size as measured by full-time student enrollment (FTE) and seventh in the number of associate degrees awarded in all disciplines. It ranks 12th in the number of degrees awarded to minority students and 22nd in the number of associate degrees awarded to Black students.

Uniquely, the five campuses represent the demographic and cultural character of the community in which HCC is located. For example, Ybor City campus, which is located in the historic Ybor City, is predominantly an urban campus, with the highest enrollment of Black students. Dale Mabry Campus, which is a suburban campus, enrolls the second highest number of Black students, even though it has been formally recognized as a Hispanic-serving institution (HSI). The remaining three campuses are a combination of rural and suburban campuses and have the least number of Black students.

Of particular importance, Hillsborough County School District is the seventh largest district in the nation and is confronted with high levels of poverty among its student body. According to the National Center for Education Statistics (2010), the majority of students who are living below the poverty line are of Black and Hispanic descent. This information has helped to guide the policies and practices of HCC in retaining the majority of low-income students and students of color. In 2013–2014, HCC served 44,941 students of which 21.4% were racially Black and approximately 28% of Hispanic origin (see Figure 3.1).

Recognizing that education is a key to reducing poverty in Hillsborough, HCC seeks to isolate factors associated with academic success by targeting Black and Hispanic students enrolled at HCC in special programs. In view of the methods employed to help our most at-risk student groups, specific strategies focusing on Black student populations with the lowest rates of attainment will be discussed in depth for the reader's review. Following are several of the key research principles, theories, and practices implemented by HCC that have brought about the greatest outcomes for Black student retention.

Figure 3.1. Hillsborough Community College profile, 2013–2014.

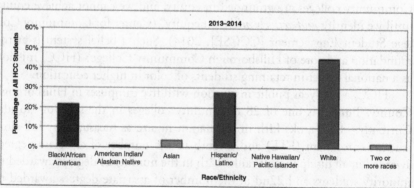

Source. Hillsborough Community College Institutional Research, 2014.

Note. Hillsborough Community College had a total annual unduplicated headcount of 44,941 in 2013–2014. The College served 43,579 students who took credit and/or clock-hour courses, and an additional 1,362 students took at least one Recreation & Leisure course (but no credit or clock-hour courses). Demographic analyses exclude Recreation & Leisure students due to extensive missing data.

Challenges: Understanding Black Student Enrollment

Amid demographic studies, national education statistics, and enrollment data, research continues to reveal that fewer Black students are enrolling in college. Questions are still unanswered about students, specifically males, who enroll in college but do not complete degrees at the rate of White students. We pose the following questions: Are there factors related to success for some populations that might also be associated with success for others? Do the lack of resources (e.g., academic advising, financial aid, and tutoring), or the lack of knowledge of how/where to access these resources, negatively impede the academic success of Black students? In response to these queries, we have concluded that because of the large number of Black students from first-generation and low-income backgrounds, intrinsic motivation to achieve academically is not the initial impetus. Specifically, Black students need to be convinced that the college experience is a "good fit" for them. That is, they are initially motivated extrinsically through the college culture by intangibles, like mutual respect, equal treatment, structured programs, and a "sense of belonging."

With this knowledge kept in mind, HCC has become increasingly successful with enrolling first-time-in-college (FTIC) Black students. For example, Florida State Equity enrollment trend data from 2012–2013 to 2013-2014 revealed that there was a sizeable increase of FTIC students. The most significant increase (60.6%) was the enrollment of FTIC Black females, from 523 in 2012–2013 to 840 in 2013–2014. The enrollment of Black males also increased from 418 in 2012–2013 to 639 in 2013–2014 (see Figure 3.2).

Much of the growth in enrollment of Black students is attributed to HCC-wide success of targeted recruitment that uses unique and cutting-edge strategies:

Figure 3.2. Black FTIC comparison of HCC enrollment data, 2012–2103 and 2013–2014.

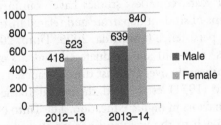

Source. Florida Department of Education (2013). *The Fact Book: A Report for the Florida College System.*

- HCC created a partnership with predominantly Black urban high schools, which in turn created a pipeline from high school directly to HCC.
- HCC established a community project called HCC L.I.F.E. (Linking In Fellowship and Education), which is an initiative designed to partner with the county's community Black churches by informing them, through a variety of presentations and workshops, of educational opportunities at HCC and of ways to achieve college access goals. As part of the partnership, HCC provides financial aid, college application workshops, and direct access to Black ministries. At least 25 Black churches are affiliated with the program.
- Black, Brown, and College Bound (BBCB) is a national conference that addresses national and local issues of access, retention, and graduation of African American and Latino males. HCC is proud to become the preeminent national voice and leader in addressing issues facing Black and Latino males for colleges and universities across the United States. HCC has begun to benefit from this national attention and more FTIC students are enrolling at HCC from other surrounding cities in Florida.

Over the past two years, HCC has been successful in attracting more FTIC Black students, whereas historically, community colleges have attracted more nontraditional Black students ages 25 and over. This nontraditional student enrollment has stabilized with no increases over the past three years, from 2012–2014. Many academic programs are designed for aiding Black students, specifically first-time students. Therefore, strategies for retention and completion are now beginning to refocus on the traditional-age students.

A Guide To Success: Theories on Retaining Black College Students

For more than 40 years, countless studies have examined the factors that lead to various forms of student departure and related institutional efforts to encourage student persistence (Guiffrida, 2006; Tinto, 2006). The theories and "best practices" to retain and graduate all students enrolled in college have increased significantly over the past three decades. Tinto (1975), Astin (1985), and Spady (1971) established theoretical frameworks to explain student-leaving behaviors in higher education. The Tinto (1975) model took a sociological approach to the issue and posited that it was the interaction between two variables that influenced staying or leaving behavior—the college and the student. The Tinto model has become the most widely accepted theoretical model concerning student attrition in higher education regardless of the type of postsecondary education. College persistence and success are determined by the student's level of structural integration (extrinsic rewards such as grades) and normative integration (intrinsic reward of intellectual development) in the college system. This means that the student must be motivated to achieve academically by extrinsic rewards (e.g., grades, recognition, scholarships) but must have a sufficiently high level of intellectual ability to navigate the college system and be successfully retained.

There is limited research and few publications focusing on the retention of Black students in community colleges. One of the most compelling analyses about what motivates Black students to succeed in college in general is a book titled *Blacks in College*, by Jacqueline Fleming (1985), which focused on factors that contributed to higher retention and completion rates of Black students based on their experiences at historically Black colleges and universities (HBCUs). Jacqueline Fleming, a psychologist from Harvard University, conducted a longitudinal research study on students enrolled in HBCUs and compared them to students enrolled in predominantly White institutions (PWIs) during the same period. Her research resulted in a psychological assessment that revealed that it was the impact of relationships and interaction that motivated Black students to succeed in college, essentially by establishing a sense of belonging among professors, advisers, counselors and their peers (Fleming, 1985). Historically, 90% of Black students were enrolled at HBCUs in 1945; however, only 18% of Black students have enrolled at HBCUs since 1991. This motivated some PWIs to establish retention strategies and develop special programs to increase Black student enrollment. The challenge to increase college retention and completion rates of Black students at PWIs during the 1990s prompted Beverly Tatum, president of Spelman College, to author the book, *Why Are All the Black Kids Sitting Together in the Cafeteria?* (1997). Tatum (1997), who is also a psychologist, provided an extensive analysis of why ethnic groups gravitate together in school and in college settings. The findings resulted in the development of a racial identity model.

The Focus on Black Males in College

In an increasingly competitive global economy, the breadth and multiplicity of education for students of color is becoming more and more essential. In 2002, Black men made up only 4.3% of students enrolled at institutions of higher education, the exact same percentage as in 1976 (Harper, 2006b; Strayhorn, 2010). As we look for the numbers of Black and Latino males who are graduating from college to increase, the goal is to have this population not only become a significant and highly sought-after population but also diversify campus communities and further institutional goals. Although racial and ethnic achievement gaps, at least between Black and White children, have been declining over time, Black and Hispanic children continue to lag behind their peers on a wide variety of academic achievement measures and other metrics related to academic success (Duncan and Magnuson, 2011; Farkas, 2011). These problems may be acute for young boys of color (Davis, 2003). Despite some recent progress, only 52% of African American males and 58% of Latino males graduate from high school in four years, compared with a rate of 78% for White males (Schott Foundation for Public Education, 2012). Furthermore, young females from all racial and ethnic groups have steadily been outpacing their young male counterparts in successfully completing college in recent years (Bailey & Dynarski, 2011).

Indeed, Black men face a number of difficulties and arguably unique challenges that may inhibit their success in college (Bailey & Moore, 2004; Noguera, 2003). Although the enrollment of Black students in undergraduate programs has increased from 10% in 1976 to 14% in 2008, Black males are not enrolling in college at the rate of Black women and their White male counterparts (Harper, 2006a; Strayhorn, 2008a). In fact, over the past 25 years, Black males have made no progress. They represent only 5% of all of the undergraduate students and only 3% of those in graduate programs. Unfortunately, recent literature review and research about Black men in college reveal that discouragement of Black males to enroll in college begins at the high school level (Ogbu & Wilson, 1990; Strayhorn, 2008b). They are almost absent from high school gifted and advanced classes, very concentrated in special education courses, and tracked into low academic ability classrooms (Palmer & Strayhorn, 2008; Jackson & Moore, 2006). For this reason, many Black males graduate from high school discouraged and with low academic preparation.

Hillsborough Community College: Four Pillars of Academic Achievement

In response to the theories surrounding Black student achievement and low enrollment of Black male college students, the Four Pillars of Academic Achievement were developed by the authors and are based on best practices and theories from an extensive literature review on college retention and completion. Furthermore, these Four Pillars of Academic Achievement were developed from extensive professional experience and leadership, with 60 years of combined college experience as faculty and administrators. The four pillars are as follows: (1) create a culture of academic achievement; (2) understand the cultural/ethnic differences; (3) expose students to new environments and opportunities; and (4) provide adequate resources and mentoring experiences. Hereafter is an overview of each of these fundamental pillars that we have deemed critical to the retention success of our Black student groups (especially male) and have been proven to work.

Pillar I: Create a Culture of Academic Achievement

Creating a culture of academic achievement for Black students must be intentional, structured, and involve cultural competency. *Culture* is defined as beliefs, customs, attitudes, and behaviors that are characterized by a group or organization. Thus, the academic or scholarly expectations, projects, and outcomes must be connected to the cultural needs of Black students. Institutions provide a wide array of special programs to help bring students together, especially students who share interests or backgrounds. These include, among other special programs, ethnic/racial affinity groups, special housing programs, and freshman interest groups. These special programs provide services and academic support that further individualize and personalize education. Typically, they provide students with guidance on course-taking and, in some institutions, special program staff serve each participant as the "advisor of record" (Muraskin & Lee, 2004). Following are key aspects of creating a culture of academic achievement:

1. **Affirm Student Potential.** The literature is replete with acknowledgment that Black students are historically and systematically confronted with low expectations to achieve in college. They experience many facets of racial microaggression from professionals, such as the professors and academic advisers who interact with them during their academic journeys. The following are examples of microaggressive statements directed at Black college students by their professors: "Did you write this paper?" and "I can't believe you earned an 'A' on that test." As a result, Black students are not challenged to excel academically, encounter low expectations and stereotypical assumptions about their academic ability to succeed, and internalize the stereotypical belief that they are weak academically.

2. **Provide for Intentional Academic Planning.** Intentional academic planning is critical in providing intrusive advising, orientation courses, and continual academic monitoring and follow-up. The majority of

community colleges have small classes, which afford the students and professor the opportunity for recognition and class discussion. Special programs focused on Black students provide academic support and give them a greater sense of belonging on campus. These types of programs should enlist dedicated full-time faculty who are easily accessible to students and who play an active role in shaping students' academic progress. Educational innovation should be employed to create unique courses that help students to acclimatize to college life and offer a wealth of support through tutoring, group study sessions, and supplemental instruction. While it may appear that students participating in special programs are isolated from the majority of the student population, the institution and the program administrators should make special efforts to provide a wide range of social and cultural activities to help them engage and to include them in college-wide events.

3. **Acknowledge Barriers.** Unlike other ethnic/racial populations, Black students are challenged with a myriad of barriers before they enter college, and they are often faced with new challenges after enrollment. Barriers while in college include institutional racism, financial constraints, and limited academic preparation. They need help with learning to balance pre-college life and family, with normalizing help-seeking behaviors, and with help and encouragement from sufficient academic and personal support systems. There are two reasons why community colleges can—and should—take the lead in this effort. First, community colleges open their doors to all students and serve large numbers of low-income, first-generation adult and minority students. Second, open access is just the first step toward attaining the equity ingrained in the mission of community colleges (CCCSE, 2014). In this regard, many Black college students have not experienced a systematic approach to learning that includes an enlightened and enriched academic, intellectual, culturally student-centered educational environment. As such, HCC has established a culture of achievement with special programs focused on the success of increasing the college completion and transfer rates with unique programs for all students, but tailored for special populations.

4. **Employ Intrusive Support Programs.** Another critical aspect to creating a culture of academic achievement is to acknowledge that the community college is a student "commuter culture" when compared to campus life at traditional colleges and universities. The lack of continued engagement with college life for Black students can create some challenges, which can be countered through intentional and structured college support. Structured intrusive programs, which require students to participate in cohort

academic activities, resonate culturally with Black students in college. The intrusive approach to academic and personal support improves the lack of understanding about the culture of college and ensures that Black students engage in the academic environment on an ongoing basis. The cohort experience provides the level of interaction, peer support, and "sense of belonging" discussed earlier in research conducted by Fleming and Tatum. The cohort model allows students (or students with similar backgrounds) to create a sense of community and a spirit of equality. Designated advisers, tutors, or related staff who have demonstrated commitment to providing individualized and personal support to Black students, should be assigned to these cohort groups.

5. **Individualized Academic Follow-up.** Black students rarely receive personal attention and privileges based on their academic pursuits. Tracking the academic progress of each student with individualized follow-up and advising is a critical best practice approach for student success. Examples of positive messages from faculty and staff are "I expect an 'A' from you next time"; "I believe you can continue on to a professional school after graduating from college"; "When you complete your associate degree from this community college, you need to transfer to a four-year college"; and "Do not give up; I believe you can be successful with some tutorial support." These messages should permeate planned educational seminars, educational activities, and challenging academic projects. The academic success of Black students should be recognized by planning programs, orientation, or ceremonies on the college campus, among peers and with college leaders, to publically recognize their academic success and improvements. Designating a professional staff member (adviser, coordinator, faculty, and administrator) who is willing to establish a relationship with the student will create a comfortable educational setting in which a student can share academic problems and questions and receive guidance.

Pillar II: Understand Cultural/Ethnic Differences

Most Black students have expressed in many ways that they are not understood. They are not understood culturally, which often impedes the efforts of academic advisers and faculty mentors in getting to know the students. In the African American culture, relationships matter. For example, Harper (2007) found that forced classroom participation and certain faculty teaching styles may have a negative impact on African American males. The following strategies have been proven efficacious to understanding ethnic and cultural differences among our students:

1. **Focus on the Intake Process.** Special programs should include opportunities for Black students to participate in individual intake or initial interviews. During the intake process, the adviser should assess the student's academic aptitude, semester course schedule, GPA, test scores, part-time or full-time work schedule, family/parent status, and so on. The adviser should inquire about the student's personal status without being insensitive and judgmental to determine if additional guidance and resources are needed. In addition, it is necessary to conduct an academic assessment of each student (transcript, grades, strengths/weaknesses, test scores, etc.) and establish realistic academic and career goals. The initial intake process is critical to the college success of Black students. Also, it provides an opportunity to create and build a relationship with them. Only after building such a relationship will the professional be able to identify critical indicators or needs for the student's success in college. If college advisers convince Black students that they are genuinely and sincerely interested in the students' success, the relationships will be strengthened, which will motivate the students to succeed.

2. **Host Motivational Forums and Seminars.** As previously discussed, many Black students are accustomed to experiencing racial microaggressive responses from persons of authority and have experienced these responses also from student peers throughout their matriculation in K–12 grades and college. As a result, microaggressive behavior creates an educational environment in which Black students feel targeted, distrust authority, and are impeded in their help-seeking behavior. Help-seeking behavior is crucial to the academic and personal success of many Black students enrolled in community colleges. Especially for Black males, help-seeking translates to internalized stereotypical beliefs that they are weak academically. This perceived belief inhibits them from seeking tutorial support, advising, counseling, financial support, and so forth. Thus, motivational forums and seminars to inform Black students on how to navigate college is a critical component to their overall college success.

3. **Understand Unique Differences.** Black college students are very diverse within their ethnic/racial groups, and they also enroll at the community college with a broad level of diversity. For example, within the Black community, there are a number of subpopulations, which include Caribbean, African, and African American backgrounds. It is important to let students know that their unique differences are recognized. Examples of appropriate inquiries from college faculty and staff relating to ethnicity are as follows: "What is your nationality?"; "Where are you from originally?"; "Tell me about yourself [background, family,

and career goals]?" and "Can you benefit from additional financial support?" Plan and schedule activities for Black students related to their cultural/ethnic heritage or background. Institutions should maximize the services available to students to help bring them together, especially students who share similar interests or backgrounds. Collaborative learning among peers fosters a community of students that leads to a significantly higher level of campus involvement, satisfaction with the college environment, personal acceptance and achievement, and social and academic development.

4. **Establish a College-Wide Diversity Council.** HCC has a college-wide Diversity Council comprising students, faculty, and staff representing all five campuses. The council composition is intentionally diverse and has been extremely effective in improving the racial and diversity college climate at HCC. The council coordinates and supports traditional ethnic/cultural celebrations and provides a series of seminars offered throughout the academic year titled "Courageous Conversations" (2016). This series promotes college-wide participation and addresses issues that affect race and diversity throughout the entire college community.

Pillar III: Expose Students to New Environments and Opportunities

A significant number of Black students are enrolled in college, especially in community colleges, from low-income and/or first-generation backgrounds. These economic realities prevent them from engaging and experiencing the type of exposure that would be beneficial for their success in college. The extent to which the individual becomes academically and socially linked into the academic and social structures of an institution determines the individual's departure decision. In other words, the leaving behavior of a student is largely dependent on how he or she integrates into the formal and informal academic and social systems of a college.

Despite the current mix of public and private subsidies, students from low-income families do not enter college at the same rate as more affluent students. Academic, cultural, or financial factors limit low-income students' educational opportunities. In fact, the graduation trend is vastly affected by this factor. Pell Grant recipients are probably more likely than higher income graduates to have financial problems that can cause them to leave school and are more likely to experience nonfinancial risk factors, such as single parenting status, delayed college enrollment after high school, inadequate academic preparation, extensive family obligations, and lack of experience with the college environment (U.S. Department of Education, 2005).

Pillar IV: Provide Adequate Resources and Mentoring Experiences

Appropriate resources should be connected to the needs of the student. Understanding the "whole student" (i.e., personal, financial, and cultural needs) is critical to the overall success of students in college. College resources include tutoring, mentoring, scholarships, stipends, financial aid, and access to technology. When Black students are convinced that the college is invested in them, they will work harder to achieve their academic goals. In this regard, community colleges should structure the following into their academic and student support services:

1. **Implement Financial Advising and Mentoring Programs.** The most critical resources related to the successful college retention and completion of Black students is connected to financial status—money. It has been documented in the *Journal of College Retention* and the *Journal of Student Financial Aid* that Black students drop out of college because they cannot afford to pay tuition and other expenses associated with college. Black students, especially Black males, rely on working during college. Examples include paid summer internships; paid leadership roles at college, such as SGA and housing; and fellowships and scholarships (Harper & Griffin, 2011). Facing these financial challenges prevents Black students from completing college within a four to five year time period. In fact, data suggest that more than 50% of Black students are enrolled in college for at least six years or more (Harper & Griffin, 2011). HCC has created many opportunities that provide financial support for low-income students, and especially for students participating in special programs. It is critical to advocate and secure sufficient funding for special programs targeted to Black students. Adequate resources, such as scholarships, technology support, tutorial services, personalized advising, college tours, and cultural activities, have a significant effect on the overall academic and personal success of Black students.

2. **Faculty and Peer Mentoring Programs.** Faculty and peer mentoring are both very powerful tools for retaining Black students. For example, Harper (2006a) found that peers play a significant role in collegiate success for African American males and that peer mentors help these students to become successfully acclimated to the college environment. In addition, Palmer and Gasman (2008) found that encouragement from faculty and administrators plays an important role in the academic success of Black males. The study also stressed the importance of mentors and role models in Black males' success. Findings suggest that those Black men who reported having frequent and varied supportive

relationships with faculty, staff, and peers were more likely than other Black males to be highly satisfied with their college experience (Strayhorn, 2008b).

3. **Establish Cohort Learning Communities.** The cohort program model has had many unintended positive outcomes with peer mentoring at the community college level. This model represents varied age levels and the vast experiences of many student participants, especially when compared to traditional-age cohort models at four-year colleges and universities. The nontraditional-aged student is more mature, older and wiser, and evolves as a positive role model and influence for many of the traditional age students. Many Black students do not have positive role models in their communities and homes to provide shared insight and wisdom, to guide them to make better decisions and choices that will affect their overall college success.

Four Pillars in Action: HCC Minority Male Programs as National Models

The Four Pillars of Academic Achievement have been a guiding force for establishing effective programs and initiatives on campus. Through solidified partnerships among administrators, faculty, and staff, HCC has made a national mark in the areas of retention and persistence of their minority male student populations. Such programs and initiatives have become a benchmark for other schools to draw from and include the following:

Black, Brown, and College Bound (BBCB) Summit

Over the past decade, HCC has developed a national dialogue surrounding the crisis facing Black and Latino males enrolling in and completing college. HCC has coordinated and sponsored a national summit called BBCB. This summit has become a national collaborative, which has included 18 college cosponsors, 18 corporate sponsors, and 70 colleges and universities from more than 25 states. Summit participants include college presidents, researchers, program directors, faculty community leaders, and more than 300 male college students. The summit provides three days of forums, plenaries, and seminars focusing on best practices, successful strategies, and cutting-edge research to address the minority male crisis in higher education. The BBCB Summit has garnered national attention and attracted some of the best experts and national speakers in the United States. The summit has been fortunate to have national speakers such as Shaun Harper, Damon

Williams, J. Luke Wood, Michael Eric Dyson, and celebrities such as Steve Harvey and Ervin "Magic" Johnson, to name a few.

Hillsborough Community College HOPE Scholars Program

HCC has also focused on the needs of their own minority males by establishing a successful minority male program called HOPE (Helping Students with Opportunities in Programs and Education) Scholars Program. This program is a college completion and four-year-college transfer program targeted to Black and Latino males. After four years of institutional support, 236 males have participated in the program, of which 60% have completed associate degrees, with an impressive 100% four-year transfer rate of those who have completed their degrees. More than 80% of the program participants are from low-income, first-generation backgrounds.

In addition to the financial support ($1,000 stipend scholarship per student), academic services, personal support, technology support, college tours, and career guidance contribute to the success of the HOPE Scholars. However, the primary factor that contributes to the overall success of the HOPE Scholars is the faculty mentors. Our dedicated faculty serve as role models, coaches, academic advisers, and big brothers/sisters and are committed to helping the students navigate the path to college completion and beyond. The mentors provide assistance in academic planning, course selection, and four-year-college preparation, which has significantly increased HOPE Scholars' college completion and transfer rates. The completion and transfer rates of Black and Latino males in the HOPE Scholars Program far exceed the completion and transfer rates of any other students enrolled at Hillsborough Community College from 2012 to 2014 (see Figure 3.3).

The word "scholar" is rarely used to designate Black men. The label of "scholar" exudes a sense of self-esteem, which ultimately translates to becoming a high achiever. This level of accomplishment is believed to lead to high expectations and compels students to sustain that scholarly status.

Hillsborough Community College Collegiate 100 (C-100) Program

Hillsborough Community College Collegiate 100 (C-100) is an auxiliary organization of 100 Black Men of America, Inc. International Brand C-100 extends the 100's mission of college and university campuses across America. Male and female students who are in academic good standing and have a passion to mentor and deliver community service are eligible to become members of a C-100 chapter. It is a district-wide initiative, open to all students on all of five campuses, designed to engage students in leadership,

Figure 3.3. Three-year graduation rates for males at HCC.

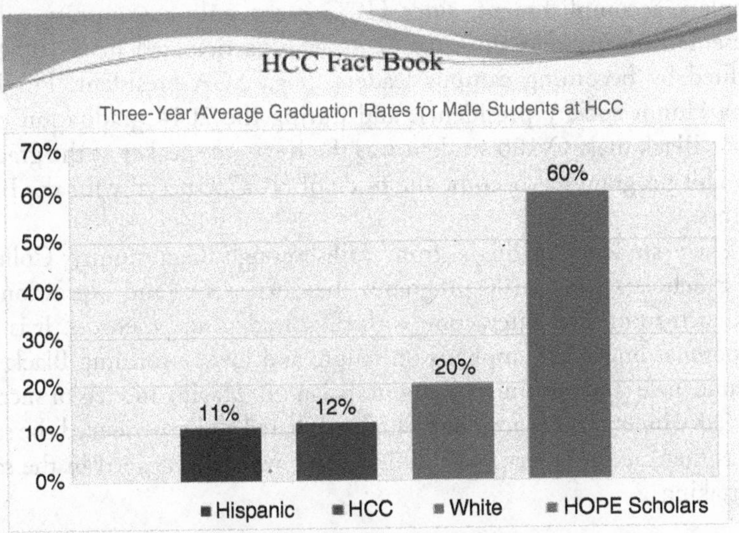

Three-Year Average Graduation Rates for Male Students at HCC

HCC Fact Book

- Hispanic: 11%
- HCC: 12%
- White: 20%
- HOPE Scholars: 60%

Source. Hillsborough Community College Institutional Research, 2014.

mentoring, and community service. College selection ranks as one of the largest decisions that Black students are asked to make. The C-100 program is designed to motivate and develop talented students as they pursue academic excellence and leadership.

HCC C-100 is the only community college represented nationally among 70 college chapters across the United States. It is within this program that every opportunity for developing student purpose is cultivated. College tours encourage students to become good decision-makers. The C-100 College Program Tour gives young Black and Hispanic males the ability to examine concerns and personal interests during the college selection process. C-100 students are assigned specific advisers with resources and guidance throughout the selection process, with the end goal in mind to select a college and a major that will lead them to successful careers. Students are prepared to handle the complexities of today's society and to enhance self-confidence and motivation throughout the community college experience. In addition to each student's development and college experience, C-100 students gain positive personal values and assistance in social skills, life skills, and good character traits. The students are expected to be academically and scholastically prepared when they transfer to four-year institutions or the trade of their choice.

Since its inception, the HCC chapter has won first, second, and third place at the National 100 Black Men conference over the past three years (first place 2013, second place 2014, and third place 2012). This is an exemplary accomplishment, since HCC is the only community college represented during that time. Students who participated in C-100 have benefited by becoming campus leaders, (e.g., SGA president, Phi Beta Kappa Honor society president), and during the 2014 graduation ceremony a Black male C-100 student was the Keynote speaker at the graduation. This program has become the pride of HCC, especially for the Black students.

When students graduate from Hillsborough Community College's HOPE Scholars and C-100 programs, their experience and expression are heightened from their interaction with their leaders and mentors. It is said that popular one-sided emphasis on failure and low-performing Black and Hispanic male students must be counterbalanced. Having models of successful bread-winners and champions who have shared and experienced the same path as they are on is very impactful to those who are engaged in the same undertaking

HOPE Scholars Summit

Hillsborough Community College's HOPE Scholars Program hosts and sponsors an annual male summit in partnership with the Hillsborough County Public School. The purpose of the HOPE Scholars Summit is to address best practices and innovative strategies to increase the number of Black and Latino males enrolled in high school who complete high school and enroll in college. The HOPE Summit drives a platform to empower, motivate, and inform Black and Latino males in 10th, 11th, and 12th grades of the value and need to enroll in and complete college. More than 700 high school males have attended this summit from 2011 to 2014. The summit provides an opportunity for these male students to experience national male role-model speakers with testimonies and motivational messages about how to overcome racism, poverty, low expectations, stereotyping, and peer pressure to complete and graduate from high school and then to complete college. The summit also provides opportunities for the students to hear testimonies from a panel of HOPE Scholars who serve as positive role models and who reinforce the reality that these young men can overcome the obstacles mentioned previously in this book and be successful in college.

The "Four Pillars of Academic Achievement" are imbedded and embraced in every aspect of the HOPE Scholars program, which is a testament to the importance of implementing the aforementioned theories and practices for improving the academic success of Black students in college.

Conclusion

Hillsborough Community College prides itself on successful initiatives and programs that have progressively improved the enrollment, retention, completion, and transfer rates of Black students over the past five years (2010–2015). These outcomes are largely due to the institutional support and leadership at HCC, which has been instrumental in coordinating academic, personal, and cultural support services that are tailored to meet the needs of Black students. This coordinated college model substantiates the theories discussed combined with the Four Pillars that have constituted this overall student success. The Four Pillars have served as foundational threads to help weave the fabric of our institution-wide success.

Black students in college have unique personal and academic challenges to complete college. However, Black students are expected to be held accountable to the same educational standards and policy for all students enrolled at HCC. As a result, HCC has been successful in launching a national platform to bring to the attention of academic professionals, and corporate and community leaders and to address this crisis and find solutions for these Black males on a local and national level. We have broadened the conversation and served as an influence to improve this national dilemma by providing opportunity for Black students to successfully complete college.

References

Astin, A. (1985). Involvement: The cornerstone of excellence. *Change* (July–August), 35–39.

Bailey, D. F., & Moore, J. L., III. (2004). Emotional isolation, depression, and suicide among African American men: Reasons for concern. In C. Rabin (Ed.), *Linking lives across borders: Gender-sensitive practice in international perspective* (pp. 186–207). Pacific Grove, CA: Brooks/Cole.

Bailey, M. J., & Dynarski, S. M. (2011). Inequality in postsecondary education. In G. J. Duncan & R. J. Murnane (Eds.), *Whither opportunity? Rising inequality, schools, and children's life chances* (pp. 117–132). New York, NY: Russell Sage Foundation.

Center for Community College Student Engagement. (2014). *Aspirations to achievement: Men of color and community colleges (A special report from the Center for Community College Student Engagement).* Austin, TX: University of Texas at Austin, Program in Higher Education Leadership.

Courageous Conversations. (2016). Retrieved from https://www.hccfl.edu/gwsc/equity-diversity-office/diversity-council/courageous-conversations.aspx

Davis, J. E. (2003). Early schooling and academic achievement of African American males. *Urban Education, 38*(5), 515–537.

Duncan, G. J., & Magnuson, K. (2011). The nature and impact of early achievement skills, attention skills, and behavior problems. In G. J. Duncan & R. J.

Murnane (Eds.), *Whither opportunity? Rising inequality, schools, and children's life chances* (pp. 47–70). New York, NY: Russell Sage Foundation.

Florida Department of Education (2013). *The fact book: A report for the Florida College System*. Deptartment of Education: Division of Accountability, Research, and Measurement. Retrieved from: http://www.hccfl.edu/media/716919/2013%20 state%20fb.pdf

Farkas, G. (2011). Middle and high school skills, behaviors, attitudes, and curriculum enrollment, and their consequences. In G. J. Duncan & R. J. Murnane (Eds.), *Whither opportunity? Rising inequality, schools, and children's life chances* (pp. 71–90). New York, NY: Russell Sage Foundation.

Fleming, J. (1985). *Blacks in college: A comparative study of students' success in Black and in White institutions*. San Francisco, CA: Jossey Bass.

Guiffrida, D. A. (2006). Toward a cultural advancement of Tinto's theory. *Review of Higher Education, 29*(4), 451.

Harper, S. R. (2006a). *Black male students at public universities in the U.S.: Status, trends and implications for policy and practice*. Washington, DC: Joint Center for Political and Economic Studies.

Harper, S. R. (2006b). Enhancing African American male student outcomes through leadership and active involvement. In M. J. Cuyjet & Associates (Eds.), *African American men in college* (pp. 68–94). San Francisco, CA: Jossey-Bass.

Harper, S. R. (2007). The effects of sorority and fraternity membership on class participation and African American student engagement in predominantly White classroom environments. *College Student Affairs Journal, 27*(1), 94–115.

Harper, S. R., & Griffin, K. A. (2011). Opportunity beyond affirmative action: How low-income and working class Black male achievers access highly selective, high-cost colleges and universities. *Harvard Journal of African American Public Policy, 17*(1), 43–60.

Hillsborough Community College Institutional Research. (2014). *HCC fact book 2014*. Retrieved from http://www.hccfl.edu/media/1060728/final%20draft%20 factbook%202014%20november21%202014.pdf

Jackson, J. F. L., & Moore, J. L., III. (2006). African American males in education: Endangered or ignored? *Teachers College Record, 108,* 202–205.

Muraskin, L., & Lee, J. (2004, December). *Raising the graduation rates of low-income college students*. Washington, DC: Pell Institute for the Study of Opportunity in Higher Education.

National Center for Education Statistics. (2010). *Digest of education statistics*. Washington, DC: Author.

Noguera, P. A. (2003). The trouble with Black boys: The role and influence of environmental and cultural factors on the academic performance of African American males. *Urban Education, 38*(4), 431–459.

Ogbu, J. U., & Wilson, J. (1990). Mentoring minority youth: A framework. (Report No. ED354293). New York, NY: Columbia University. Retrieved from http:// eric.ed.gov/?id=ED354293

Palmer, R., & Gasman, M. (2008). It takes a village to raise a child: The role of social capital in promoting academic success for African American men at a Black college. *Journal of College Student Development, 49*(1), 52–70.

Palmer, R. T., & Strayhorn, T. L. (2008). Mastering one's own fate: Non-cognitive factors associated with the success of African American males at an HCBU. *NASAP Journal, 11*(1), 126–143.

Schott Foundation for Public Education. (2012). *The urgency of now: The Schott 50 state report on Black males and public education 2012.* Cambridge, MA: Author.

Spady, W. (1971). Dropouts from higher education: Towards an empirical model. *Interchange, 2,* 38–62.

Strayhorn, T. L. (2008a). Fittin' in: Do diverse interactions with peers affect sense of belonging for Black men at predominantly White institutions? *NASPA Journal, 45*(4), 501–527.

Strayhorn, T. L. (2008b). The role of supportive relationships in facilitating African American males' success in college. *NASPA Journal, 45*(1), 26–48.

Strayhorn, T. L. (2010). When race and gender collide: Social and cultural capital's influence on the academic achievement of African American and Latino males. *Review of Higher Education, 33*(3), 307–332.

Tatum, B. (1997). *Why are all the Black kids sitting together in the cafeteria? And other conversations about race.* New York, NY: Basic Books.

Tinto, V. (1975). Dropouts from higher education: A theoretical synthesis of the recent literature. *Review of Educational Research, 45,* 89–125.

Tinto, V. (2006). Research and practice of student retention: What next? *Journal of College Student Retention, 8*(1), 1–19.

U.S. Department of Education. (2005). Federal Pell Grant program end-of-year report. Submitted by Pearson Government Solutions. Retrieved from https://www2.ed.gov/finaid/prof/resources/data/pell0405.pdf

PART TWO

HISPANIC/LATINO STUDENT POPULATIONS

4

VOICE OF THE NATIONAL RESEARCHER

Community College Data Trends for Latino Student Populations

Deborah A. Santiago

I am a firm believer in education and have worked very hard to tell young Latinos that they must go to college and that, if possible, they should pursue an advanced degree. I am convinced that education is the great equalizer.

—Jimmy Smits

A country's most precious resource is its human capital, and in today's knowledge-driven economy, a college degree is critical to the success of an engaged citizenry and competitive workforce. It is projected that by 2020, 65% of all jobs in the United States will require some college education and training beyond high school (Carnevale, Smith, & Strohl, 2013). Therefore, leaders in the federal government and philanthropy have articulated national goals to increase college degree completion and regain the international lead in the proportion of the population with a college degree. Given Latinos' current population representation, growth, relative youth, and levels of educational attainment, the data show the nation's success in reaching its degree completion goals will rely on its ability to accelerate the degree completion of Latinos as part of all who complete a degree (Santiago, 2010).

Community colleges are the nation's gateway to postsecondary education for many Hispanics[1] because of their location, accessibility, and affordability. Community colleges are often overlooked or derided in public policy, in part because of policymakers' general emphasis on traditional students in traditional postsecondary pathways, a preference for supporting institutions

63

offering bachelor's degrees, and both low expectations and low completion and transfer data for students at community colleges. As public attention evolves from a focus on access to college to degree completion, some community colleges are increasingly transforming their policies, practices, and resources in a manner that can significantly increase Latino college completion and contribute to the nation's goals for a more educated workforce and citizenry.

Why focus on Hispanics? While the majority of the U.S. population is still non-Hispanic White, Latinos are the youngest and among the fastest growing racial/ethnic group in the United States. The median age for Latinos in the United States is 27 compared to 42 for non-Hispanic Whites (Excelencia in Education, 2014). From this statistic alone, one can infer that Latinos already make up a large number of students being educated today in secondary and postsecondary institutions across the country. In fact, Hispanics are currently the second-largest racial/ethnic group in the United States overall (17%) as well as in early childhood, K–12 education, and postsecondary education. Hispanics represented 25% of children under 9 years of age (U.S. Census Bureau, 2013), 22% of students in K–12, and 16% of students in postsecondary education (Santiago, Calderon Galdeano & Taylor, 2015). Further, the Hispanic population is projected to continue growing. While the enrollment of Latinos along the educational pipeline is significant, their educational attainment is lower than that of adults overall. In 2013, 22% of Latino adults had earned an associate degree or higher, compared to 31% of African Americans, 42% of Whites, and 60% of Asians (U.S. Census Bureau, 2004, 2013). There is a clear opportunity for institutional efforts and public policy to improve the educational attainment for Latinos, and community colleges are well positioned to contribute to this national goal.

Many people are uncomfortable talking about race/ethnicity in policy and practice. They would rather the focus be on "educating all students" and not disaggregate by race/ethnicity. However, data show persistent educational attainment gaps among racial/ethnic groups that contradict an assumed focus on educating all. If the nation were effectively educating all students, these persistent educational attainment gaps would not exist. Acknowledging racial and ethnic trends *describes* our society in constructive ways and thus helps us to understand it. The use of data and analysis to identify factors affecting the success of specific student populations establishes a base of information from which to develop more effective policies, engage diverse stakeholders, and enhance tactical responses to better target limited resources to meet the nation's education goals. Given this fact, it is worth articulating the profile of Latino students in postsecondary education overall, and in community colleges specifically, in order to shape the policies and practices that can better serve community college students. This chapter provides an overview of the Latino population in community colleges, some challenges and opportunities within the sector, and some considerations and recommendations that set the context for leaders and practitioners accelerating Latino student success in community colleges.

Latinos in Community Colleges: Enrollment Growth and Concentration

Latinos' participation in postsecondary education has increased in the last several decades, and much of this is attributable to increased participation in community colleges (Snyder & Dillow, 2015). The growth of Latinos enrolled in community colleges has more than doubled over the last 22 years (230%) and has outpaced increases in total enrollment in community colleges (36%). From 1990 to 2012, Latinos increased their representation in community colleges from 8% to 20% of all students enrolled. In fact, in the last four years alone, while enrollment at community colleges overall has decreased by 5%, Latinos' enrollment in community colleges has continued to increase by 10%. Latinos were also more likely to enroll in community colleges than all other groups. In 2012, 46% of Latinos in postsecondary education were enrolled in community colleges, compared with 34% of African American students, 32% of Asian students, and 31% of White students. This enrollment has also been increasingly concentrated. The majority of Latinos enrolled in community colleges (62%) was also concentrated in two states—California and Texas—and in a relatively small number of community colleges identified as Hispanic-serving institutions (HSIs) (Excelencia in Education, 2013).

HSIs are defined in federal law as accredited and degree-granting public or private nonprofit institutions of higher education with 25% or more total undergraduate Hispanic full-time equivalent (FTE) student enrollment (Title V, 2008).[2] In 2013–2014, 60% of Latino undergraduate students were enrolled in 12% of institutions (409 institutions) in the United States. Almost half of HSIs (190 institutions) and another 109 emerging HSIs (15–24% undergraduate Hispanic FTE) were community colleges. HSI community colleges were concentrated in two states and in urban areas, were relatively large, and were growing in number. About two-thirds (121 institutions) of HSI community colleges were in California (86 institutions) and Texas (35 institutions). Further, almost half (93) of HSI community colleges were in cities; 27% were in suburbs, and 24% in towns or rural areas. HSI community colleges are large institutions with the average enrollment size by headcount of about 11,500 students, as compared to 6,655 for other HSIs. Hispanics create HSIs because of concentrated enrollment, but what are HSI community colleges doing to go beyond access to college to increase Hispanic degree attainment? Using data to identify institutions where Latinos enroll is important, as it reveals opportunities to target constrained resources at HSI community colleges and reach a larger segment of Latinos. Such a strategy will help to address institutional quality and support access to degree completion.

The Evolving Pattern of Latinos and Community Colleges

Both the Latino population and community colleges in the United States continue to evolve. Latinos represent a mix of people from over 20 Latin American countries of origin, all with historical Spanish language, values, and customs. The Latino population will continue to evolve in the United States at the same time other generations of Latinos influence, and are influenced by, the current society. In similar ways, community colleges are continually evolving their offerings and strategies to meet the shifting educational and economic demands in their community, region, and state. This evolution complicates the presentation of a generalized profile of both Latinos and the community colleges that enroll them. In this state of movement is strength, flexibility, adaptability, and new opportunities, but also a myriad of challenges to effectively address policy and practice as a constantly evolving target.

The profile of Latinos in education is increasingly representative of the growing majority of students—a post-traditional profile (Santiago, 2012). They may not be college-ready; may delay initial postsecondary enrollment while entering the workforce; may enroll at a community college; often need remedial education; take courses part-time, online, and at multiple institutions; live off-campus with their parents or with their own dependents; and take more than four years to complete a degree. Many work 30 hours or more a week. They make college choices on the basis of cost of attendance, location, and accessibility. Further, they are self-motivated to work toward the American Dream of economic well-being by balancing family and work responsibilities with education. Those who know the postsecondary education process know this requires a challenging reconciliation of high aspirations for college with actual attendance and completion at many institutions that are not funded or structured to ensure every students' success. Many Latino students have a goal to do better than their parents and have a pragmatic, if sometimes naïve, perspective about postsecondary education.

From Deficit to Asset Profiles

Both Latinos and community colleges have another characteristic in common: a general deficit-based profile. For both Latinos and community colleges, this evolution is occurring within the existing societal, economic, and governance opportunities and constraints.

While Latinos make up a growing share of those enrolled in postsecondary education, they are rarely mentioned in discussions. If they are included, gross generalizations and limited facts—often based on individual experiences, a media story, or clichés shared by others—limit constructive discussions on how to serve Latino students well. For example, Latinos are generally described as immigrants, high school dropouts, and English language learners (ELL) who do not value education. While Latinos are more likely than other ethnic groups to fit some of this profile, the majority of Latinos do not. In fact, the majority of Latinos in the United States are native-born, high school graduates, English language proficient, and value postsecondary education. Consider these facts:

- The majority of Hispanic adults (64%) in the United States are native-born (U.S. Census Bureau, 2012, Table 13). School-age Hispanics are even more likely to be U.S.-born. Only about 7% of all students in K–12 education had unauthorized immigrant parents and were thus potentially unauthorized immigrants, and not all were Latino (Pew Research Center, 2014).
- The majority of Latino students (66%) spoke a language other than English at home, but 84% of these students still spoke English without difficulty (Aud, Hussar, Kena, Bianco, Frohlich, Kemp, et al., 2011).
- Census data show that in 2012, 65% of Latinos 25 years of age and over had completed high school. While this is lower than other groups, it is still the majority of that population (U.S. Census Bureau, 2012, Table 9).
- For many years, surveys from Public Agenda (Immerwahr, 2004) have consistently shown Latinos believe a college education is important, and Latino voters consistently rate education among their top three most important issues. However, many Hispanics are concerned about the lack of opportunity for qualified students (Immerwahr & Johnson, 2007).

This profile varies from state to state and school district to school district, but data show the national profile of Latinos is more asset-based than is often articulated. Clarifying the profile of Latinos does not imply the issues of immigration, language acquisition, and high school completion are not important or relevant policy issues. These are critical issues to address. And recognizing that Latinos highly value education does not signify that this value alone guarantees enrollment to completion. However, characterizing the majority of Latinos in education today by a deficit-based and limited profile can marginalize efforts to serve the population well. Institutions seeking to improve Latino educational attainment should contextualize issues and develop strategies to accelerate Latino success with this more accurate profile in mind.

In this same vein, community colleges are important institutions in postsecondary education, often seen from a deficit-based profile. Community colleges are relatively lower in cost than public colleges and universities, are more accessible (most are open access and enroll all who apply), are responsive to community needs, and serve students with low income and varying academic preparation levels. Community colleges also have multiple missions such as providing community and economic development through workforce training and community enrichment; preparing students academically to transfer to a college or university; conferring terminal academic credentials, including certificates, associate degrees and, on a more limited basis, bachelor degrees; offering English as a Second Language and adult basic education programs; and collaborating with high schools in dual enrollment and early college high school programs to allow students to earn college credit. Yet community colleges are often perceived as institutions of last resort and of low quality, while continuing to receive lower funding per student than other types of institutions and at the same time being asked to meet ever-increasing public expectations of access, retention, and completion (College Board, 2013).

From Access to Completion

As open-access institutions that enroll all who register, low-cost institutions with limited resources to serve their students, and institutions with multiple missions, community colleges are both engines of opportunity and limited agents of Latino student success. Historically, the measure of the colleges' success was ever-expanding student enrollments. While access to college is a necessary precursor to degree completion, access alone does not guarantee degree completion for Latino and other students. In fact, the prevailing perspective that once students have been admitted, it is completely up to them to complete—"*Que vayan con Dios* (Go with God)"—has slowly but increasingly become passé with the increased focus on the role of the community college in degree completion. In 2012, 17% of all degrees earned in the United States were from community colleges. For Latinos, about 25% of all degrees earned in 2012 were from community colleges (U.S. Department of

Education, 2013). Further, Latinos significantly increased associate degrees in the last 10 years compared to other groups. From 2003–2004 to 2012–2013, the number of Latinos receiving an associate degree increased 75%. In that same time frame, African Americans increased 44%, Asians increased 39%, and non-Hispanic Whites increased 37% (U.S. Census Bureau, 2004, 2013, Table 1).

Community colleges provide broad access to postsecondary education for many but confer a smaller proportionate number of degrees or sufficient credits to transfer to baccalaureate programs. Still, community colleges are a critical postsecondary pathway of opportunity for Latino students, and some of their perspectives and profiles, described later are important considerations for policy and practice to serve these students well.

Many Latino students in community colleges are first-generation college-goers who value higher education and balance work, family, and education to persist to completion. Data show about 22% of Latino adults have an associate degree or higher, and about 20% of Latinos at community college have parents with bachelor's degrees, compared to 30% of all community college students (U.S. Census Bureau, 2004, 2013, Table 1). As the first in their family to go to college, Latino students cannot be assumed to have sophisticated knowledge about college. Further, whether Latino students' parents have gone to college or not, they are clear motivators for their children's pursuit of a college education. Many of these students also work and live at home, with either their parents or their own families, while enrolled. For these students, their persistence in college is the result of balancing work, family, and education. They are working to "have it all," and few are aware of research indicating a decreased likelihood of completion for those who attend college in nontraditional patterns.

Affordability, rather than accountability measures, generally affects Latinos' college choices and persistence. The majority of Latinos in community colleges (53%) are financially independent. About 75% work while enrolled, and 30% work full-time while enrolled. Furthermore, about 30% of Latino community college students have dependents, 26% have independent income less than $20,000, and 25% have dependent income less than $40,000 (National Center for Education Statistics [NCES], 2013). Latino students at community colleges considered college costs when deciding which college to attend and their enrollment intensity. The "sticker price" was one of the primary factors determining their enrollment. About 25% of Hispanics lived below the poverty level, compared to 13% of non-Hispanic Whites (U.S. Census Bureau, 2012, Table 41). For these students, knowing the sticker price allowed them to plan their work and attendance patterns to pay for their education on a semester-to-semester basis. However, Latino students shared stories of having to choose between taking more courses or paying for basic necessities. Latino students were more likely than other undergraduates to be enrolled part-time (45% versus 38%) (Ginder, Kelly-Reid, & Mann, 2014). Research shows that students enrolled part-time are less likely to complete a degree in a timely manner than students enrolled full-time. They might "stop out" to earn money and then re-enroll or "pay as they go" with limited knowledge of other financial options. In contrast, with surveys and focus groups, Latino students at community colleges did not consider measures like graduation rates, yield rates, or research funding levels in selecting their college. Overall, Latinos were more likely to make their choices based on location, cost, and access than other measures of institutional success generally discussed as critical in public policy.

Students believe that a quality education does not have to cost more. For many Latino students at community colleges, their college choices were based on practical factors such as cost, location (proximity to their family), and accessibility. Many Latino students do not ascribe to conventional assumptions that the cost of an education represents the quality of the institution. In focus groups, students mentioned their belief that they could get a good education anywhere if they were motivated. Some students shared the perspective that the first two years of college were basic and therefore preferred to go to a community college and then pay more (including borrowing) for the final two years of college (Santiago, 2007). Other students shared the perspective that "college was college"; they did not see significant distinctions between the quality of different institutions. These students did not see the need to pay more than what they saw was necessary to secure a quality education. In fact, several high-achieving Latino students who chose to attend community colleges thought the quality of education at the institution they selected was comparable to other more selective and distant colleges and universities. While providing greater access, community colleges are often funded at much lower levels than public colleges or universities, thus resulting in lower levels of student support services, academic support, or financial aid than better-resourced institutions.

Considerations and Recommendations

Both population projections and current educational attainment levels show the nation has a great opportunity to reach its educational attainment goals with a tactical plan that intentionally includes Latinos. Thoughtful educators and policymakers understand the persistent educational attainment gaps disaggregated by racial/ethnic group show both postsecondary institutions and public policies can be improved to serve all students better. This awareness has led many to consider what and who needs to change to more effectively serve Latino students and thus expand the country's human capital and leadership.

Latinos' increased enrollment in postsecondary education creates the potential of closing long-standing educational attainment gaps if more of these students complete a degree. As community colleges have created real opportunities for Latinos to increase their access to postsecondary education, these institutions can continue evolving to increase Latinos' degree completion. The following considerations and recommendations very briefly address the importance of change in the current policy and institutional environment to improve the success of Latino and other community college students:

- Community colleges can improve their knowledge of the students they enroll and evolve to serve these students well according to the strengths and needs of the students they serve, especially Latinos.
- Public policy and funders can incentivize and support more effective practices and innovative models at community colleges for support services tied to degree completion.
- Public policy and funders can incentivize community colleges' capacity building as well as completion strategies in more targeted ways.
- Public policy can align federal and state postsecondary education and skill development funding for low-income students at community colleges.
- Public policy can increase flexibility for institutions to serve students.
- Public policy and funders can incentivize expanded, coordinated student services at community colleges.
- Public policy and funders can improve transfer and completion of bachelor degrees by replicating and scaling effective strategies at community colleges.
- Public policy can expand eligibility for other public financial aid, beyond Pell Grants, aligned to students' needs.
- Public policy can increase community college participation in federal work-study programs.

Recommendation 1: Community Colleges Should Know Who They are Serving

Both community college leaders and funders should know who they are enrolling and serving to degree completion. Too many well-intentioned but ineffective policies and practices exist that are based on broad and inaccurate assumptions of who is being served and their needs, and this can have an adverse impact on Latino students. Community colleges that acknowledge and invest in policies and practices that serve the post-traditional student profile they actually serve, rather than the traditional profile many assume, will develop more appropriate services and strategies more representative of Latino and other groups of students. Institutional profile reports, internal assessments of gateway courses, tracking of students from adult programs and feeder high schools, and economic and social profiles of the diverse students served may facilitate this awareness to inform policy and practice.

Recommendation 2: Incentivize and Support More Effective Practices and Innovative Models for Support Services Tied to Community College Completion

The completion agenda has radically altered the way that community colleges look at what can be done outside the classroom to support that goal. Low completion rates at community colleges are due in part to the absence of resources that can provide support outside the classroom. What works to increase Latino student success at community colleges? The same thing that works for most students in postsecondary education—an intentional focus on their individual strength and needs supported with one-on-one mentoring and advising. However, few institutions can afford to offer one-on-one support for all of their students. Over the last 10 years, some cost-conscious strategies with an intentional focus of including and serving Latinos, as part of all served, have shown some evidence of effectiveness in improving Latinos' progress in community colleges. These programs include cohort models of support services, mentoring, and academic engagement, in which groups of students are guided and counseled through the entire process to graduation; family and parental involvement in orientations and outreach; aligned pathways between K–12, community colleges, and colleges/universities that prioritize student participation; supplemental instruction for more time on task for academic enrichment; integrated financial literacy programs; sophisticated and even automated education planning tools that enable students to plot more efficient academic routes; and in between peer support cohort models and mandatory counseling, among other ideas. These approaches have some evidence of effectiveness for Latino students and have been recognized and highlighted by various national organizations, such as the League of Innovation, the American Association of Colleges and Universities, and Excelencia in Education. Moreover, they have potential to be replicated and scaled to serve more students at community colleges. Scaling up to wider implementation from limited evidence-based practices requires incentives for community colleges to adopt new strategies. It is also imperative to generate faculty buy-in, as faculty members play an essential role, whether in the classroom or in an advising capacity, in encouraging students to stay on their education path.

Recommendation 3: Incentivize Community Colleges' Capacity Building and Completion Strategies in More Targeted Ways

Concentrated enrollment in HSI community colleges creates opportunities to invest limited resources in more targeted ways to ensure Latinos receive access to more services and support. To better implement initiatives that continue providing access while also enhancing student outcomes, community colleges need practical financial incentives and support for themselves and their students. One way to incentivize measured improvements in degree completion at community colleges is to build on existing federal institutional development programs (e.g., Title III, Part A, and Title V, Developing Hispanic-Serving Institutions [HSIs], of the Higher Education Act) with supplemental funds. These competitive grant programs provide additional resources for institutions with a high enrollment of needy students and insufficient revenue to increase their institutional capacity and educational quality over five years. Community colleges meet both criteria; they have limited resources from the state and local levels and enroll a high percent of needy (low-income) students. As a result, federal support to increase their capacity and quality can improve the support services and strategies to completion for Latino students.

Capacity-building and quality improvement investments, however, do not necessarily translate immediately to increased degree completion. Therefore, one strategic solution to consider is to use the existing programs and develop a set-aside within the program (or explicit components of the program) for community colleges to supplement their capacity-building grants with degree completion grants. Community colleges could be asked to submit a measureable plan to increase degree completion and/or transfer performance within the grant period, taking into account the student population served. In its FY 2015 budget, the Obama administration proposed a Pell "bonus" grants program that has features similar to this strategy.

Recommendation 4: Align Federal and State Postsecondary Education and Skill Development Funding for Low-Income Students

There are numerous federal and state programs for which low-income students at community colleges are eligible, including workforce development, human resource and income-maintenance support, postsecondary and adult education, and career and technical education. Given the many Latinos who are low-income, this alignment could improve their financial engagement in community college. The lack of integration among these education and human resource programs is a major drag on the system. The rules that govern these programs, unfortunately, limit their efficient administration and implementation. Furthermore, the onus is usually on the students to discover the programs, and they are required to apply separately for each one in order to receive support. Therefore, aligning the administration and funding for at least some of these programs and simplifying application procedures can help ensure that students and trainees complete programs and progress toward earning postsecondary credentials. The political, policy, and administrative hurdles entailed in effecting this change are worth surmounting. One model gaining in popularity across the country is one in which community colleges partner with a variety of government offices and community organizations: Single Stop USA. Single Stop works with students and administrators to help students with multiple financial needs—such as applying for a multitude of government benefits, filing their taxes, and receiving financial and legal counseling from community organizations. This model provides access to low-income and first-generation students who often lack college and financial knowledge about the benefits of a wide variety of government community services and programs.

Recommendation 5: Increase Flexibility for Institutions to Serve Students

The institutions serving low-income, first-generation, and Latino students are continually challenged to keep up with the changing and growing numbers of regulations to administer financial aid and serve the needs of their students. Too often, services for students are crowded out by the need to meet administrative requirements. This is one reason that more community college students are not maximizing their use of programs intended to provide them with financial opportunities for college access and completion. Streamlining the federal regulations imposed on institutions to access and manage financial aid will increase institutions' flexibility to better serve their students.

Recommendation 6: Incentivize Expanded and Coordinated Student Services

Increasing college completion will require student services that solve key barriers to college completion. Foremost among these barriers is increasing costs and financial challenges for Latinos and other students. Programs that guide low-income students to existing resources they are eligible to receive are among several promising models that merit replication, creating concrete and replicable opportunities to make community college more affordable. The upcoming reauthorization of the Higher Education Act (HEA) provides the opportunity to incentivize colleges to rethink the services they offer to their students and to make sure funding helps to address barriers to key educational outcomes like retention, completion, and employment measures. Bolstering competitive grant-making and demonstration funding linked to promising practices is one way HEA reauthorization can seed more student service innovation. Similarly, state policymakers should use their higher education appropriations to encourage community college reform that addresses barriers to college completion.

Recommendation 7: Improve Transfer and Completion of Bachelor Degrees by Replicating and Scaling Effective Strategies

Currently, transfer policies and information about them are decentralized and not uniform or standardized. Fortunately, there are examples of states and institutions that have successfully dealt with the transfer issue. Policies must be implemented that better inform prospective students, especially low-income and first-generation students, about the transfer process and ways to more effectively achieve transfer and, ultimately, completion. The lack of clearly defined, explicit pathways to transfer and degree completion beyond the community college must be rectified for many community college students, including Latino and low-income students.

In California, two pieces of legislation have been enacted to establish a guaranteed pathway for students to transfer from community colleges to California state universities, along with support services to facilitate degree completion or transfer. Further, the University of California system has placed a renewed emphasis on transfer from community colleges. In Virginia, students who graduate from one of the state's 23 community colleges with an associate degree and a minimum grade point average are guaranteed admission to more than 20 of the commonwealth's colleges and universities. In addition, eligible community college students may receive a college transfer grant to help subsidize additional costs incurred by attending the four-year college. There are also efforts at the institutional level to improve the transfer process. For example, El Paso Community College and University of Texas at El Paso coordinate along with their feeder school districts to have early college high school linked to the institutions, as well as joint admissions and financial aid applications and shared data to support students' transfer and completion. As compelling as these examples are, there needs to be a national standard, rather than isolated instances of state or institutional transfer and completion efforts. Improved transfer needs to be catalyzed, in particular at the state level, because the federal government lacks the means by which to stimulate needed reform.

Recommendation 8: Expand Eligibility for Other Public Financial Aid Aligned to Need

Accessing the financial safety net can require students to meet challenging work requirements that make it more difficult to complete their college program. Too often Latino and other low-income students encounter difficult trade-offs when identifying the financial aid that will allow them to access and persist to degree completion. State and federal policies can give welfare agencies more flexibility to provide benefits to individuals moving through educational programs that will enhance their employability and reduce their dependence on safety net programs in the long term. The federal government should follow the example of states that allow a college education to count toward the work requirements of benefits like SNAP (Supplemental Nutrition Assistance Program) and TANF (Temporary Assistance for Needy Families). Massachusetts, for example, has increased the flexibility of its food stamp program to allow college students who are enrolled at least part-time to more easily qualify for and apply for SNAP. This reform can serve as an example for how public benefits can be used to support college completion.

Recommendation 9: Increase Community College Participation in Federal Work-Study programs

Affordability for a community college education is a factor in the choices and retention to completion for Latino and other students. While most of the attention in financial aid is on Pell Grants, increasing and then sustaining community college participation in the federal work-study program provides an opportunity to increase representation in existing financial aid opportunities while supporting a student's need to work. However, this participation requires two things. First, there must be geographic/sector alignment of the campus-based program funding formula to better target students with extreme financial need. Second, the current cumbersome campus-based program administration (i.e., match requirements, allocation of community services, and other placements) must be simplified.

This is important because in 2010, community colleges enrolled 34% of all students (as measured in FTE) but were allocated only 16% of federal work-study funds. In comparison, private four-year institutions enrolled 18% of all students in higher education and were allocated 40% of federal work-study funds. Further, institutions in the West and South (where many Latinos enroll) received lower percentages of work-study allotment relative to their enrollment of students than the Mid-Atlantic and Northeast.

In the last 10 years, there has been a decrease of community college students participating in federal work-study, while there has been an increase of students at four-year institutions. Some community college administrators have stated that the process for participating in the program and the administrative costs for its implementation have constrained their ability to participate. Simplifying the regulations and requirements for participation may encourage more community colleges to participate and provide work-study aid to their students. In addition, more explicit targeting of the support to needy students may be necessary.

Notes

1. The terms *Hispanic* and *Latino* are used interchangeably throughout the chapter.
2. To be eligible for the "Developing HSIs Program," the law further requires that an HSI have a high enrollment of needy students and low educational and general expenditures.

References

Aud, S., Hussar, W., Kena, G., Bianco, K., Frohlich, L., Kemp, J., & Tahan, K. (2011). *The condition of education 2011* (NCES 2011-033). Table A-6-2. Washington, DC: U.S. Department of Education, National Center for Education Statistics.

Carnevale, A. P., Smith, N., & Strohl, J. (2013). *Recovery: Job growth and education requirements through 2020*. Washington, DC: Center on Education and the Workforce, Georgetown University. Retrieved from https://cew.georgetown.edu/wp-content/uploads/2014/11/Recovery2020.FR_.Web_.pdf

College Board. (2013). *Trends in student aid 2013*, Figures 8A and 8B. Retrieved from http://trends.collegeboard.org/sites/default/files/student-aid-2013-full-report-140108.pdf

Excelencia in Education. (2013). *Hispanic serving institutions 2012–13*. Retrieved from http://www.edexcelencia.org/hsi-cp2/research/hispanic-serving-institutions-2012-13

Excelencia in Education. (2014, April). *Latino college completion: United States*. Retrieved from http://www.edexcelencia.org/research/college-completion/united-states

Ginder, S., Kelly-Reid, J., & Mann, F. (2014). *2013–14 Integrated Postsecondary Education Data System (IPEDS) methodology report*. Washington, DC: U.S. Department of Education, National Center for Education Statistics. Retrieved from http://nces.ed.gov/pubs2014/2014067.pdf

Immerwahr, J. (2004). *Public attitudes on higher education: A trend analysis, 1993 to 2003*. New York, NY: Public Agenda and the National Center for Public

Policy and Higher Education. Retrieved from http://www.publicagenda.org/files/public_attitudes_on_higher_education.pdf_

Immerwahr, J., & Johnson, J. (2007). *Squeeze play: How parents and the public look at higher education today*. National Center Report #07-4. San José, CA: National Center for Public Policy and Higher Education. Retrieved from http://www.highereducation.org/reports/squeeze_play/squeeze_play.pdf

National Center for Education Statistics. (2013, December). *2011–12 National postsecondary student aid study (NPSAS: 12): Price estimates for attending postsecondary education institutions—first look*. Washington, DC: U.S. Department of Education, Institute of Education Sciences. Retrieved from http://nces.ed.gov/pubs2014/2014166.pdf

Pew Research Center. (2012). *Unauthorized immigrants in the U.S.* Washington, DC: Author. Retrieved from http://www.pewhispanic.org/interactives/unauthorized-immigrants-2012/

Santiago, D. (2007). *Voces (Voices): A profile of today's Latino college students*. Washington, DC: Excelencia in Education.

Santiago, D. (2010). *Ensuring America's future: Benchmarking Latino college completion to meet national goals: 2010–2020*. San Jose, CA: National Center for Public Policy and Higher Education. Retrieved from http://www.uky.edu/ie/sites/www.uky.edu.ie/files/uploads/ACC_Ensuring%20Americas%20Future%20Benchmarking%20Latino%20College%20Completion%20.%20.%20.pdf

Santiago, D. (2012). *Using a Latino lens to reimagine aid design and delivery*. Washington, DC: Excelencia in Education. Retrieved from http://www.sheeo.org/sites/default/files/publications/6_excelencia_latinolens_whitepaperfeb2013.pdf

Santiago, D., Calderon Galdeano, E., & Taylor, M. (2015). *The condition of Latinos in education: 2015 factbook*. Washington, DC: Excelencia in Education. Retrieved from http://www.edexcelencia.org/research/2015-factbook

Snyder, T. D., & Dillow, S. A. (2015). *Digest of education statistics 2013*. Table 306.20. Washington, DC: U.S. Department of Education. Retrieved from http://nces.ed.gov/pubs2015/2015011.pdf

U.S. Census Bureau. (2004). *Current population survey, annual social and economic supplement, 2004*. Retrieved from https://www.census.gov/hhes/www/poverty/publications/pubs-cps.html

U.S. Census Bureau. (2012). *Current population survey, annual social and economic supplement, 2012*. Retrieved from https://www.census.gov/hhes/www/poverty/publications/pubs- cps.html

U.S. Census Bureau. (2013). *Current population survey, annual social and economic supplement, 2013*. Retrieved from https://www.census.gov/hhes/www/poverty/publications/pubs-cps.html

U.S. Department of Education. (2013). *Postsecondary institutions and cost of attendance in 2013–14; degrees and other awards conferred, 2012–13; and 12-month enrollment, 2012–13*, Table 3. Washington, DC: National Center for Educational Statistics. Retrieved from http://nces.ed.gov/pubs2014/2014066.pdf

5

VOICE OF THE NATIONAL LEADER

Equal Opportunity for All Students: Are We There Yet?

Maria Harper-Marinick

Equal opportunity for all persons, to the maximum of their individual abilities and without regard to economic status, race, creed, color, sex, national origin, or ancestry is a major goal of American democracy. Only an informed, thoughtful, tolerant people can develop and maintain a free society.

—President's Commission on Higher Education, 1947

The quote from the President's Commission on Higher Education appointed by President Truman to examine the functions of higher education in our democracy has always resonated with me. I believe the findings of the commission are as relevant today as they were in 1947, especially the focus placed on access, equity, and democracy. According to the authors of the report, the role of education is to ensure equal opportunity for all individuals so that access is not a function of the family and community into which individuals are born or the color of their skin. Community colleges were identified as the institutions of postsecondary education better suited to deliver the promise of equal opportunity, and that is still the mission today of the more than 1,000 community colleges in our nation.

I have been part of the Maricopa Community Colleges in Arizona for over 20 years and have served in a senior leadership role for almost a decade. I have responsibility for all academic and student support areas as well as institutional research and effectiveness, so I am very familiar with the demographics of our students, retention and success rates, and issues impacting Latino students in community colleges. On an annual basis, our system of 10 colleges serves about 230,000 credited students; 27% identify themselves as Hispanic. Even though I believe we should continue to improve our recruitment and retention efforts, we have seen increases in the number of Latinos attending our colleges and in all measures of college success. I am involved in college and career readiness work at the state and national levels and with national organizations whose goals are to create dialogue about what matters most regarding Latino education; to support research and data analysis about student engagement and success; and to promote social justice, inclusion, and equality.

I believe that the educational issues affecting our Latinos and Latinas should be everyone's concern. Many reports have been published highlighting the problems. In some cases, these reports include very compelling data about demographic shifts and trends and the state of Latino education. The issues seem to be clear: the number of Latinos in the United States has grown steadily for the last decade and is projected to continue to grow, and yet not enough Latinos are graduating from high school, entering higher education, and attaining college degrees. What is less clear is whether or not there is an understanding of the consequences of maintaining the status quo. At risk is the economic prosperity of our nation. As stated in the Truman Commission report, "Only an informed, thoughtful, tolerant people can develop and maintain a free society" (President's Commission for Higher Education, 1947, p. 3); and I add that only those with the ability to think critically will be truly engaged citizens; only those with an education beyond high school will prosper and benefit from social mobility. Community colleges will continue to be the institutions that provide affordable access to all individuals, and those of us who work in community colleges have a responsibility to make courageous decisions about institutional policies and practices that, without compromising access, help all students to achieve success. Doing nothing, waiting for the "problem" to go away, is not the responsible choice. As Martin Luther King Jr. said, "Our lives begin to end the day we become silent about things that matter" (Good Reads, 2016).

What We Know

Latinos are the fastest growing group in the United States, and not solely because of immigration growth. In many states, Latinos are the increasing majority in the K–12 education system; and in some states, like Arizona, more than 90% of the Latinos in grades K through 6 were born in the United States. Student performance continues to improve even though ethnic and racial gaps still exist in regard to attainment. According to the Pew Research Center (Krogstad & Fry, 2014), in 2012 young Latinos were less likely to drop out of high school and more likely to graduate from high school than they were in 2000; Latinos have increased their college-going rate immediately after graduating from high school—69% of the graduating class of 2012 was enrolled in college in the fall of 2012.

While the performance data are promising and we celebrate that more Latinos are going to college, we still have much work to do to improve college completion rates of our students, which remain lower than those of other groups. Only 37% of Latino high school completers between the ages of 18 and 24 are enrolled in college, compared to 40% of Black and 49% of White. In 2012, only 20% of Hispanic adults had earned at least an associate degree, compared with 36% of all adults. Inarguably, 20% is not an acceptable rate when we know that the majority of the jobs that pay a livable wage require a postsecondary credential. According to a report commissioned by the American Association of Community Colleges (2012), the primary advocacy organization for the nation's community colleges, "What we find today are student success rates that are unacceptably low, employment preparation that is inadequately connected to job market needs and disconnects in transitions between high schools, community colleges, and baccalaureate institutions" (p. viii). For our communities to prosper, we need more Latinos completing high school and earning a college degree. We are especially anxious for Latinos to earn undergraduate degrees in science, technology, engineering, and mathematics (STEM) fields where most high-wage jobs will be available.

Access to all postsecondary institutions has increased, but not equally at all institutions. Latinos are underrepresented in four-year institutions, especially in the more selective institutions. Yet they are well represented in two-year public institutions, where currently about 56% of Latino undergraduate students enroll. Community colleges are the institutions of choice for many Latinos; and for some, that is the only option to transition into postsecondary education. Latinos are attending community colleges for a variety of reasons: affordable tuition, proximity to home and family, flexibility in the schedule and instructional delivery, and breadth of curriculum and program offerings. Community colleges offer transfer pathways to universities; occupational programs for work skills development and career enhancement; adult basic education; and evening, weekend, and online courses. As previously stated, with open-access policies and low tuition rates, community colleges are sometimes the only choice some individuals have to access higher education. Community colleges can be the gateway to new and better opportunities.

The challenge that community college leaders face and struggle to change is the low retention and completion rates of many students who attend community colleges, especially our Latino and African American males. While about 80% of those entering community college as first-time college students say they plan to earn at least a bachelor's degree, only about 12% actually do so within 6 years (Century Foundation, 2013). Outcomes are not much different for highly qualified students from low-income families: 69% of those students who began at four-year institutions earned a bachelor's degree compared with just 19% of those who started in a community college (Haycock, 2010).

We want to and must help a greater proportion of students attain their goals to complete an associate degree and/or transfer to a baccalaureate-granting institution to increase their chances to obtain a job with good to high wages. The reality is that more than half of all students who begin at two-year institutions do not achieve a postsecondary degree. Almost half of all first-time community college students are not enrolled in any institution and have not received a degree or certificate six years after getting started. Close to half of Latinos in community colleges do not transfer to a four-year institution. The persistence, completion, and transfer rates of Latinos are among the lowest. My comments are not intended to place blame on or give undue criticism to community colleges; many institutions are doing what they can with the resources available, and some have had great success with initiatives designed specifically to support Latinos. However, I believe that we have a moral responsibility to fully understand why our Latino students do not have equal access to more selective institutions, why they are not completing high school and college at the same rate as other groups, and why they are overrepresented in remedial courses, which are community college courses designed to teach students the basic skills they should have learned in high school. We must find multiple solutions to what is without a question a complex problem.

Why We Should Care

The success of Latinos is essential to our nation's social and economic prosperity. If we are to achieve President Obama's goal of having, by 2020, the highest proportion of college graduates in the world, we must increase substantially the number of Latinos who graduate from high school and successfully attain a college degree or credential. "For the US to regain the top ranking in the world for college and degree attainment, Latinos will need to earn 5.5 million more degrees by 2020" (Santiago & Galdeano, 2014).

The agenda is not about promoting a single ethnic group; it is not about politics or ideology; it is not even just about education for its own sake. It is about maintaining a strong democratic society and developing a robust national economy. "Lower levels of educational attainment constitute a serious impediment to the future prosperity of all residents regardless of their views on immigration, public education, or on the proper role of government in society" (Hart & Hager, 2012, p. 10). We know that education matters and that low educational achievement often correlates with low earning. Low earning means less purchasing power, less investment in the community, lower tax revenues, and greater reliance on public services and benefits.

Over the next decade, jobs requiring education and training beyond high school will grow faster than those that do not. It has been predicted that there will be 55 million job openings in the economy through 2020 and about 65% of them will require some level of postsecondary education (Center on Education and the Workforce, 2013). We need an educated population that can perform the highly skilled, better-paying jobs of the new economy. We want Latinos to have the preparation and capacity to perform in jobs that will pay higher wages to support their families and enhance the quality of their lives. We want our young Latinos to be ready to take an active role in the community and participate fully in government, business, education, or whatever path they choose. The conditions under which they are born should not determine who they have the potential to become. But unless we do something differently to make sure more Latinos are graduating from high school and college, these jobs will be out of reach. "At the very moment that our knowledge economy demands far more highly educated workers than are currently being produced, our institutions of higher education are letting the fastest growing part of the population fall dramatically behind" (Guttierez, 2011, p. 19).

What Are the Realities for Latino Students?

First-generation college students face significant challenges from the moment they start at a community college, even if they have the capacity and aspirations to complete a degree and the motivation to do so, and the situation is not different for Latinos. They may come from disadvantaged families and lack the resources and support to attend college; they may not have the academic preparation to succeed in higher education; they may have to deal with competing life priorities such as holding full-time jobs and providing financially for their families; or they may have limited English language proficiency.

The gaps in academic achievement do not manifest themselves just when students enroll in college; they begin in the earlier grades of the educational pipeline for low-income students who may not have had access to early childhood education and support services, who most likely attended schools with inadequate resources, who did not have access to or were not encouraged to take honors and Advanced Placement (AP) courses, and who were not advised to consider attending college as the pathway to a job or career.

Not all Latino students face these challenges, however, so we should avoid generalizing, stigmatizing, or blaming the students or their families. We should not think of these conditions as either destiny or insurmountable barriers; they are just a reality that may prevent students from engaging fully in college life. Given the appropriate conditions for learning and adequate support, Latinos do have the potential to succeed as much as any other group. They have the same aspirations: to have an education and improve their quality of life.

Academic Preparation

Even though the high school graduation rate of Latinos has increased, as have college participation rates, Latinos often begin college with lower levels of college readiness and are overrepresented in remedial courses, which is concerning. Lack of readiness for college courses has been correlated with low completion rates. A high percentage, about 60%, of students entering community colleges have test scores that place them in one or more remedial courses in three disciplines: English, mathematics, and reading. These students are deemed not to be ready for college-level course work because of placement scores and are required to take remedial courses that are known in most community colleges as developmental education courses, which are designed to help academically underprepared students gain the skills necessary to successfully complete college-level courses. These courses are offered primarily at community colleges, and more often than not, they are not free. They are credit courses that cost the students the same tuition as college-level courses, yet they are not transferable or applicable to a degree at the community college or a university. Students who are not ready for college-level courses will need to invest money—including their financial aid—and time to take the required remedial courses. These courses can be gatekeepers that prevent students from moving on and persisting in college. The more remedial courses students need to take, the less likely it is that they will stay in college through the completion of a degree. If students are immigrants for whom English is a second language, then they will be required to take English as a second language (ESL) classes in addition to the remedial courses.

The question we must ask is, why are so many of our entering Latino students placed in remedial courses? Are they just not as prepared and ready for college work as other students? Is their academic experience in high school vastly different? Are they influenced by the low expectations we have had of them in school? Is it test bias? Is it poor advising? Is it the language spoken at home? If we know the answers, the questions for leaders then are: What are we going to do differently to change the outcomes? How will we use existing data and reports on effective practices to redesign our institutions, to invest in innovative practices, and to provide incentives for success and not just access?

Access and Affordability

A high-achieving, low-income student has about the same statistical chance of going to college as does a low-achieving high-income student. Almost 25% of low-income students who score in the top quartile of standardized tests never go to college. And of those who do, many never earn a degree. (Merisotis, 2014, p. 1)

Although there are many factors that affect college attendance and success, without question a major barrier is cost of attendance. Tuition at public and private institutions, two- and four-year, continues to increase. Students from high-income families have a greater probability not only of going to college but also of graduating (Tough, 2014). Students from low-income families, as are many Latinos, are less likely to enroll in college and stay enrolled until completion of a degree. For many families, the cost of attendance determines where students can and will go, which makes access to higher education not as equitable as it should be. More than six decades after the Truman Commission report, *Higher Education for American Democracy,* was issued, our nation continues to "deprive itself of a vast pool of potential leaders and socially competent citizens by allowing access based on economic status to be perpetuated" (President's Commission for Higher Education, 1947). Access to a high-quality college education is still too dependent on family income and social circumstances.

Given the high cost of attending college, it should not be surprising that Latino students from low-income backgrounds are less likely to stay enrolled in college, attend full-time, and complete a degree. We know that attending college full-time makes a positive difference in course completion, persistence, transfer, and completion of degrees. Students who attend community colleges full-time succeed in all measures at a much higher rate than those who attend part-time. I believe that if all students could afford to attend college full-time, they would. Unfortunately, for many of our Latino students this is not feasible. Some have to work more than 20 hours a week to support their family and pay for their college expenses. They may not be eligible for financial aid, grants, or institutional scholarships and may be reluctant to take a loan. Working an excessive number of hours while attending college affects students' ability to perform well and make progress toward the completion of a degree.

Many low-income families do not have enough information about what financial resources exist that could help their family members pay for college. Some find federal student-aid documents complicated and intimidating; some may not be aware of institutional grants and scholarships. According to a report of the Advisory Committee on Student Financial Assistance (2008), "millions of community college students who appear to be eligible for need-based financial aid are not applying for aid. Some think they are not eligible for financial aid and some find the application form too complex" (p. 7).

It should be the responsibility and obligation of the institutions of higher education, working with social services and governmental agencies, to ensure that financial barriers do not prevent our Latino students from accessing the opportunity for a college education.

Pathways to Success

In 2009, President Obama asked "every American to commit to at least one year or more of higher education or career training. This can be community college, a four-year school, vocational training, or apprenticeship. But whatever the training may be, every American will need to get more than a high school diploma" (Obama, 2009). In the next decade, jobs requiring post–high school education and training will grow more rapidly than jobs that require only a high school diploma or less. A high school diploma, while necessary, is not sufficient anymore; jobs in high-demand, high-paying fields will require, at minimum, an associate degree or vocational certification. This message needs to be communicated to our Latino students and their families. It is critical they understand that with a strong educational foundation and a college credential, they will have more and perhaps better options for employment. Education is indeed the foundation for social mobility and economic progress; and we should demand high-quality education for our Latino students.

A school culture of high expectations for all students, including Latinos, should be the norm. Our Latino students need to believe that they are as capable as other students of doing good work; that their choices for a career or profession are limited only by their interest and abilities; that going to college is not out of reach. Intended or unintended messages to the contrary are unacceptable. Our schools should be counseling students about all the opportunities that could be available in academic or vocational programs, starting with the courses students take in high school. A rigorous, relevant, and broad curriculum should prepare the students for college and career and lead to multiple pathways, including vocational certifications, associate degrees, and/or bachelor's degrees. The choice should be made by the student and his/her family, and not predetermined by the courses students are advised to take. While vocational certifications or degrees will lead to gainful employment, students should be encouraged to broaden their focus and aspire to complete a bachelor's degree. And to facilitate the transition, we must improve the articulation between community colleges and universities. Transfer rates for Latinos continue to be a challenge in many states. However, it is of critical importance to ensure that the pathways from community college to baccalaureate-granting institution are designed to be efficient, seamless, and cost-effective and allow for maximum applicability of credits.

What Is Next?

Inarguably, the economic prosperity of our nation and the preservation of democratic principles we value will depend on what we do to ensure that a larger number of Latinos, especially those in low-income households, have access to high-quality educational opportunities beginning in preschool and continuing through college. It is our collective responsibility to ensure that our students receive the academic foundation and support services that will help them be ready for college-level work and then enter the workplace in jobs that pay at minimum a livable and decent wage. All levels of our educational systems, social services agencies, and governments need to work together to remove barriers and make it less burdensome for Latino students to attain a college degree or certificate. We need to fully address the achievement gaps that exist and "acknowledge that systematic disparities in opportunity and privilege characterize the lives and educational experiences of people of color" (Center for Community College Student Engagement,, 2014, p. 30).

Those of us who work in community colleges perhaps cannot solve all or most of the problems affecting the Latino students, but there is much we can do to provide a safe and supportive environment conducive to learning and personal development. We can implement strategic initiatives, based on research and proven effective practices, that we know work for all students and some that may be especially beneficial to Latino students. We must start by sharing information with the community about the opportunities that exist and raising awareness of the value of a college education. The community should demand that all students get the best education possible. Educational practices matter. Environments matter. Expectations matter. Following is a list of specific recommendations that leaders should consider implementing at the institutional level:

1. **Strengthen partnerships between high schools and community colleges to establish a college-going culture.**
   a. Communicate to students and families what the college-readiness standards are and why we have high expectations for *all students*.
   b. Offer access to early college experiences (e.g., dual or concurrent enrollment).
   c. Offer early placement assessment and remediation courses while students are still in high school at no cost to students and their families (e.g., after-school and summer bridge programs).
   d. Encourage all students to enroll in college immediately after completing high school.
2. **Improve access to and information about financial support.**
   a. Communicate increased federal aid eligibility widely and effectively.
   b. Make applying for financial assistance and scholarships easier.
3. **Make student retention and successful attainment of goals the focus of institutional policies and practices.**
   a. Require orientation, advising, college success courses, and establishment of a program of study for degree-seeking students.
   b. Offer flexible schedules and structure programs to encourage completion of shorter-term, stackable credentials along the pathway to completion of degrees.
   c. Establish an environment of high expectations, engagement, and strong personal connections.
   d. Create multicultural centers and Latino studies centers.
4. **Work with business partners to offer opportunities for work experience while in college (e.g., internships and externships).**
5. **Establish clear, effective, and efficient transfer pathways between community colleges and baccalaureate-granting institutions.**
   a. Develop articulation agreements that maximize the transferability of courses and applicability of credits.
   b. Provide easy access to comprehensive information about program options, cost, and potential financial assistance.
   c. Have dedicated advisers that can work with students and their families.

Someone asked me not too long ago what I think about when I go to work in the morning. It didn't take long to find the answer. I am grateful for the opportunities I have had to live a full, productive, and engaged life, and I think of how many people in my community may not have had the same opportunities. I feel empathy for those who struggle every day to provide a meal, a house, and education for their family because of the circumstances surrounding their lives. I hope for a day when all people are treated fairly and equitably regardless of where they come from, what they look like, or how they sound; when all people have access to quality public education; when all people can engage in learning and develop to their full potential. And in many ways, this is precisely why community colleges were founded and why I have chosen a life of service in a community college system.

References

Advisory Committee on Student Financial Assistance. (2008, September). *Apply to succeed: Ensuring community college students benefit from need-based financial aid.* Retrieved from http://files.eric.ed.gov/fulltext/ED502886.pdf

American Association of Community Colleges. (2012). *Reclaiming the American Dream: Community colleges and the nation's future.* A report of the 21st-Century Commission on the Future of Community Colleges. Washington, DC: Author. Retrieved from http://www.aacc.nche.edu/21stCenturyReport

Center for Community College Student Engagement. (2014). *Aspirations to achievement: Men of color and community colleges.* Retrieved from http://www.ccsse.org/docs/MOC_Special_Report.pdf

Center on Education and the Workforce. (2013). *Recovery: Job growth and education requirements through 2020.* Washington, DC: Georgetown University, Center on Education and the Workforce. Retrieved from https://cew.georgetown.edu/recovery2020

Century Foundation. (2013, April). *Bridging the higher education divide: Strengthening community colleges and restoring the American Dream.* New York: Author. Retrieved from http://tcf.org/assets/downloads/20130523-Bridging_the_Higher_Education_Divide-REPORT-ONLY.pdf

Good Reads. (2016). Martin Luther King, Jr. quotes. Retrieved from http://www.goodreads.com/quotes/6407-our-lives-begin-to-end-the-day-we-become-silent

Gutierrez, R. A. (2011). "The promise of our democracy." In Association of American Colleges and Universities, *The drama of diversity and democracy: Higher education and American commitments* (pp. xiii–xxi). Washington, DC: Association of American Colleges and Universities. Retrieved from http://www.aacu.org/sites/default/files/files/publications/DramaofDiversity_2011.pdf

Hart, B., & Hager, C. J. E. (2012). *Dropped? Latino education and Arizona's economic future.* Tempe, AZ: Morrison Institute for Public Policy, Arizona State University. Retrieved from http://pipertrust.org/wp-content/uploads/_my_publications_pdf/4847-a8027bf2.pdf

Haycock, K. (2010, April 7). Community colleges are not a silver bullet for closing completion gap. *Higher Ed Watch*. Retrieved from http://higheredwatch
.newamerica.net/blogposts/2010/guest_post_community_colleges_are_not_a_
silver_bullet_for_closing_our_completion_gap-

Krogstad, J. M., & Fry, R. (2014, April 24). *More Hispanics, Blacks enrolling in college, but lag in bachelor's degrees*. Washington, DC: Pew Research Center. Retrieved
from http://www.pewresearch.org/fact-tank/2014/04/24/more-hispanics-blacks-
enrolling-in-college-but-lag-in-bachelors-degrees/

Merisotis, J. P. (2014, Spring). *Focus*. Lumina Foundation. Retrieved from http://
focus.luminafoundation.org/spring2014/

Obama, Barack. (2009, February 14). *Remarks as prepared for delivery dddress to joint
session of Congress*. Retrieved from http://www.whitehouse.gov/the_press_office/
Remarks-of-President-Barack-Obama-Address-to-Joint-Session-of-Congress

President's Commission on Higher Education. (1947). *Higher education for American democracy*, Vol. 2, *Equalizing and expanding individual opportunity*. Retrieved
from http://babel.hathitrust.org/cgi/pt?id=mdp.39015082042329;view=1up;seq=8

Santiago, D. A., & Galdeano, E. C. (2014). *Latino college completion: United States*.
Washington, DC: Excelencia in Education. Retrieved from http://www.edex
celencia.org/research/college-completion/united-states

Tough, P. (2014, May 15). Who gets to graduate? *New York Times Magazine*. Retrieved
from http://www.nytimes.com/2014/05/18/magazine/who-gets-to-graduate.html

6

CUTTING-EDGE MODELS FOR BEST PRACTICE

"I Do Belong": Cultivating Hispanic and Low-Income Student Success

Eduardo J. Padrón

The ultimate goal of the educational system is to shift to the individual the burden of pursuing his education.

—John W. Gardner

In 1960, Miami meant tourists. The region's economy thrived on sun and sand, drawing Americans from every corner of the country. Families took their precious vacation days on Miami Beach, retirees escaped the winter forever, and college students stormed the beaches in the spring.

These traditions have endured and even flourished, but they take place in a Miami that 1960 offered little hint of at the time. Fidel Castro's forces rolled into Havana on New Year's Day in 1959, launching one of the more prolific immigration sagas in U.S. history. In the year that followed, 50,000 Cubans arrived in Miami, setting in motion a stunning demographic makeover of an iconic American city. By 1962, 1,500 to 2,000 Cuban refugees were landing in Miami each week, and by 1970, Miami-Dade County had been transformed. A community of 80% non-Hispanic Whites had become 45% Hispanic, 32% White, and 23% African American (University of Miami Cuban Heritage Collection, 1978). Today, the county is nearly 66% Hispanic, including not only Cubans but also transplants from every country in Central and South America. The once-prevailing White population is a mere 15% of the total, with African Americans at 19% (U.S. Census, 2012).

I was among the multitudes in 1962, one of nearly 15,000 children who departed Cuba through Operation Pedro Pan. I was equipped with fervent instructions from my mother to gain a college education in America. I learned math and science and social studies at Miami High as I learned English. Following instructions, I applied to Harvard, Princeton, and several other elite schools, but when the returns were in, I had one acceptance: the local community college then known as Dade County Junior College (Dade Junior).

Dade Junior opened its doors in 1960, just months after the first wave of Cuban arrivals. The inaugural class of 1,428 students reflected the beginnings of what has become the most diverse student population in the nation. It included seven Black students, making Dade Junior the first integrated junior college in Florida and the first integrated public college in the old Confederacy (Miami-Dade Community College [MDCC], 1988). For the many Cubans seeking a foothold in very foreign surroundings, the college became a second home. For most students, it was the only option because of English language competency, affordability, and the college's location, allowing families to maintain close connections. In the early years, the lingering notion of returning to Cuba was also motivation for families to keep their college-going children close.

Dade Junior marked the first appearance of public higher education in South Florida. The Cuban influx, combined with needs of the homegrown population, created phenomenal growth. By 1964, enrollment had swelled to 13,000, and by 1967, the college was the largest college or university in the state, with more than 23,000 students. It was the fastest growing junior college in the nation, enrolling more freshmen than the University of Florida, Florida State University, and the University of South Florida combined (MDCC, 1988).

Today, Miami Dade College (MDC) is the largest public college or university in the nation, enrolling 170,000 students at seven campuses and several outreach centers. MDC's Virtual College accounts for more than 13,000 of the total enrollment via online and blended courses.

One of MDC's locations is the InterAmerican Campus (IAC), located in the heart of Miami's Little Havana neighborhood. Today, IAC offers students the full range of degree and short-term options and is the home campus for MDC's School of Education. The bachelor of science in education prepares teachers for secondary math and science as well as K–12 exceptional education. But IAC began as a bilingual outreach center of MDC's downtown Wolfson Campus. By 1980, it was the largest bilingual facility in all of higher education, just in time to accommodate the latest wave of immigrants via the Mariel boat lift.

The college's diversity has long been a defining characteristic. Today, students from 180 countries, speaking 90 languages, bring the world's cultures and viewpoints to our classrooms and campuses. Students of Hispanic origin make up more than 70% of the total, and while students with roots in Cuba remain a dominant aspect of the college's makeup, all the countries in Central and South America are now represented. Among these and other students with international origins, 29% overall are not U.S. citizens. The remaining students are 17.6% African American and 7% White.

The Challenge of Poverty: Its Impact on Student Success

The aspects of the MDC demographic that pose the greatest challenge to student success are well beyond national origins. As community college educators know too well, the core of the challenge is nothing other than poverty, a tenacious root element with branches that further complicate the lives of students. At MDC, 67% of students are classified as low income, and 46% live beneath the federal poverty guideline (Miami Dade College Institutional Research, 2014). Exit polls performed by the college on each departing student confirm financial need as the overwhelming reason.

Those branches of poverty extend into nearly every corner of a student's life and ultimately weigh on the ability to succeed in college. Sixty-two percent of MDC students attend part-time, and 70% work while in school, with nearly 30% working at least 35 hours per week (Miami Dade College Institutional Research, 2014). Those are hours that cannot be spent studying or, just as important, being on campus in connection with other students, faculty, and staff.

Other factors also contribute to the student success challenge. Most of our students—72% as of 2013—enroll at MDC in need of at least one developmental course in basic skills of math, reading, writing, or English language. To make matters more difficult, the Florida legislature recently enacted legislation that allows students to enter college-level courses regardless of skill level. The same legislation prevents Florida colleges from assessing those levels for entering students. This experiment has just begun to play out, and addressing this hurdle is part of an overall strategy the college has implemented (see "Student Achievement Initiatives").

Lastly, and perhaps most telling of the generational stubbornness of poverty, 56% of MDC students are the first in their families to attend college. This statistic alone speaks to the significance of the community college mission and the supportive environment we're able to create for students.

Across the country, colleges are confronted by the most inveterate of societal stumbling blocks, and recent studies demonstrate the very un-American reality that prosperity and the fruits of the wealthiest nation on Earth depend on who your parents are and how much they earn. About a quarter of college freshmen born into the bottom half of the income distribution will earn a bachelor's degree by age 24, while almost 90% of freshmen from families in the top income quartile will complete their degree, according to the Georgetown Center on Education and the Workforce (Carnevale & Strohl, 2010). Factor in the recent study by economists from Harvard and University of California–Berkeley that indicates social mobility is no worse than it was in 1971 (Chetty, Hendren, Kline, & Saez, 2014). But that amounts to faint praise when the finding is combined with the widening gap between wealthy and low-income Americans. Stagnant mobility equates with another young generation hamstrung by the economic frustrations of their parents and grandparents.

Changing Student Attitudes That Limit Academic Success

For community college educators in classrooms and student support touch points, these circumstances translate well beyond demography and data. They have seeped into the attitudes that our students bring to campus. In too many instances, students harbor limits that become self-fulfilling, listening too closely to stories they tell to themselves, stories born amid the circumstances of their lives. For the community colleges that host these students—Hispanic, African American, White, and almost always poor—student success demands an embrace of the whole student. The formula is simple if demanding: rigorous standards, high expectations, and a support environment nothing short of extraordinary.

A 2014 article in the *New York Times Magazine* titled "Who Gets to Graduate?" (Tough, 2014) offered a poignant expression of the challenges these students and their colleges confront. The author recounted the work of education researchers at Stanford who began from a point of view familiar to what we at MDC have observed for years: that students fell short of their potential due to the presence of doubts about their ability. Further, the researchers found these feelings to be especially virulent at transition points that included the freshman year of college. And finally, such feelings were expressly problematic among students who might view themselves as having something to prove, which certainly includes low-income, first-generation students in a new cultural environment.

While the doubts varied for individuals, the researchers pointed to two primary stumbling blocks. Doubts about whether the students could ever truly belong at their institution collaborated with misgivings about their intelligence: they weren't smart enough for college. They believed in an "entity theory" of intelligence, as the researcher Carol Dweck named it; they had a fixed quantity of intelligence that wouldn't budge no matter how hard they studied.

While it may sound simplistic, much of what we do to assist students, both academically and via student support, is aimed at disabusing them of these two beliefs. Doubts amount to trip wires at the starting line, falsehoods that lower expectations, derail momentum, and reinforce a relentless cycle of poverty.

A Call for Completion: Reinventing Miami Dade College

Entering Miami Dade College's Wolfson Campus in downtown Miami, the first thing you see is the flags. They wind upward for five floors, encircling the central atrium. If you are a student from Cuba or Haiti or Guyana, or even Turkey or the Ivory Coast, you can find your flag any day of the week. These are the same flags that serve to ignite the several campus commencement ceremonies the first week of May. When "Pomp and Circumstance" concludes the processional, one by one, the flags of the graduates parade across the stage. The shouts and songs of the Pedro Pans, the Marielitas, the Haitians, the Colombians, and all the others are the declarations of long journeys fulfilled in an environment where they did belong, where they felt at home.

If lives are reinvented in this atmosphere, then surely the institution itself has set the precedent. MDC's history has been a series of reinventions, always seeking to confirm the axiom of "access with excellence." The early years opened the door to a new generation of American college students, including ever-growing numbers of Hispanic and Caribbean students. When classes began in 1960, the college presented a new alternative to the course work and standards of Florida's state universities. Programs offered broad choice and freedom to invent independent study.

From the very beginning, it was obvious that our students had significant needs. Language, culture, financial pressures, prior preparation, and the rigors of higher education combined to present enormous challenges to college completion. In the mid-1970s, the college had become host to many students who were inching along the completion path. Between 1975 and 1978, MDC initiated a college-wide review, underlined by the question of whether open access could be successfully combined with excellence and high standards. The result was a set of general education requirements in the arts and sciences for all students and a new Standards of Academic Progress, or SOAP, which held students to specific progress objectives.

Workforce innovations and partnerships with industry and regional economic development linked MDC, its faculty, and its students to workforce projections and jobs. In recent years, MDC's Learning Outcomes Project and Student Achievement Initiatives have intensified the focus on student success. And as rigor and academic expectations have been reinforced, the corresponding support mechanisms have grown alongside.

The Learning Outcomes Project

MDC began the Learning Outcomes Project in 2005. After much consideration, the faculty arrived at 10 college-wide outcomes to be infused into the preparation of all students, regardless of major or program. The 10 outcomes reflected a liberal learning agenda for the twenty-first century and a working definition of what it means to achieve a Miami Dade College education. The learning outcomes address competency as follows:

1. Communicate effectively using listening, speaking, reading, and writing skills.
2. Use quantitative analytical skills to evaluate and process numerical data.
3. Solve problems using critical and creative thinking and scientific reasoning.
4. Formulate strategies to locate, evaluate, and apply information.
5. Demonstrate knowledge of diverse cultures, including global and historical perspectives.
6. Create strategies that can be used to fulfill personal, civic, and social responsibilities.
7. Demonstrate knowledge of ethical thinking and its application to issues in society.
8. Use computer and emerging technologies effectively.
9. Demonstrate an appreciation for aesthetics and creative activities.
10. Describe how natural systems function and recognize the impact of humans on the environment.

The Learning Outcomes Project also includes two essential components of assessment and mapping. Faculty have crafted real-world, scenario-based assessments that call on students to exercise several competencies. The mapping project employs an intricate evaluation of the more than 2,000 MDC courses for the presence and depth of each learning outcome. Together, assessment and mapping allow the disciplines and programs to gauge student success and adjust curriculum and cocurricular activities.

The paragraphs that follow offer a range of targeted programs that address the completion gap for Hispanics in particular. But other factors that serve as an underpinning to the college environment have a pervasive impact on student success for Hispanics as well as all our students.

Student Achievement Initiatives

According to the accumulated data, both national and in Miami-Dade County, Hispanics of all origins are playing catch up in regard to educational achievement. The collection of targeted programs at MDC is certainly responsive to these data, but a much grander approach exists because of the special circumstances that have evolved in South Florida and at MDC. The second decade of the twenty-first century in Miami is host to the early years of a fourth Hispanic generation. Cubans and other Hispanics have both embraced and transformed the America they found in this community. They are the new majority of the Miami they discovered.

Hispanic Access to College Education Resources (HACER), Si Puedo, the National Science Foundation (NSF) STEM project, and several additional targeted Hispanic programs afford much-needed attention. All of these projects fall within the larger Student Achievement Initiatives (SAI) and borrow many of the holistic approaches that are, once again, reinventing the student experience at MDC. Initiated in 2010, with a grant from the Completion by Design initiative of the Bill and Melinda Gates Foundation, SAI has evolved as the college's most ambitious effort to embrace the totality of student need while also aiming to address individual students' academic paths and personal barriers to completion.

MDC's SAI and HACER reflect the college's belief in the value of following each student's progress very closely, in effect, assuming an intrusive posture toward student success. And of course, our efforts seek to scale and coalesce all the impressive small projects that have brought success to various handfuls of students.

Hispanic Access to College Education Resources

While Hispanics represent the mainstream of students at MDC and benefit from the college's overall success strategies, specific initiatives have taken aim at Hispanics' historical deficits in college success. Today, just 61% of Hispanics in Miami-Dade County have a high school diploma, and 38% hold a post–high school degree. But just 22% have completed a bachelor's degree, compared to 45% of non-Hispanic Whites.

Miami-Dade County Public Schools (M-DCPS) is the nation's fourth largest public school system, with more than 350,000 students, 65% of whom are Hispanic. MDC has partnered with M-DCPS since its inception to establish a feeder system for high schools to MDC's several locations, as well as Summer Bridge and other college preparatory programs. MDC enrolls just over 47% of all M-DCPS graduates (Miami Dade College Institutional Research, 2014), and 76% of those graduates who move on to colleges and universities in Florida (Florida Department of Education, 2012). MDC's enrollment of college-going students reflects the highest draw from the local public school system of any higher education institution in Florida.

HACER is a unique partnership in support of Hispanic students and their families that has evolved in recent years. It includes not only the public school system but also nonprofit and business participants. HACER is not only an acronym for this program but also the Spanish word for "to do." By engaging both students and families, the program addresses a thorough range of needs in support of college readiness. For Hispanic students and families, the notions of belonging and capability are still accompanied, albeit to a much lesser degree than in years past, by additional doubts about even the possibility of attending college and the ability to afford the costs.

The program originated with support from the Lumina Foundation, with the intention to create a more robust college-going culture for Hispanics in Miami-Dade County. The substantive goals of the project are to increase the number of Hispanic students who graduate from high school and are properly prepared for postsecondary studies and, ultimately, to increase the proportion of Hispanics who achieve high-quality college degrees or work-force certifications to 60% by the year 2025.

Partnerships are a central tenet of HACER. In addition to M-DCPS, 16 partners work with MDC across key sectors of the community:

- **Community-Based Organizations:** College Readiness Institute, College Summit, Education Fund, iMentor, Single Stop USA, and UAspire
- **Hispanic-Serving Organizations:** South Florida Hispanic Chamber of Commerce, Univision
- **Higher Education:** College Readiness Institute, Florida International University, Single Stop USA
- **Business:** Bank of America, Beacon Council, Greater Miami Chamber of Commerce, South Florida Hispanic Chamber of Commerce
- **Policymakers:** City of Miami, Miami-Dade County, Miami-Dade County District School Board

More than 100 events with six target high schools occurred during the 2012–2013 academic year. More than 9,000 students and parents participated in the activities.

- **Financial Aid Literacy Workshops:** More than 30 workshops were conducted at local area high schools to help guide students and parents through the financial aid processes while increasing awareness of resources and increasing college affordability.

- **Free Application for Federal Student Aid (FAFSA) Marathon Sessions:** With the prerequisite of the financial aid workshops, more than 100 marathon sessions have been conducted at local high schools to assist students in completing and submitting the FAFSA form. More than 1,000 students and parents were served during the 2013–2014 academic year.
- **HACER Website:** Launched to support South Florida students and their parents as they prepare for college, the site provides information and resources regarding access and college readiness via computer or smart phones.
- **Teacher Collaboration Professional Development Project:** Semester-long training with Miami-Dade County Public Schools offered professional development during the spring 2013-2 semester to 50 high school content area teachers (math, reading, and writing) to strengthen articulation and high-school-to-college curricula. Course shadowing and faculty-to-faculty exchanges were held to foster the alignment. In addition, M-DCPS and MDC staff collaborated to identify students' needs and challenges, articulate long-term student-centered instructional goals, and adopt responsive classroom pedagogies.

Additional HACER activities, in collaboration with the various partners, included academic tutoring and mentoring; college tours; student workshops on organization and time management, college awareness, and success planning; summer bridge programs; career planning workshops; and test prep boot camps.

SAI has taken aim at restructuring academic, social, and financial processes—in effect, the entire realm of student experience. This college-wide project has engaged hundreds of faculty and staff on design and implementation teams, with the purpose to make these processes as efficient as possible in regard to degree or certificate completion, while maintaining access and quality. MDC was the only single institution to gain the Gates Award, with the other three awards to cadres of several institutions in the same state. We are in the process of producing a model that can serve to advise other institutions throughout the country in regard to student completion and success.

Our planning seeks to improve the student experience according to how ready—or not—students might be for college. *One of the most salient points uncovered in our research is that students who complete at least half of their required course credits and 25% in their major area in their first year are twice as likely to finish their degree.* Clearly, we recognized the need to reinvent developmental education, shorten its duration, and help students to identify a major area of study and remain consistent with it over time. All of this and more needs to be accomplished at the level of quality demanded by the 2006 Learning Outcomes Project.

The following is a summary of further elements within SAI that span the entire student experience at MDC, from early outreach to graduation and continued education and workforce engagement.

- **Three-Tiered Coaching and Mentoring Model:**
  - *Pre-college advising* (PCA) in the 56 public high schools in Miami-Dade County, provides collaboration with high school staff and one-on-one work with MDC applicants. Through PCA, MDC is able to provide advising, career counseling, admissions, financial aid, and academic enrichment services during the high school senior year.
  - *Senior academic advisers* conduct *Shark Start orientations* and engage one-on-one with new students to help them register for classes and plot an individual education plan (IEP). They manage student caseloads and follow student progress from orientation through the 25% completion of major study benchmark.
  - *In academic coaching and mentoring,* staff and faculty team to guide students from the 25% benchmark to graduation. Staff and faculty are linked to students according to program and career aspirations.
- **Online Orientation:** Begins academic planning and financial aid applications. Includes *Shark Bites* video vignettes, MDC through the eyes of fellow students.
- **Shark Start Orientation:** Mandatory in-person orientation; students are required to register for classes. Includes introduction of assigned advisers, registration for classes, and completion of an IEP. A critical takeaway for students attending Shark Start is the opportunity to meet their assigned adviser in person. Students are then required to meet with an assigned senior adviser during their first semester in college for an in-depth discussion of the IEP, career options, review of the Student Success Inventory results, a noncognitive assessment, and available campus resources.
- **Developmental Education:** Modularized, accelerated, and co-curricular instruction, paired with in-class tutoring support, is the approach in math, reading, and writing. MDC and high school developmental education teachers work together on 12th-grade remediation courses.

- ***Shark Academy:*** Concentrated one-week enrichment option for students who are not college ready in math, reading, or composition. Since the inception of this program, over half of the participants improved their initial placement by at least one level, with 25% becoming college ready.
- ***Mathematics Support Model:*** Developmental math is the foremost stumbling block for underprepared students. The Academic Support Plan for MDC's gateway college-level math course was developed to build a more supportive learning environment to serve students at varying skill levels. A learning assistant is assigned to each section of the course, coordinating review sessions and providing one-on-one and small group support. Online supplemental support is also made available to students using a combination of monitored assignments and pretest review sessions.
- ***Integrated Planning and Advising Services (IPAS):*** Suite of integrated Web-based platforms support case management; document campus engagement; and provide data collection and student dashboards. Platforms enable risk targeting and intervention, counseling and coaching, and education planning.
- ***MDC Single Stop:*** MDC's partnership with Single Stop USA provides students access to an online platform that assesses eligibility for the full range of federal and state benefits. Over three years, more than 25,000 students and their families have accessed more than $28 million in benefits and services, including tax preparation, legal, and financial counseling. Development of a self-screener platform offers potential to expand reach to all incoming students.
- ***Case Management:*** The reality at MDC, long committed to open enrollment, is that the college will never have enough advisers to effectively relate face-to-face with each student. But technology solutions can be employed to help advisers prioritize and focus their energies where need is apparent. The system will allow advisers to set early alerts and updates in a student's profile and maintain a real-time inventory of student progress, challenges, and accomplishments in academics, campus engagement, financial aid needs, and more.
- ***Student Success Inventory (SSI):*** A range of noncognitive elements, including motivation, academic discipline, and social engagement are the focus, with predictive indexes for achieving a 2.0 GPA and a student's return for year two. Results appear on student's dashboard.
- ***Academic Pathways:*** Thirty-three sequential pathways providing advisers essential tools to help students clarify choices, chart a path, and avoid excess credits.

- *Communities of Interest (COI):* COIs aim to provide students with a surrounding academic and personal support milieu based on major area of study. Financial aid, academic support, faculty mentors, special events, and speakers offer a ready community for each student.
- *Focus 2 Career Assessment:* Self-paced, online, interactive career and education planning system to explore occupations and career planning maps.

Progress Report

Two years into the implementation of SAI and HACER, the student experience at MDC is changing. Results suggest that the college is not only seeing results from the various program and support elements but also observing the beginnings of scaling these programs to affect significant numbers of students and data-based success. The following captures several of the progress indicators (Miami Dade College Institutional Research, 2014):

- More than 30 financial aid literacy workshops were held at local high schools for students and parents.
- More than 100 FAFSA Marathon sessions were held at local high schools, and more than 1,000 students and parents were served during the 2013–2014 academic year.
- Pre-college advisers and multiple outreach efforts resulted in an increase in the on-time graduation rate of approximately 10.8% in Miami-Dade County Public Schools, up from 23,125 in 2011–2012 to 25,622 in 2012–2013.
- Enrollment from high schools with MDC pre-college advisers increased by 14% over the previous year.
- Mandatory in-person orientations (Shark Starts) have welcomed more than 20,000 first-time-in-college direct-entry-from-high-school students over a two-year period. Such orientations have been enhanced by an online, self-paced component.
- All students who attended the mandatory Shark Start orientations have been assigned a student services adviser. Fall-to-spring retention for these students has risen to 90%. This represents a significant increase over earlier admitted students without an assigned adviser.
- The percentage of students entering college enrollment needing remediation decreased 7.03% between 2011–2012 and 2012–2013.
- About 2,600 students completed the Shark Academy one-week enrichment programs in developmental math, reading, and

composition. As indicated earlier, more than half improved their initial placement by at least one level, with 25% becoming college ready.

- About 97% of first-time-in-college direct-entry students had first semester IEPs created prior to orientation.
- Since 2012–2013, approximately 10,000 students have reached the 25% benchmark in their major area of study and have transitioned to more than 250 academic coaches and mentors.

New Curriculum, New Opportunities

The challenge for every higher education institution today is to be relevant. MDC has long been a proponent of the tenets of liberal learning, and the college has strived to apply those principles to meet the demands of a changing society and workforce. The Learning Outcomes Project reflects that requirement directly and remains the centerpiece of the learning process for students. But a number of other elements round out the effort to provide low-income and minority students with a full menu of opportunities to continue their education or move into high-paying employment with workforce-ready skills.

Aligning With Regional Workforce Goals

In 1996, Miami-Dade County's Beacon Council, the economic development arm of the county, launched the One Community One Goal (OCOG) initiative. OCOG identified several target industries, with the aim of reinforcing existing businesses and drawing new commercial ventures to the community. MDC, in turn, realigned its workforce and professional programs to match OCOG's target industries. This process has become an ongoing endeavor to identify and develop programs that meet the continually changing demands of the emerging South Florida economy. Since 1996, MDC has developed close to 100 new bachelor's and associate degrees, as well as numerous short-term certifications, all in high-demand areas of the economy.

MDC is home to 13 professional schools today, spanning the range of both long-standing and newly emerging workforce needs. The MDC schools include the following:

- Architecture and Interior Design
- Aviation
- Business

- Continuing Education and Professional Development
- Engineering and Technology
- Education
- Entertainment and Design Technology
- Science
- Funeral Service Education
- Miami Culinary Institute
- Health Sciences
- Justice
- Nursing

Examples of new in-demand workforce programs are the 16 bachelor's degrees now available at MDC. The earliest was in education, preparing students who were often in their 30s to return to neighborhood schools with which they were only too familiar. The program prepared teachers for K–12 exceptional education, as well as a broad scope of secondary science majors to encourage STEM expertise. The Bachelor of Science in Nursing soon followed, preparing students for consistent demand in the region. The remaining four-year degrees included Public Safety Management; Physician Assistant; Supervision and Management; Electronics Engineering Technology; Film, TV, and Digital Technology; Early Childhood Education; Biological Sciences; Information Systems Technology; and Logistics and Supply Chain Management.

All of the students who earn these degrees become immediate contributors to the local economy. They are ready to contribute because the academic programs have been crafted in concert with industry leaders. The Biological Sciences degree is a perfect example, having originated with an appeal from the biotechnology industry to provide graduates who were ready beyond the traditional academic training in the sciences. The MDC program, with help from these industry professionals, is delivering graduates ready to support the biotechnology and bio-pharmacology businesses in the region.

MDC's Honors College

The Honors College provides students with a rigorous and challenging two-year experience. For Hispanic and low-income students, it has become a doorway to academic and life achievement that would not have otherwise been possible. Each entrant to the Honors College is awarded a full tuition scholarship for two years of full-time study. In addition to academic programs that challenge and engage, students take advantage of opportunities beyond the classroom, including the Salzburg Seminar in Austria and the Washington Center seminars on politics and the media. MDC Honors College graduates have proved their mettle at the nation's finest universities, including Harvard, Yale, MIT, Stanford, and many more. These and other institutions continue to reach out to MDC for the rich diversity that our students bring to these universities.

Ideas and the Miami Animation and Gaming International Complex

The South Florida region is driven by small business activity. The industriousness of a strong immigrant population began a redefinition of the region, and new energy supplied by businesses in biotechnology, entertainment, information technology, the growth of the health-care and banking industries, and more has strengthened the region. In fact, the 2014 rankings for best small business metros by the *Business Journals* (Business Journals, 2014) list Miami–Fort Lauderdale as number two among 101 U.S. markets for starting and growing a small business. And that means that the skills and ingenuity of entrepreneurship are crucial for those aiming to turn ideas and start-ups into successful ventures.

Enter MDC and the new Idea Center. The Idea Center will serve as a hub for innovation and entrepreneurship for students and the larger community. From a range of disciplines, students will collaborate with faculty and business experts in a high-tech environment. Program elements that include the Idea Factory, the Startup Challenge, the Pioneers Speaker Series, CREATE Miami, and Phase II Ventures will provide guidance and skill-building at every stage of development, from concept to start-up to flourishing enterprise. In addition, MDC is infusing entrepreneurial skill building across the full range of its curriculum.

Just a few floors down from the Idea Center, MDC is also introducing the Miami Animation and Gaming International Complex (MAGIC). This training and innovation center will prepare students in a state-of-the-art, industry-inspired learning environment to be ready contributors in this burgeoning realm. MAGIC will include an interactive gallery of student projects; an interdisciplinary living lab featuring the Brain, a collaborative interconnected gamer environment; a motion capture studio, where objects take flight; sound engineering and color correction suites; classrooms equipped with the latest technology that will feature dual-touch screen interfaces and hands-on learning experiences that promote an exploratory, high-tech approach; and lastly, a screening hall, where enthusiastic audiences will find much to cheer during screenings of semester-long student animation projects.

Conclusion

The United States in 2014 embodies long-standing contradictions—contradictions that are inherent for a country invested deeply in both a market-driven, bottom-line economy as well as a democratic ethos. And with great fervor, all manner of political and economic arguments accompanies this partnership. Suffice it to say, maintaining a healthy tension is a delicate balancing act.

No government or institution can guarantee prosperity. Equality of incomes has never been the aim of this democracy, but as the Nobel economist Joseph Stiglitz wrote in a *New York Times* article in 2013, "Inequality of opportunity is indefensible." Stiglitz pointed out that economic mobility in the United States is now lower than in most of Europe and every country in Scandinavia (Stiglitz, 2013). And the Pew Research Center posits inequality at the highest levels since 1928 (Desilver, 2013).

This circumstance has enormous effect on educational opportunity. The achievement gap for college completion between rich and poor children born in 2001 was 30%–40% larger than it was for those born 25 years earlier, according to Stanford sociologist Sean F. Reardon (2011). And we know, from many sources, that Hispanics and African Americans are still paid substantially less than Whites.

In this context, is there any doubt of the value America's community colleges deliver to low-income and minority students? First and foremost, they have the chance to attend college when their finances would have prevented it at any other institution. And the payoff is clear: In Florida, both the associate in science and bachelor of science from the Florida College System (community colleges) provide graduates higher salaries, on average, than the bachelor's degrees from the state's universities and private institutions (Florida College System, 2011). And those degrees cost much less not only to students but also to the state coffers.

While community colleges have earned their high marks for academic and workforce sophistication, it is not at all unflattering to assign them safety-net status. The accolade for MDC, as the most important institution in the Miami community, is easily assigned to community colleges in hundreds of locales across the country. These institutions have achieved the balance of economic focus and individual opportunity that our larger society still struggles to rediscover.

The imbalance is reflected, glaringly so, in state houses across the country. Education funding continues to be vulnerable in the face of what seems to be perpetual funding constraints and reduced revenue streams. Support for these open-access institutions that address the opportunity gap is labeled as discretionary in state budgets and, as the largest discretionary item absorbs, critical cuts far too often.

The battle for balance will likely rage for years to come. No doubt, the remedies are complicated and further exaggerated by a society and economy in constant and often overwhelming transformation. But this is not a challenge of keeping up with change; quite the contrary, the issue of balance rests on what we value. And if we don't value the inalienable opportunity to learn, to gain an education on this day in history, then all the change in the world risks being worthless and without direction. This is not the conversation we're having today, and it's long overdue.

References

Business Journals. (2014). *Small business ranking, 2014.* Retrieved from http://www.bizjournals.com/bizjournals/gallery/10721

Carnevale, A. P., and Strohl, J. (2010, June). *Rewarding strivers.* Washington, DC: Georgetown University, Center on Education and the Workforce.

Chetty, R., Hendren, N., Kline, P., & Saez, E. (2014). *Where is the land of opportunity? The geography of intergenerational mobility in the United States.* NBER Working Paper No. 19844. Cambridge, MA: National Bureau of Economic Research. Retrieved from http://www.nber.org/papers/w19843

Desilver, D. (2013). *U.S. income inequality on rise for decades.* Pew Research Report. Retrieved from http://www.pewresearch.org/fact-tank/2013/12/05/u-s-income-inequality-on-rise-for-decades-is-now-highest-since-1928/

Florida College System. (2011). *Zoom,* Edition 2011-02. Retrieved from http://www.fldoe.org/core/fileparse.php/7724/urlt/0072375-zoom2011-02.pdf

Florida Department of Education. (2012). *High school feedback report: 2012 Florida public high school graduates.* Retrieved from http://data.fldoe.org/readiness/default.cfm?action=view_report_alldistricts&DisplayYear=2012&ItemNumber=17&SubItem=b.2

Miami Dade College Institutional Research. (2014). *Fact book.* Retrieved from http://www.mdc.edu/ir/Fact%20Book/MDC%20Highlights%20and%20Facts_Nov2014rvd.pdf

Miami-Dade Community College. (1988). *Under construction: 25 years of Miami-Dade Community College, 1960–1985.* Tulsa, OK: Lion & Thorne.

Reardon, Sean F. (2011). The widening academic achievement gap between the rich and the poor: New evidence and possible explanations. Retrieved from https://cepa.stanford.edu/sites/default/files/reardon%20whither%20opportunity%20-%20chapter%205.pdf

Stiglitz, J. (2013, February 16). Equal opportunity, our national myth. *New York Times.* Retrieved from http://opinionator.blogs.nytimes.com/2013/02/16/equal-opportunity-our-national-myth/

Tough, P. (2014, May 15). Who gets to graduate? *New York Times Magazine.*

University of Miami Cuban Heritage Collection. (1978). *Cuban Refugee Center records, 1960–1978*. Retrieved from http://proust.library.miami.edu/findingaids/?p=collections/findingaid&id=46&q=&rootcontentid=5552#id55521500.html

U.S. Census. (2012). *Quick facts: Miami-Dade County*. Retrieved from http://www.census.gov/quickfacts/table/PST045215/00

PART THREE

NATIVE AMERICAN/AMERICAN INDIAN STUDENT POPULATIONS

7

VOICE OF THE NATIONAL RESEARCHER

National Data Trends on Native American/American Indian Student Retention at Community Colleges

Wei Song

We will be known forever by the tracks we leave.

—Dakota

merican Indian/Alaska Native students are the least-researched student group in higher education. According to the 2010 Census, 5.2 million people in the United States identified themselves as American Indian and Alaska Native, either alone or in combination with one or more other races. Out of this total, 2.9 million people identified as American Indian and Alaska Native alone (U.S. Census Bureau, 2012). In 2013, only 154,000 Native American[1] students enrolled in degree-granting postsecondary institutions; 64,000 of these students enrolled at public two-year institutions. In both categories, Native American students account for less than 1% of the total enrollment (U.S. Department of Education, 2014). Many federal surveys and studies, such as the Census Bureau's American Community Survey (ACS) and Current Population Survey (CPS), do not report results on Native Americans because of small sample sizes or statistical insignificance. As a result, information on Native Americans' postsecondary education and labor market outcomes is scattered and hard to find.

This chapter gives an overview of Native American students' enrollment patterns, characteristics, progress, and challenges at community colleges and their postsecondary education outcomes. The author hopes to provide readers a better understanding on Native American students in community colleges.

National Enrollment Trends

The enrollment of American Indian/Alaska Native students in U.S. postsecondary institutions has more than doubled in the last several decades, from 76,000 in 1976 to 173,000 in 2012 (see Figure 7.1), exceeding the pace of the overall postsecondary enrollment growth (88% over the same period). American Indian/Alaska Natives are also more likely to enroll at two-year public colleges than the general population. Although the proportion of the American Indian/Alaska Native students enrolled at two-year colleges decreased from 52% in 1976 to 41% in 2012, this proportion has always been higher than the proportion of public two-year college enrollment in total enrollments at degree-granting institutions, which is relatively stable around one-third in the last several decades.

In 1976, the American Indian/Alaska Native males enrolled in degree-granting colleges and universities slightly outnumbered American Indian/Alaska Native females (38,500 and 37,600, respectively). However, the number of Native American females enrolled quickly exceeded the number of males enrolled, with at least 10 percentage points difference since 1980. As of fall 2013, 93,000 American Indian/Alaska Native females (60%) and 62,000 males (40%) enrolled at degree-granting postsecondary institutions, with a difference of 20 percentage points, which is only second to the gender gap among African American students (26%).

Although the number of American Indian/Alaska Native students enrolled at postsecondary institutions has increased significantly in the last several decades, the enrollment rate of 18-to-24-year-old American Indian/Alaska Natives has been lagging behind the postsecondary enrollment rates of youths of other races/ethnicities and, far behind those of Whites and Asians (see Figure 7.2).

During 1989 and 2012, the average enrollment rate of 18-to-24-year-old Native Americans was 24%, similar to that of Hispanics. As a comparison, the enrollment rate is 40% for Whites, 59% for Asians, and 31% for Blacks. This suggests that access to postsecondary education is still a challenge to Native American youth.

Characteristics of Native American Community College Students

There are only a few large-scale surveys or databases providing information on community college student characteristics beyond gender and race/ethnicity. One of the data sources is the Beginning Postsecondary Students Longitudinal Study (BPS) by the U.S. Department of Education, which selects nationally representative samples of beginning postsecondary students

Figure 7.1. Fall enrollment of American Indian/Alaska Native students in degree-granting postsecondary institutions: 1976–2012.

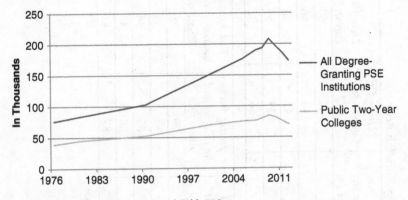

Source. U.S. Department of Education, 2014, Table 306.

Figure 7.2. Enrollment rates in degree-granting institutions, by race/ethnicity.

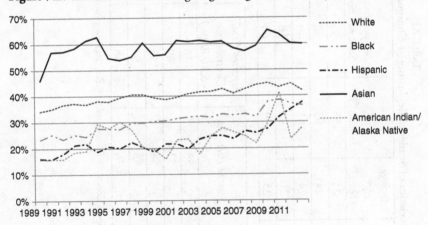

Source. U.S. Department of Education, 2014, Table 302.

and tracks them over six years. The latest three student cohorts examined are those who started postsecondary education in 1989, 1995, and 2003. According to the 2003 BPS, the average age of American Indian/Alaska Native students when they first enrolled at community colleges was 25 (see Table 7.1), slightly older than the average age of other race/ethnicity groups. Of Native American students, 60% were independent students, and 66% lived off campus by themselves. As a comparison, the proportions of

TABLE 7.1
Characteristics of Students Beginning at Community Colleges by Race/Ethnicity

	Average Age (Years)	Female (%)	Independent Student (%)	Parents Had Postsecondary Education (%)	Living Off Campus by Self (%)	Living With Parents (%)
White	24	55	35	60	42	50
Black or African American	24	62	46	54	45	46
Hispanic or Latino	24	61	40	42	43	53
Asian	21	42	18	55	25	59
American Indian/Alaska Native	25	59	60	48	66	32

	Started Part-Time (%)	Expected Family Contribution <$3,000 (%)	Received Pell Grant in First Year (%)	Expecting Bachelor's Degree and Above (%)	Took Remedial Course(s) in First Year (%)
White	53	36	22	79	28
Black or African American	52	69	53	83	33
Hispanic or Latino	58	57	31	85	34
Asian	58	52	27	88	36
American Indian/Alaska Native	76	68	41	87	41

Source. U.S. Department of Education, National Center for Educational Statistics, Beginning Postsecondary Study 2003.

students of other races or ethnicities being dependents or living with parents were much higher than those of Native American students. Less than half of the American Indian/Alaska Native students' parents had postsecondary education experiences, while a higher proportion of White, Black, or Asian students had postsecondary educated parents. More than two-thirds (68%) of the Native American students started their study at community college with expected family financial contribution less than $3,000 in the first year, while a much larger proportion of White, Hispanic, or Asian students expected more financial support from their families. In their first year, 41% of the American Indian/Alaska Native students received Pell Grants.

Three-quarters of American Indian/Alaska Native students started at community college as part-time students. This percentage is much higher than any other race/ethnicity group. The proportion of American Indian/Alaska Native students who took remedial course(s) (41%) is also higher than those of other race/ethnicity groups. However, when asked about their educational goals, 87% of American Indian/Alaska Native students reported that the highest degrees they expected to obtain were bachelor's or above on par with the percentage of Asian students who expected such degrees, higher than the expectations of White, Black, and Hispanic students.

The 2003 BPS is a national sample of students who began their post-secondary education in 2003. It represents the characteristics of the students who first enrolled in 2003 and may not reflect the changes in the last 10 years. Further, due to the small sample size of Native Americans, a lot of information on Native American students, particularly progress and completion, is not reported by National Center for Educational Statistics (NCES) out of concerns of reliability. Therefore, the author examined the data collected by Achieving the Dream, Inc., to provide another perspective for the Native American students' community college experiences.

Achieving the Dream (ATD) is a national reform network for community college student success. Since the launch of the initiative in 2004, it has grown to a network of over 200 community colleges in 34 states and the District of Columbia. ATD promotes the use of longitudinal cohort-based student data to inform decision making. To facilitate that process, each participant college is required to submit student-level data to the ATD database to track academic progress. The ATD database contains longitudinal records of 2.8 million students who started at an ATD college for the first time from fall 2004 to fall 2012. Table 7.2 presents their demographic and college readiness information.

Among the students who first attended community colleges in the ATD network, the average age of Native Americans was 24 years, the same as that of the African American students but older than the average age of other

TABLE 7.2
Characteristics of Community College Students in the ATD Network

	Total Students (N)	Average Age (Years)	Female (%)	Referred to Any Developmental Ed (%)	Referred to Developmental Math (%)	Referred to Developmental English (%)
White	1,424,624	23	53	46	41	19
Black/African American	605,369	24	59	62	55	37
Hispanic	589,665	22	55	53	47	27
Asian	154,711	23	51	44	32	25
Native American	31,042	24	56	56	51	33

Source. Achieving the Dream, Inc., 2011

race/ethnic groups. Of Native American students, 56% were referred to a remedial course. Specifically, more than half of the Native Americans were referred to developmental math and about one-third were referred to developmental English. Only African Americans have a slightly higher percentage of students who were referred to remedial courses.

Progress and Completion

How do Native American students progress through community college? As discussed earlier, more than half of the Native American students were referred to remedial courses when they first started. Community colleges usually require that students who do not meet certain achievement metrics complete remedial course sequences before they can take any credit-bearing courses. For Native American students who were referred to remedial courses, about one-third completed developmental math within two years, and half completed developmental English within two years (see Table 7.3). Their completion rates are higher than those of Blacks and Latinos, but lower than those of Whites and Asians.

Less than 60% of the Native American students persisted to the next year, comparable with the proportion of African American students who persisted, but lower than the porportion of White (65%), Asian (71%), or Hispanic students (66%). Only 12% of the Native American students graduated with a credential within four years, on par with Hispanic and Black students, but lagging far behind the graduation rates of White (17%) and Asian students (18%).

TABLE 7.3
Persistence and Completion at Community Colleges

	Completed Dev Math in Two Years (%)	Completed Dev English in Two Years (%)	Persisted to Next Year (%)	Completed Credential in Four Years (%)
White	41	56	65	17
Black/African American	28	47	58	10
Hispanic	36	48	66	13
Asian	40	53	71	18
Native American	32	51	59	12

Source. Achieving the Dream, Inc., 2011.

Figure 7.3. Graduation rates at two-year public postsecondary institutions by race/ethnicity, 2000–2009.

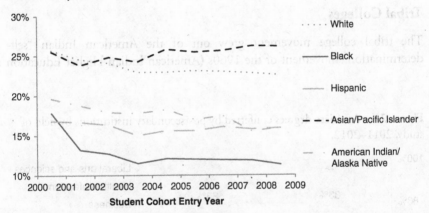

Source. U.S. Department of Education, 2014, Table 326.

According to the IPEDS data, the graduation rate of student cohorts from 2000 to 2009 within 150% of normal time averages 18% for Native American students (see Figure 7.3), 24% for Whites and Asians, 13% for Blacks, and 16% for Hispanics. However, the IPEDS graduation rates are based on first-time, full-time, degree-seeking students, which is a smaller cohort among community college students, who are more likely to study part-time than students enrolled at four-year colleges. For example, according to the 2003 BPS, more than half of the students started community college part-time.

Regardless of data source, the completion rates at community colleges are low, particularly for Native American, Black, and Hispanic students.

Many students start higher education at community colleges and then transfer to other colleges. The 2003 BPS data show that about a third of students transferred to other colleges by the end of the sixth year after initial enrollment at a community college. The Native American students had the lowest transfer rate of 25%[2] among all race/ethnic groups.

What subjects do American Indian/Alaska Native students study at community colleges? According the numbers of associate degrees conferred in 2011–2012 (see Figure 7.4), 33% of the degrees conferred to American Indian/Alaska Native students are in liberal arts and sciences, 18% in health professions, 15% in business, 5% in engineering or mechanic technologies, and 4% each in computer sciences and social sciences. This distribution is very similar to the distribution of all associate degrees conferred, suggesting that the academic or career interests of American Indian/Alaska Native students do not differ much from the overall pattern of community college students' academic or career choices.

Tribal Colleges

The tribal college movement grew out of the American Indian "self-determination" movement of the 1960s (American Indian Higher Education

Figure 7.4. Associate degrees conferred by postsecondary institutions by field of study, 2011–2012.

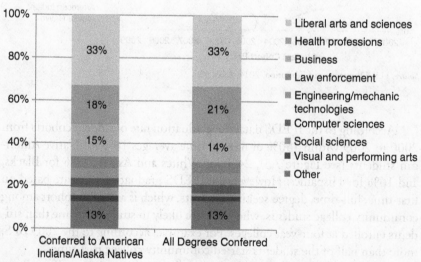

Source. U.S. Department of Education, 2014, Table 320.

Consortium [AIHEC], 2014). In 1968, Navajo Community College (now Diné College) was established by the Navajo Nation in Arizona and became the first tribal college. In 2014, there were 37 tribal colleges and universities, 34 chartered by the tribal nations and 3 chartered by the federal government. Tribal colleges started as two-year public institutions, but now 13 of them grant bachelor's degrees and 5 have been approved to grant master's degrees.

As of fall 2013, the 34 accredited tribal colleges and universities enrolled 18,000 students, among which over 13,000 were enrolled at public two-year or public four-year colleges that primarily grant associate degrees (IPEDS; U.S. Department of Education, 2013). About three-fourths of the students enrolled at tribal colleges and universities are American Indian/Alaska Natives.

Although Native American student enrollment at tribal colleges and universities is a small percentage (less than 10%) of the Native American enrollment at all postsecondary institutions, tribal colleges play a significant role in educating Native Americans. Tribal colleges were created in response to the higher education needs of American Indians and generally serve geographically isolated populations that have no other means to access education beyond the high school level. According to AIHEC (2014), the typical one-way commute for students enrolled at tribal colleges is 30 to 100 miles.

In addition to providing programs of study in disciplines and of academic rigor that are accepted by the mainstream of higher education, the tribal colleges are charged with the unique missions of reinforcing and promoting traditional native culture (AIHEC, 2014; Badwound & Tierney, 1988). The tribal colleges have developed and implemented curriculum from unique tribal perspectives; their academic structure reflects tribal culture; they make efforts in restoring, writing, and revitalizing native languages; and they are actively engaged in community-based activities.

Tribal college researchers have cited geographic isolation, chronic underfunding, and underprepared students as the most severe challenges for tribal colleges (His Horse Is Thunder, 2012). For example, 66% of students who registered at tribal colleges required some developmental education according to the data reported to AIHEC; one tribal college reported that nearly 95% of entering freshmen required remedial courses in at least one content area (His Horse Is Thunder, 2012).

Challenges for Native American Students at Community Colleges

Researchers (Brayboy, Fann, Castagno, & Solyom, 2012; McAfee, 2000; Hoover & Jacobs, 1992; Falk & Aitken, 1984; Bowker, 1992) have identified a number of factors related to Native American students' persistence and success at higher education institutions. These factors include academic preparation, access to financial aid, cultural differences, institutional support services, and support from family and the larger Native communities.

Many existing studies have established pre-college academic preparation as a major predictor of college GPA and financial resources as an important predictor of college persistence. In previous sections, data have shown that Native Americans started community colleges with lower academic preparedness, particularly when compared with White, Asian, or Hispanic students. Financial aid data also show that Native American students disproportionately come from economically challenged families and require financial assistance to pursue higher education. Despite their dire need for financial aid, many Native American students fear that they will incur too much debt if they rely on loans to fund their higher education (Tierney, Sallee, & Venegas, 2007). In addition, the average amount of financial aid awards Native Americans received was several hundred dollars below the national average (Tierney, Sallee, & Venegas, 2007). Having unmet financial need is a significant barrier to Native students' enrollment and persistence at colleges.

In addition to low academic preparedness and financial difficulty, which is not unusual for low-income minority students when they start at community colleges, Native American students face another major challenge—the cultural differences between tribal cultures and the mainstream postsecondary institutions. Many Native American students grow up in a community of Indigenous people separated from the mainstream society; thus, it is highly likely that these students experience more acute cultural differences when they attend non-tribal higher education institutions. They need to make a big effort to learn to navigate through the college administrative and academic system and learn to understand or perceive everything from the mainstream point of view, which is sometimes contrary to their tribal worldviews (Watson, Terrell, Wright, & Associates, 2002; Carney, 1999).

Providing support to Native Americans at the institutional level is vital to Native Americans as they battle with lower academic preparedness and insufficient financial resources through college. Involving and connecting Native students can bring a sense of belonging. Studies have shown that engagement in student social groups, participation in first-year programs, and peer mentors played an important role in Native American students' academic success (Harrington & Hunt, 2010; Lundberg, 2007; Shotton, Oosahwe, & Cintron, 2007). Furthermore, having role models and interaction with faculty members outside the classroom also contributes positively to Native American college student success (Harington & Hunt, 2010; Jackson, Smith, & Hill, 2003).

It is essential to accommodate Native American students' cultural differences and alleviate their sense of isolation when institutional services are designed and implemented. For example, Guillory and Wolverton (2008) showed that Native American students have different, sometimes contrary views on factors affecting persistence. Very often the faculty and administrations failed to recognize students' connection to their families and tribal communities and on-campus social support as key persistence factors. Institutions should create social networks that are aimed at supporting Native American students and best utilize their family support and tribal connections.

Postsecondary Education Outcomes

In 2013, 50% of Native Americans age 25 or older had at least some postsecondary education (see Figure 7.5), this proportion is lower than that of Whites (64%), Blacks (52%), or Asians (71%), but higher than that of Hispanics (38%). However, only 15% of Native Americans had a bachelor's degree or above, the same as Hispanics, but much lower than the proportion of adults who had such degrees among Whites (34%), Blacks (19%), and Asians (52%).

Historically, the unemployment rate of American Indians/Alaska Natives has been higher than that of Whites, Asians, and Hispanics and very often higher than that of Blacks. For example, for nine years from 1997 to 2007, the unemployment rate of Native Americans was over 10%, peaking at

Figure 7.5. Educational attainment of adults age 25 and older, by race/ethnicity.

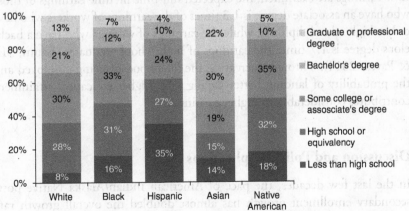

Source. U.S. Department of Commerce, Census Bureau, 2013. American Community Survey, 2013. Table generated by author by using American FactFinder (http://factfinder2.census.gov).

14.5% in 2003; for eight years the Native American unemployment rate was the highest among all race/ethnicity groups (DeVoe & Darling-Churchill, 2008). In 2013, the overall unemployment rate in the United States was 7.4% (U.S. Bureau of Labor Statistics, 2014); however, rates were highest for Blacks (13.1%) and Native Americans (12.8%), far exceeding the unemployment rates of Asians (5.2%), Whites (6.5%), and Hispanics (9.1%).

When employment rate is examined,[3] Native Americans also lag behind other race/ethnic groups in terms of employment status. In 2013, the employment rate of Native Americans was 52%, compared with over 60% for Asians, Whites, and Hispanics (U.S. Bureau of Labor Statistics, 2015). Particularly, the employment rate of Native American women was 47%, the lowest among all adult women.

Studies have shown that groups with higher educational attainment are associated with lower unemployment rates (DeVoe & Darling-Churchill, 2008). For Native Americans, higher educational attainment is the factor most likely to increase their odds of being employed (Austin, 2013). Compared with those who have less than high school education, Native Americans with some college education are three times more likely to be employed, while those who earned an associate degree are four times more likely to be employed.

In 2012, the median annual earnings of full-time year-round workers 25 to 34 years old who had an associate degree was $35,720, which is 1.2 times higher than that of the workers who had only a high school diploma (U.S. Department of Education, 2014). The earning gap between associate degree holders and high school degree holders is even bigger for female workers and minority workers (especially for Hispanics and Asians). When projected lifetime earnings are examined, the expected full-time lifetime earnings of those who have an associate degree is 1.3 times of the earnings of workers who have only a high school diploma; while the earnings of workers who have a bachelor's degree is 1.7 times the earnings of high school graduates (Baum, Ma, & Payea, 2014). Through increasing the likelihood of being employed and the probability of landing better-paying jobs, higher education attainment contributes considerably to higher earnings.

Discussion and Policy Implications

In the last few decades, the pace of American Indian/Alaska Native postsecondary enrollment growth has almost doubled the overall growth rate in higher education enrollment. However, compared with the enrollment rates of 18-to-24-year-olds of other races/ethnicities, the postsecondary enrollment rate of Native Americans is still low. On average, Native American adults also have lower educational attainment than adults of other races/ethnicities. Furthermore, even though Native Americans have higher educational aspirations than other students when they first start at community colleges, their graduation rates are low compared with those of students of other races/ethnicities. This suggests that the postsecondary education system not only needs to help expand Native American access to higher education but also persist and graduate.

The first step is to improve Native American students' college readiness, academically, financially, and mentally. Many Native American students are not academically ready for college—the high percentage of Native American students in need of developmental education is a major barrier to their persistence and completion. They are not mentally ready—many are first-generation college students without much knowledge on college life, which may be at odds with their traditional values or worldviews. They don't have adequate financial resources to start college—the poverty rate of Native Americans is highest among all race/ethnicity groups (DeVoe & Darling-Churchill, 2008); two-thirds of Native American students' families were unable to provide more than $3,000 for their first year's study. They didn't get much help from high school counselors either—many navigated the college application and financial processes alone or with the help of their families (Waterman, 2007).

Having timely access to school counselor guidance plays an important role in students' college aspiration, particularly for first-generation students who rely almost exclusively on counselors and school staff for information about going to college. To provide meaningful academic and career guidance for Native American students, schools counselors should have a good understanding of Native Americans' cultures and values (Shutiva, 2001).

Building a strong partnership between community colleges and high schools is an effective strategy to help students transit into postsecondary education. Postsecondary outreach programs, particularly early-intervention programs like TRIO programs, Gaining Early Awareness and Readiness for Undergraduate Programs (GEAR UP), and College Horizon, which focus on college awareness and readiness, have served a considerable number of Native American high school students and have provided them with much-needed support for transition into college. Early-college high schools for Native youth have also been successful in improving academic performance and college enrollment substantially (Brayboy et al., 2012).

Once Native American students enroll at community colleges, colleges serving a sizable number of Native American students need to conduct a thorough review of the students' challenges, needs, and protective factors for success. Colleges need to address questions like, Why do so many Native Americans leave after their first year of study? How can Native Americans be more involved in college life? How can tribal nations and student families help to support student success work? Particularly, given an overwhelming proportion (three quarters) of Native American students start as part-time students, how can colleges ensure these students also make firm academic progress despite their part-time status?

Finally, there needs to be more research on Native American students' postsecondary education experiences and labor market outcomes. For example, why are there fewer Native men pursuing higher education? What are their experiences navigating the postsecondary pipeline? Are the Native students working in fields relevant to the degrees they earned? In addition to quantitative research, qualitative studies are highly needed to understand the diversity among Native students, to breakdown the perception of Native students as a monolithic group.

Higher education is a major vehicle for personal financial prosperity and social upward mobility. A larger number of postsecondary graduates benefit the society as a whole through increased productivity and broader participation in civic life. Native American students are more likely than the general population to start their postsecondary education from community colleges, which are more accessible and affordable compared with four-year institutions. Community colleges also provide students a good foundation for further education if they choose to continue in school. By working with communities, researchers, and policymakers, community colleges can help students of all races and ethnicities succeed.

Notes

1. Throughout this chapter *American Indian/Alaska Native, Native American, Native,* and *Indigenous* are used interchangeably.

2. Interpret with caution. Owing to the small sample size of Native American students, the standard error represents more than 30% of the estimate.

3. Although unemployment rate is the most commonly used measure of job market performance, employment rate is considered a better measure for populations suffering from chronically high unemployment (Austin, 2013). To be classified as unemployed, a person must be without work, be available for work, and have actively searched for work (U.S. Bureau of Labor Statistics, 2008). Once a person stops looking for work, he/she is no longer counted in the labor force. Employment rate is calculated as the ratio of employed to population and is not affected by the proportion of people who are not job seeking voluntarily or involuntary.

References

Achieving the Dream. (2011). Data notes: Sept/Oct 2011. Retrieved from http://achievingthedream.org/resource/12930/data-notes-septoct-2011

American Indian Higher Education Consortium. (2014). *Overview of AIHEC*. Retrieved from http://www.aihec.org/our-stories/docs/2014_AIHEC-Overview .pdf

Austin, A. (2013, December 13). *Native Americans and jobs: The challenge and the promise.* Economic Policy Institute Briefing Paper. Retrieved from http://www .epi.org/publication/bp370-native-americans-jobs/

Badwound, E., & Tierney, W. G. (1988). Leadership and American Indian values: The tribal college dilemma. *Journal of American Indian, 28*(1). Retrieved from http://jaie.asu.edu/v28/V28S1lea.htm

Baum, S., Ma, J., & Payea, K. (2014). *Education pays 2013: The benefits of higher education for individuals and society.* New York, NY: College Board.

Bowker, A. (1992). The American Indian female dropout. *Journal of American Indian Education, 31*(3), 3–20. Retrieved from http://jaie.asu.edu/v31/V31S3ame.html

Brayboy, B., Fann, A., Castagno, A. E., & Solyom, J. A. (2012). *Postsecondary education for American Indian and Alaska Natives: Higher education for nation building and self-determination.* Hoboken, NJ: Wiley Periodicals.

Carney, C. M. (1999). *Native American higher education in the United States.* New Brunswick, NJ: Transaction Publishers.

DeVoe, J. F., & Darling-Churchill, K. E. (2008). *Status and trends in the education of American Indians and Alaska Natives: 2008* (NCES 2008-084). Washington, DC: National Center for Education Statistics, Institute of Education Sciences, U.S. Department of Education. Retrieved from http://nces.ed.gov/ pubs2008/2008084.pdf

Falk, D., & Aitken, L. (1984). Promoting retention among American Indian college students. *Journal of American Indian Education, 23*(2), 24–31. Retrieved from http://jaie.asu.edu/v23/V23S2pro.html

Guillory, R., & Wolverton, M. (2008). It's about family: Native American student persistence in higher education. *Journal of Higher Education, 79*(1), 58–87.

Harrington, C. F., & Hunt, B. (2010). The impending education crisis for American Indians: Higher education at the cross roads. *Indigenous Policy Journal, 21*, 1–13.

His Horse Is Thunder, D. (2012). *Breaking through tribal colleges and universities.* Briefing paper prepared for American Indian Higher Education Consortium. Retrieved from http://www.aihec.org/our-stories/docs/reports/BreakingThrough.pdf

Hoover, J., & Jacobs, C. (1992). A survey of American Indian college students: Perceptions toward their study skills/college life. *Journal of American Indian Education, 32*(1), 21–29. Retrieved from http://jaie.asu.edu/v32/V32S1sur.htm

Jackson, A. P., Smith, S. A., & Hill, C. L. (2003). Academic persistence among Native American college students. *Journal of College Student Development, 44*, 548–564.

Lundberg, C. A. (2007). Student involvement and institutional commitment to diversity as predictors of Native American student learning. *Journal of College Student Development, 48*, 405–417.

McAfee, M. (2000). From their voices: American Indians in higher education and the phenomenon of stepping out. *Research News on Graduate Education, 2*(2), 1–10.

Shotton, J. J., Oosahwe, E. S., & Cintron, R. (2007). Stories of success: Experiences of American Indian students in a peer-mentoring retention program. *Review of Higher Education, 31*, 81–107.

Shutiva, C. (2001). *Career and academic guidance for American Indian and Alaska Native youth.* ERIC Digest (EDO-RC-01-2). Eric Clearinghouse on Rural Education and Small Schools.

Tierney, W. G., Sallee, M. W., & Venegas, K. M. (2007, Fall). Access and financial aid: How American Indian students pay for college. *Journal of College Admission, 197*, 14–23.

U.S. Bureau of Labor Statistics. (2008). The unemployment rate and beyond: Alternative measures of labor underutilization. *Issues in Labor Statistics, June 2008.* Retrieved from http://www.bls.gov/opub/btn/archive/the-unemployment-rate-and-beyond-alternative-measures-of-labor-underutilization-pdf.pdf

U.S. Bureau of Labor Statistics. (2015). Labor force characteristics by race and ethnicity, 2014. BLS Reports: November Report 1057. Retrieved from http://www.bls.gov/opub/reports/race-and-ethnicity/archive/labor-force-characteristics-by-race-and-ethnicity-2014.pdf

U.S. Census Bureau. (2012). The American Indian and Alaska Native population: 2010. *2010 Census Briefs.* Retrieved from http://www.census.gov/prod/cen2010/briefs/c2010br-10.pdf

U.S. Census Bureau. (2013). American Community Survey, 2013. Table generated by author by using American FactFinder. Retrieved from http://factfinder2.census.gov

U.S. Department of Education. (2013). Integrated postsecondary education data system fall enrollment survey (IPEDS-FE). Washington, DC: Author.

U.S. Department of Education. (2014). *Digest of education statistics 2013.* Retrieved from http://nces.ed.gov/programs/digest/2013menu_tables.asp

Waterman, S. (2007). A complex path to Haudenosaunee degree completion. *Journal of American Indian Education, 46*(1), 20–40. Retrieved from http://jaie.asu.edu/v46/46_1_%202007%202%20Waterman.pdf

Watson, I., Terrell, M., Wright, D., & Associates. (2002). *How minority students experience college: Implications for planning and policy.* Hampton, VA: Stylus Publishing.

8

VOICE OF THE NATIONAL LEADER

American Indian Voice: A National Perspective

Cynthia Lindquist, Ta'Sunka Wicahpi Win (Star Horse Woman)

Tell me and I'll forget. Show me, and I may not remember. Involve me, and I'll understand.
—Native American saying

I am obligated to explain a few things so that the reader might better understand who I am and where I came from before I became a tribal college president in 2003. Star Horse Woman is my second Dakota name, given to me by a medicine man from Canada at a point in time when I was working for the Indian Health Service at the national level and on a traditional medicine initiative for the agency. My elders taught me that when I introduce myself with my Dakota name, I must explain that I speak the truth as I understand it and that I speak from my heart. A Dakota *win* (woman) does not put herself "out front" or tout herself as a leader, let alone as a national leader. Of the seven Dakota values of life, humility is greatly admired and still recognized as an important characteristic one should exemplify.

I am a member of the Spirit Lake Dakota Nation, and I was asked (by elders) to apply to become the president of Cankdeska Cikana (Little Hoop) Community College. I had worked for my tribe off and on over the years and have a public administration background. Cankdeska Cikana Community College (CCCC) had been put on accreditation probation in late 2002, and by the time they hired me in the fall of 2003, the college had 18 months until the comprehensive visit by the Higher Learning Commission to restore its accreditation status. We were successful and granted 10 years' accreditation. Having grown up in the era without plumbing and running water on the reservation and also as the eldest of 13 children, I am very good at cleaning up messes. However, I do have a master's degree in public administration; a doctorate in education leadership; and extensive development, management, and political work experience.

As a tribal member and now as an elder, I believe I have greater compassion and responsibility to "help my people." In being a tribal college president, my passion is derived from my students as well as from our community. It is a most challenging role, with complex issues and minimal resources, and yet, tribal colleges and universities (TCUs) do phenomenal work. If we (tribal colleges) were not here, our people would not be college students, nor would they have access to opportunities to help themselves, to dream and aspire, and to hope for things to be better. TCU success is not mainstream success. The following chapter is written with these perspectives in mind, as well as insights from my 30-plus years working with Native people and particularly my experiences from the past 12 years as a tribal college president.

Historical Context, Treaties, and Education

First and foremost, it must be understood that American Indians and Alaska Natives (AI/ANs) have a unique relationship with the United States of America. It is a relationship that is embedded in the colonization and settling on the homelands of America's indigenous people. This relationship is neither honestly explained in history books nor taught accurately in the classrooms. It is rooted in treaty law, legal wranglings, and federal policy meant to "deal" with the Indians (or the "Indian problem") but primarily to take ownership of the lands. This relationship is political—not race-based—and it continues today, but it is greatly misunderstood by the American public and compounded by stereotypes like "free" education or health care, Indians are lazy drunks, we get checks every month, or are now millionaires from the casinos. Besides the stereotyped beliefs of the American public, AI/ANs are less than 1% of the population and thus are politically marginalized. There are many documented disparities in Indian country that include health, education, and socioeconomic status. Most of the Indian reservations are located in geographic areas that are isolated, have severe weather extremes, and generally are at double the U.S. poverty rate of 14%.

It must be understood that AI/ANs are members (citizens) of their respective tribes, but we are also state citizens and citizens of the United States (per federal legislation granting that status in 1924). This tri-citizenship can be confusing, and at times it muddles the "who is responsible?" question. States often push off to the federal government anything that deals with Native people within the state. Tribes continue the struggle to have the federal government honor the treaty provisions that were promised, and, of course, the federal response has been piecemeal at best or nonexistent at worst. Not one treaty has been honored, and the various federal policy eras (currently self-determination) have only provided themes for issues that require a significant infusion of resources, let alone a focused and comprehensive response.

Education was one of the items promised in the treaties by the federal government in exchange for the taking of the land, minerals, and other natural resources, as well as for the confinement of Native people to the reservations. During the era of treaty-making, there were various philosophies as to "what to do with the Indians," which included termination, containment, and assimilation. Education was one of the "tools" toward the latter goal of assimilation. The education of the indigenous people was cruel in that the heart of it was to break up the family. Children were taken away to various boarding schools, and churches were assigned geographic areas to convert the "heathens." There are many writings on this subject, but it is important for educators and education policymakers to understand this history and the context of "Indian" education. Today's cultural perspective on education is a coercive tool to punish or change people; AI/ANs are still suspicious of Western education. It is only recently that my tribe—Spirit Lake Dakota—has begun to embrace education as a "good" thing and the bridge to helping us address the plethora of historical trauma issues and today's devastating poverty. Being an educated Indian does not diminish or negate my being Dakota.

History of Tribal Colleges and Universities

There is a lack of a coordinated focus on AI/AN college students due to the complexity of Indian issues as well as differences among higher education institutions. In the 1960s, within the context of the many social awakenings and unrest occurring in the United States, and because of the failure of Native students at mainstream institutions, many gifted and visionary people conceived the idea to create a tribal higher education system. This is a system that is controlled and managed by Natives and has as its core mission the teaching, learning, and perpetuation of the respective indigenous culture and language.

According to federal law, a "tribal college or university" is an institution that qualifies for funding under the Tribally Controlled College or University Assistance Act of 1978 (25 U.S.C. § 1801 et seq.). To qualify for funding under the TCU Act, an institution of higher education must (a) be chartered by the governing body of a federally recognized Indian tribe or consortium of tribes; (b) have a governing board composed of a majority of American Indians; (c) demonstrate adherence to stated goals, a philosophy, or a plan of operation that is directed to meeting the needs of American Indians; (d) if in operation for more than one year, have students, a majority of whom are American Indian; and (e) be accredited, or have achieved candidacy status, by a nationally recognized accreditation agency or association.

Of the 37 existing TCUs, 34 are designated as land-grant colleges through the Equity in Educational Land-grant Status Act of 1994 and are commonly known and referred to as the "1994s" within the U.S. Department of Agriculture system and by other land-grant institutions.

TCUs Today

Supporting and strengthening tribal identity is the core of a tribal higher education system that was established in 1968, when Diné College was founded as the first tribal college. There is a very rich, yet frustrating, close to 50-year history for today's 37 TCUs. These institutions vary in size (from 50 students to up to 2,000 students), focus (liberal arts, education, technical, and sciences), and location (rural reservation, urban, desert, frozen tundra, woodlands, or the Great Plains). All TCUs offer associate degrees, 13 offer multiple bachelor's degrees, and 5 offer master's degree programs (American Indian Higher Education Consortium [AIHEC], 2014).

The current tribal college system has 77 campus sites in 16 states and covers approximately 80% of Indian country. TCUs serve about 19,300 degree-seeking students (full- and part-time) plus another 50,000 through community-based education and support programs. Most of our institutions are reservation based and have been chartered by our respective tribal governments, though there are several anomalies, such as Haskell University, Southwest Indian Polytechnic Institute (SIPI), or the Institute of American Indian Arts (IAIA), which are federal institutions. Each tribal college serves its respective tribal community; thus the majority of students are AI/ANs (AIHEC, 2012).

TCUs serve a unique role as rural and urban education providers, and all have open enrollment policies. Nationally, 20% of the students attending TCUs are non-Indian. Tribal institutions are public, nonprofit institutions accredited in the same manner and by the same regional accrediting body as state institutions. The TCUs receive federal funding only for *American Indian students* (defined as students who are enrolled members or the biological children of enrolled members of federally recognized tribes). TCUs are authorized by Congress to receive $8,000 per Indian student; however, they actually receive only $6,355 per Indian student (fiscal year 2015). In comparison, another minority-serving institution (MSI) that receives federal operating funds, Howard University, is funded at nearly $22,000 per student, not limited by race/ethnicity.

TCU Leadership

One becomes president of a TCU by applying. It is that simple, and yet it is also complicated in that most tribes and tribal organizations have Indian preference hiring policies. While being a tribal member where the TCU is located is a good thing, it can also be very political and stressful. TCU presidents must be adept at managing politics, including the art of communication in keeping the tribal government, respective boards of regents/trustees, and various stakeholder groups informed. A TCU president must also be very good at financial management and networking the very limited resources. TCU presidents must have a strong understanding of the student learning process and the assessment of student learning—within the context of AI/AN students.

Of the 37 TCU presidents in June 2014, 34 were American Indian or Alaska Native. Of these, 27 were presidents at TCUs wherein they were tribal members. There were 14 female presidents. One president had a JD degree, 22 had doctoral degrees, 5 were working on doctorates, and the remaining nine TCU presidents all had master's degrees. Six presidents were tribal college graduates.

TCU Student Profile

A "typical" TCU student is a single mother who works full-time. She is, on average, 28 years old, is Pell (federal financial aid) eligible, and is more likely to be a first-generation college student (59% of all TCU students are first-generation). The demographics for TCU students are changing, however—for example, the percentage of female students in 2004 was 66%, but dropped to 63% in 2011. Besides gender, similar shifts are seen for age and first-generation status. TCUs are experiencing a significant increase—23% in enrollment from 2008 to 2012—as Native people see higher education as the pathway to independence and self-sufficiency (AIHEC, 2012).

Degree Completion

Pertinent issues regarding Indian education include the facts that AI/AN youth face some of the lowest high school graduation rates in the nation, and educational attainment rates for AI/ANs are the lowest of all ethnic and racial groups (see Table 8.1).

TABLE 8.1

Educational Attainment: 2006–2010 American Community Survey Five-Year Estimates

	Spirit Lake	ND	US
High school graduates, % of persons age 18+	72.3	89.4	85
Bachelor's degree or higher, % of persons age 18+	7.4	26.3	27.9

Source. U.S. Census Bureau, 2010.

Note. ND = North Dakota; US = United States.

There are many factors related to the issue of educational achievement for American Indians and Alaska Natives, and although each is described separately in this chapter, all are interrelated and connected. One affects another, and each is a part of the history of how and why Native people live the way we do.

Economic Status

Severe poverty is a contributing factor for low education attainment for AI/ANs. Median household income for North Dakota is $35,590, while for Spirit Lake reservation it is $18,000. Seven of the 10 poorest counties in the United States have a tribal college. A majority of reservations where most TCUs are located have double the U.S. poverty rate of 14% and unemployment rates greater than 50%. For the Spirit Lake Dakota Tribe, unemployment is 57%, as compared to North Dakota's rate of less than 2.4%, or the U.S. rate of 6.1%. The Spirit Lake Tribe is located in Benson County, which is one of the three counties in North Dakota with double the U.S. poverty rate. On the Spirit Lake Reservation, 80% of the *employed* population lives below the poverty guidelines (U.S. Bureau of Indian Affairs 2013).

The national average for all college students receiving Pell Grants was 36% for the academic year 2012–2013. For TCU students, approximately 80% received Pell Grants, and that number is closer to 90% at many TCUs. And though Pell helps fill the gap for our students, it is not nearly sufficient. The maximum Pell award per year is $5,645, and with the average annual cost of TCU education at $13,800, that leaves an unmet need of $8,155 or 60%. Federal student loans are offered at only two TCUs, and therefore TCU students struggle to fill the unmet need. The average annual income of students entering tribal college for the first time is $15,262, as contrasted with the average cost of a TCU education at $13,800 (including the average annual tuition cost of $2,964) (AIHEC, 2012).

Serious Health Disparities

According to the Indian Health Service AI/ANs (IHS, 2004–2006), American Indians and Alaska Natives experience disproportionately high mortality compared to all races in the United States. Age-adjusted mortality rates per 100,000 are discussed in this section (see Table 8.2).

Death rates are significantly higher for AI/ANs than for all other Americans: tuberculosis, 500%; alcohol-related, 514%; diabetes, 177%; unintentional injuries, 140%; homicide, 92%; and suicide, 82%. Nationally, from 2009–2011, substance-use disorders were higher among American Indian youth than all youth (12.9% versus 7.1%) and American Indian adults (16.9% versus 8.5%). Unmet need for substance abuse treatment among American Indian adults was consistently higher than for all adults, ranging from 19.1% to 9.8% versus 8.7% to 7.6% (Substance Abuse and Mental Health Services Administration [SAMHSA] 2012).

According to results of the 2012 North Dakota Behavioral Risk Factor Surveillance System (BRFSS), 36% of American Indians in North Dakota reported that their mental health (including stress, depression, and problems with emotions) was not good at some time in the past 30 days, compared with 32% of non-Indians. It was also noted that 23% of the Native population reported being told they had a depressive disorder, as opposed to 14.7% of non-Indians in North Dakota; between 2006 and 2011, American Indian adults perceived unmet need for mental health services and substance abuse treatment as consistently higher than all North Dakota adults (SAMHSA, 2012).

There is no specific research being conducted regarding Native college students attending tribal colleges and universities and the issues of alcohol,

TABLE 8.2
Comparison of Mortality Rates per 100,000

Health Related Issue	AI/AN (%)	U.S. All Races (%)
Alcohol Use	43.0	7.0
Diabetes	68.1	24.6
Homicide (Assault)	11.7	6.1
Motor Vehicle Crashes	47.9	15.2
Pneumonia/Influenza	27.1	20.3
Suicide	19.1	10.9
Tuberculosis	1.2	0.2
Unintentional Injuries	93.8	39.1

Source. Indian Health Service, 2004–2006.

drug, or mental health problems. In 2012, 27 of the 37 TCUs collaborated with the Center for Indigenous Health Research, Indigenous Wellness Research Institute, National Center of Excellence, University of Washington, to conduct a needs and capacity assessment survey to document what is known about (a) alcohol and other drug use; (b) risk, protective factors, and outcomes; (c) best practices; and (d) organizational capacity and readiness. Students, faculty, and staff at TCUs completed the initial assessment on key perceptions in the four areas.

As one of the 27 participating TCUs, CCCC is an engaged and vested member of the Spirit Lake Dakota community. Over 70% of our employees are Native and primarily Spirit Lake Dakota tribal members, and approximately 97% of our student population is Native. The collaboration with the Indigenous Wellness Research Institute is a long-term partnership that is establishing benchmark data regarding perceptions on alcohol and other drugs and the role the tribal college is playing in response. Preliminary findings from the assessment are that alcohol or drugs are being used for escapist or social reasons and that use does have a negative impact on the success of a college student. The perceptions noted from the assessment are also validating the important role of a tribal college as a safe haven, as a referral source, and as a place to strengthen identity and self-worth.

College Readiness

Many TCU students need remediation help with math (74%) or reading and writing (over 50%); thus, academic readiness is a constant struggle at institutions that do not have the resources for adequate support services (AIHEC, 2012). In a report released in March 2014, 52% of 2013's American Indian high school graduates who took the ACT college readiness assessment met none of the four ACT College Readiness Benchmarks (English, math, reading, and science) that indicate likely success in credit-bearing first-year college courses (ACT, 2013).

Lack of Buildings and Faculty

Many TCU campuses began in buildings that were abandoned or condemned, although improvements were being made prior to the sequestration of federal budgets a few years ago. Unfortunately, there are no primary funding sources for rehabilitation or construction projects for the tribal colleges or for other tribal construction needs. Construction or rehabilitation funding continues to be a priority for AIHEC, but the lack of adequate facilities and appropriate classrooms for the tribal colleges continues to be an issue contributing to poorer student outcomes.

Recruiting qualified faculty and in particular Native faculty is another significant disparity for Indian education outcomes. As of academic year 2011–2012, only 41% of faculty at TCUs were Native; of those, 56% were women (women were 72% of all faculty). Fewer than half (48%) of Native faculty had a master's degree or higher (73% for non-Native faculty). Full-time Native faculty earned an average of 13% less than non-Native faculty (AIHEC, 2012).

Violence in Indian Country

Another relevant educational issue is that AI/ANs are victims of sexual assault at much higher rates than any other race of people in the United States. According to the U.S. Department of Justice (2012), Native women are more than 3.5 times more likely to be raped or sexually assaulted than women of any other race in this country. AI/ANs are less likely to get the services needed after a crime occurs and are more likely to suffer long-term effects of violence. Nationally, one out of four women will be assaulted physically or sexually by the time she is 18, but for Native women that number rises to one out of three. Since many crimes are not reported, the count is probably much higher. For males nationally, one out of six will be assaulted by the time he is 18, but for Native men that figure rises to one out of five.

Student Transportation

The average commute for a tribal college student is 30 to 100 miles one way, and most reservations do not have public transportation options (AIHEC, 2014). When living in poverty, a car (or money for gas) is another "luxury" that makes attending college impossible without adequate financial assistance. Several tribal colleges provide transportation services for their students as part of retention strategies; however, this puts additional strain on limited budgets.

Technology

While most of America is "plugged in," for most Native people, distance education options are not realistic due to a lack of home computers and low bandwidth on the reservations. The Federal Communications Commission (FCC) in 2011 reported that 65% of all Americans use broadband, while less than 10% of AI/AN communities have broadband access and only 68% of the Native population have access to telephones. According to the FCC, the actual percentage, based on anecdotal evidence, may be even lower for AI/ANs.

Strong collaborations have developed excellent technology systems for most of the TCUs. These collaborations are with the National Science

Foundation, NASA, and state programs and are related to STEM (science, technology, engineering, and math) projects. CCCC is completely wired and wireless and provides its students with community Internet access via its library services, but people have been known to sit in the parking lot to access WiFi.

Family-Orientated Education

All tribal colleges and universities have as their core mission the teaching, learning, and perpetuation of Native culture and language. For Native college students, family and the extended family are paramount to the foundation of indigenous identity. For Dakota people, aunts and uncles were the traditional educators for the children, while parents and grandparents were guides within a structured kinship system. This system had formal and informal rules, taboos, and protocols, but, most important, it conveyed the teachings of common sense living in the natural environment as well as the important boundaries of roles and responsibilities.

Colonization and assimilation policies broke down this system, and Native people (families) were forced into alien dynamics (boarding schools, religious dogma, capitalism, and a democratic form of governance versus consensus) that were nearly successful in eradicating the American Indian family. However damaged or fractured our families are today, we are in fact survivors and resilient human beings. Most Native families today are intergenerational and live together due to poverty, unemployment, and a lack of housing. So the typical TCU student has added responsibilities in that, as adult children, they are supposed to help their families—that might be a nephew, an auntie, or a cousin—who live in the home along with children, parents, or grandparents.

Student Retention

With the pervasive stereotypes and misunderstandings about AI/ANs, most TCU students need help with self-confidence; they need people who believe in them and who reinforce their belief in their abilities. As place-based institutions, TCUs provide a family-centered foundation and culturally rich academic program. Our excellent but limited faculty are specialists in creating a nurturing learning environment that is conducive to the education process, but from a cultural context. TCUs understand the important role we play in modeling behaviors, supporting change, and providing an environment that promotes understanding of our students and families, as well as our communities. TCUs have established research-based data that support the premise that a Native college student, who is rooted in his or her identity and has a support network, has more positive outcomes related to academic achievement and college success.

The TCU overall institutional retention rate is 43% and has improved 32% in eight years. The tribal college graduation rate is up 17%. The actual number of graduates has increased by 15%, and the number of students earning degrees has increased by 13%. These numbers alone do not capture the success of TCU students. Those who attend to gain skills and knowledge for employment or for enrichment, but who are not in school for a certificate or degree, are part of our success. For non-degree-seeking students, the overall TCU *course completion rate* (defined as finishing what they wanted to accomplish) was 63% for the academic year 2011–2012 (AIHEC, 2012).

TCUs were created to provide higher education opportunities for Native peoples and communities. We understand the issues described previously because most of us "live it"—we come from the background that our students face each and every day. The environment is still one of day-to-day survival, but slowly, and through our students, change is happening, one student at a time. CCCC had 37 graduates in May 2014, double the number from 12 years ago. All but two achieved an associate degree; those two earned certificates. The graduating class cumulative GPA was 3.5, and almost all had job offers, were employed, or were transferring to other institutions for bachelor's programs. According to IPEDS, CCCC's graduation rate hovers between 14% and 16%, which is viewed as "not good." From our perspective and calculations (according to our definitions) the rate is closer to 25%. What must be understood is that if CCCC was not here, these 37 students would not have become college graduates. There are many exceptional TCU student success stories that speak to what our students have overcome to achieve their college educations.

Education is touted as the way to improve quality of life. Without tribal colleges and universities, our people would not have that opportunity. There are many reports and articles that discuss how TCUs have filled a void for AI/ANs. Through the TCU organization, AIHEC, we have developed our own database system and are collecting trend analysis on the success of our institutions and achievement of our students. The AIHEC American Indian Measures for Success (AIMS) is documenting the human, social, and financial impact of the TCU system, which currently serves over 80,000 students and community members.

Next Steps

There is no single solution to our challenges beyond an infusion of funding and the professional development of Native people. I offer the follow suggestions based on my many years of working for Indian health and Indian higher education:

- Higher education is the pathway for AI/ANs, and it has taken hold via the tribal colleges and universities system. Unified support and investment for AI/AN higher education opportunities must be acknowledged and supported by national education leaders and organizations as well as by the federal and state governments.
- There must be a more coordinated focus locally for a pre-K–16 education program for each and every tribal nation. This includes increased services for adult learners (e.g., GED certificate holders), literacy, and early childhood education. Tribal leaders must direct and demand this focus from their education administrators as well as governing boards and then advocate with education policymakers for programs that support the local ideas. There are many models of excellence to be followed, but resources are needed to accomplish the task.
- While TCUs do very well with very limited resources, the inequities of funding for higher education opportunities for AI/ANs must be addressed. Expanded student support services, such as career and skills advising, college readiness and academic preparedness, and financial aid that meets the needs of the student, contribute to positive Native student outcomes in college.
- TCUs must partner better and assist our students in transferring to other TCUs for terminal degrees. A stronger TCU alliance with articulation agreements could be accomplished through distance education initiatives. This means strengthening the existing TCU system's academic, career, and technical education programs for a variety of career paths and skill levels, integrating technology as a resource for student learning and institutional advancement for student success. It also includes cultural integration, apprenticeships, internships, and programs that support Native student outcomes for terminal degrees in disciplines needed by the tribal community. Mentoring and leadership projects, along with professional development for Native faculty, are all components of a more comprehensive and focused response to the unmet need for Native higher education.
- Mainstream institutions should expand their outreach to TCUs, but on our terms. We no longer want (or need) the "Great White Father" mentality when it comes to educating Native students. TCU students who transfer to the state system need more personal support and attention in addition to adequate financial aid. There are working models at most TCUs regarding this type of true collaboration and many in the STEM disciplines, as well as dual credit programs with the high schools.
- Education policy leaders and organizations should help in minimizing stereotypes by promoting literacy and discussions on history from

Native people's point of view, as well as more in-depth education on racism, prejudice, and bias for all college students.

Final Comments

In a 2009 report, *The State of the World's Indigenous Peoples*, the United Nations articulates that education is a fundamental human right:

> Education is recognized as both a human right in itself and an indispensable means of realizing other human rights and fundamental freedoms, the primary vehicle by which economically and socially marginalized peoples can lift themselves out of poverty and obtain the means to participate fully in their communities. Education is increasingly recognized as one of the best long-term financial investments that States can make. (p. 130)

As educators, we must practice what we teach, including the joy of learning—academic learning as well as everyday learning, which is the fundamental basis of indigenous education and is science-based. As a Dakota grandmother, educator, and a modern-day "leader," I must continue to incorporate cultural knowledge with our academic programs of study. We believe, and have a saying, *taku wakan ska ska*—something holy moving. Life is something holy moving. It is a healing and learning journey that we must do a better job of, as our time is so very brief. Having a safe environment to ask the questions and to search for solutions, all the while promoting cooperation, are components of an education process for all. We should do our best to better understand each other and to live together in a good way. This is education.

References

ACT. (2013). American Indian students. *The Condition of College and Career Readiness 2013*. Retrieved from http://www.act.org/newsroom/data/2013/states/americanindian.html

American Indian Higher Education Consortium. (2012). Equity in Educational Land-Grant Status Act of 1994 (7 U.S.C. §301). *AIHEC AIMS Fact Book, 2009–2010*. Alexandria, VA: Author.

American Indian Higher Education Consortium. (2014). *Overview of AIHEC*. Retrieved from http://www.aihec.org

Federal Communications Commission. (2011, July 29). *Chairman Genachowski address to National Congress of American Indians*. Washington, DC: Author. Retrieved from https://www.fcc.gov/events/chairman-genachowski-address-national-congress-american-indians

Indian Health Service. (2004–2006). *Indian health disparities*. Retrieved from http://www.ihs.gov/newsroom/factsheets/disparities/

Substance Abuse and Mental Health Services Administration. (2012). *National survey on drug use and health* (2009–2010, revised 2012). Rockville, MD: Author.

United Nations. (2009). *State of the world's Indigenous peoples*. New York, NY: Author. Retrieved from http://www.un.org/esa/socdev/unpfii/documents/SOWIP/en/SOWIP_web.pdf

U.S. Bureau of Indian Affairs. (2013). *Labor force report*. Retrieved from http://www.bia.gov/cs/groups/public/documents/text/idc1-024782.pdf

U.S. Census Bureau. (2010). Educational attainment. 2006–2010 American community survey 5-year estimates. Retrieved from https://www.census.gov/programs-surveys/acs/data/race-aian.html

U.S. Department of Justice. (2012). *American Indians and Crime* (2/14/1999) and *American Indians and Crime: A BJS Statistical Profile*, 1999–2002 (12/1/2004). Retrieved from http://www.bjs.gov/index.cfm?ty=pbdetail&iid=386

9

CUTTING-EDGE MODELS
FOR BEST PRACTICE

The Intersection of Education and Culture: Utilizing
Symbols, Relationships, and Traditions to Improve
Enrollment Management of American Indian Students

James Utterback

*Loneliness . . . to many people, no family, few Indians for support. We run to the ocean, camp in
the mountains when we can. Call our families often. . . . We can spend a day looking into the
campus mirror and see no Indian face but our own.*

—G. Clever, 1983

T he plight described by Clever is all too common among American
Indian students today. American Indians still graduate from high
school at lower rates, seek college at lower rates, and persist in college
at lower rates than any other ethnic group (Creighton, 2007; Schmidtke,
2009; Shotton, Oosahwe, & Cintron, 2007). As with the poor success rates
of other underrepresented students, the mass attrition of American Indian
students can cost valuable institutional resources and negatively affect the
institution's ability to meet its mission. In many ways, the lack of success
of these often underprepared, low-income, first-generation, and otherwise
at-risk students may also demonstrate a failure on the part of the institution
to meet a variety of special student needs (Creighton, 2007). Seminole State
College (SSC) has been particularly successful in enrolling Native American
students in higher percentages than they appear in the general population.
While 8.6% of the population in Oklahoma is Native American, Native students comprise roughly 25% of the SSC student population.

SSC is a public, state-supported, open-door, two-year institution located
in Seminole, Oklahoma. The college's service area covers 3,819 square miles

and is home to just over 140,000 people. As the only open-door college in the area, SSC has historically educated rural, economically disadvantaged, first-generation students with low levels of academic preparedness and high levels of academic need. The students from SSC's service area typically come from very small rural localities, with 44 of the 55 communities in the five-county service area having populations under 1,500 (U.S. Census Bureau, 2015). On average, 60% of the annual SSC student population is classified as low-income individuals.

The college is a Native American–serving non-tribal institution. SSC averages roughly 35% minority enrollment. The greatest percentage of the SSC minority population (70%) is American Indian. SSC is located in the heart of the Seminole Nation in central Oklahoma, the home of the Seminole tribe of Native Americans. Ten Native American tribes have affiliations in the SSC service area. Students at SSC typically come from as many as 25 to 30 different tribes.

At SSC, Native American heritage is taken seriously. Prior to statehood, Oklahoma was known as Indian Territory. The name "Oklahoma" was derived from two Choctaw words, *Okla Huma*, meaning "Red People." The Great Seal of the state of Oklahoma consists of a five-pointed star, with each point containing the official seal of one of the so-called Five Civilized Tribes: the Choctaws, Chickasaws, Cherokees, Creeks, and Seminoles. The SSC campus community is proud to be *Seminole* State College, in the city of *Seminole,* in *Seminole* County, in *Okla Huma*, in the heart of the land originally assigned to the *Seminole Nation*—tribally known as "The Land Between the Rivers." It is a proud heritage that is actively appreciated at SSC.

As a Native American president of a rural community college in Oklahoma, the author of this chapter possesses a personal vested interest in helping American Indian students succeed. The author's maternal family name is LeFlore. Family members are descendents of Greenwood LeFlore, the first principal chief, or Mingo, of the Choctaw Nation, who led the Choctaws during the signing of the Treaty at Dancing Rabbit Creek, containing the now-famous language giving Oklahoma to the American Indians "for as long as the grasses grow."

The history of American Indians now located in Oklahoma reflects the mistreatment of Indians across this country and serves to highlight some of the challenges still facing Native people. Indians located in what is now the southeastern United States were forcibly removed from their homelands to Oklahoma along a path that has come to be known as the Trail of Tears.

The generational effects of the mistreatment that occurred along the Trail of Tears are still seen today in college access and persistence rates. High levels of mistrust, fear, depression, alcoholism, and other social issues remain among the nearly 350,000 Oklahomans with documented Native American ancestral ties. Such social issues create challenges for the enrollment and success of Native American students (Cunningham, 2007).

Recruitment and Retention

Students drop out of college for a wide variety of reasons, including being underprepared academically, financial constraints, family concerns, employment conflicts, lack of engagement, and a host of similar reasons (Laskey & Hetzel, 2011; O'Keeffe, 2013; Turner & Thompson, 2014). The plight of Native American students becomes even more complicated. While the demoralizing socioeconomic status of Native Americans is certainly a primary cause of attrition, Agboo (2001) has discussed "cultural discontinuity," particularly as related to concepts of time and space, as a major reason for the lack of academic success of Native Students (Agboo as cited in Creighton, 2007).

So, SSC reaches out to Native students in secondary schools in higher numbers, assists those students in coming to college, and strives to help them achieve their educational goals. SSC has not tackled these challenges alone. The Seminole and Chickasaw Nations have made major contributions to the college's Educational Foundation to support services to at-risk students.

One of the targets of the relationship with the Seminole Nation has been to increase the number of Native students living on campus. This is an important goal in that studies show that students who live on campus during their freshman year are much more likely to graduate than students who live in any other arrangement. In highly quoted longitudinal studies of more than 500,000 students, Astin (1975, 1982, 1993) discussed numerous positive effects of living in residence halls, including students' showing lower attrition rates, achieving higher cumulative grade-point averages, and realizing greater persistence to graduation.

Cultural Environment

Making students feel welcome and connected on campus is an important aspect of cultural sensitivity. Special ceremonies are held every year on the campus of SSC to make Native students feel welcomed. In addition to events like these that may involve students, their families, counselors, and tribal leaders, SSC proudly displays on campus a seven-foot-tall "artist's proof" statue of *The Guardian*, which stands on top of the Oklahoma State Capital building.

Demonstrating for everyone the value placed on SSC's Native heritage, one of the buildings on campus is named for a world-famous artist, former

Oklahoma state senator, and former chief of the Seminole Nation, Enoch Kelly Haney. As people enter the Haney Center, they are greeted with a seven-foot statue of an Indian warrior, *Standing His Ground*. The story of this statue is based on a tradition made famous by Comanche warriors. These fighters were known for choosing a spot in a battle and staking themselves to the ground. At that point, their commitment was that no matter how the other side attacked them, no matter what the odds, they would not move from that spot.

Chief Haney has suggested that everyone does this in life. Whether against employers, spouses, the government, or some other such entity, at some point people decide on certain convictions from which they will not be moved (Haney, 2014).

As chairman of the powerful Appropriations Committee in the Oklahoma Senate, then-senator Haney was always known for standing his ground for education, on every level. His belief was that no entity was ever more deserving of funding than education. The *Standing His Ground* statue, the Comanche warrior story, and Chief Haney's legacy for education serve as models for young Indian students. College officials try to make the point to traditional-age students that people have stood their ground to give them a chance at an education. Their parents, their tribal guidance counselors, their tribal leaders believe in them and have sacrificed time and resources to help them be successful.

Two of the most recent buildings constructed on the Seminole State College campus are publicly associated with the Native American community. In 2008, a new three-story, 150-bed, state-of-the-art residence hall was dedicated as the Seminole Nation Residential Learning Center. A partnership with the local tribe led to financial assistance with the construction of the building. In addition to sleeping and small group-living areas, the living-learning center includes a computer lab, group study rooms, a laundry, and large recreational common areas. Prominent signage in both English and Seminole languages identifies the connection to the Seminole Nation. Artwork by Native American artists decorates the interior. Photos are displayed from the facility's ribbon-cutting ceremony, which featured comments from tribal leaders and a large attendance by members of the Seminole Nation. The event photos also show a Seminole tribal member playing a handmade traditional flute and a ceremonial "cedar fire blessing" on the building from a Kiowa medicine man.

The Ben and Bonnie Walkingstick Student Services Center, opened in 2010, honors a prominent state Native American business leader and long-time supporter of the college, Ben Walkingstick, and his wife. The building houses business and admissions offices, an area for student computer use, academic testing, counseling, the campus police headquarters, and student meeting areas. It was designed to allow these various areas to be housed under one roof to better serve students. Native American art, including paintings and sculptures, are displayed throughout the center. In addition to the cultural climate created by these buildings, Ben and Bonnie Walkingstick reached out to financially help Native American students attending the school. They established a scholarship in honor of Ben's late aunt, a Cherokee, who was a longtime social worker in the area. Again, this legacy and the associated scholarship assistance help Native students see that they can be successful.

Support from community donors illustrates for Native students the strong ties SSC maintains with its cultural heritage. Throughout campus, significant buildings, meeting rooms, and outdoor areas are named for prominent Native American donors or are adorned with the artwork of noted local artists. The distinct and determined use of artwork, cultural activities, and Welcome Week events demonstrates to students from their very first days on campus that SSC values their cultures. In addition, SSC welcomes several tribes on campus to hold events for their members. These have included college fairs, job fairs, graduation ceremonies, festivals, and celebrations. Whenever possible, SSC strives to participate in major off-campus tribal events, such as the annual Seminole Nation Days celebration.

Utilizing Special Programs

There are a number of federal grant programs designed to help underrepresented or underprepared students finish high school, make a transition to college, and complete college. At the time of this paper, SSC had nine of these federal programs including the following:

Gaining Early Awareness and Readiness for Undergraduate Programs (GEAR UP)

- three Upward Bound programs
- two Talent Search programs
- two Student Support Services Programs
- one Native American-Serving Nontribal Institutions (NASNTI) Program

Using a tiered approach, these programs target at-risk students from elementary school through college. Taken as a whole, these special programs help students complete high school and continue that success through college. Many of these projects help provide funds for traditional student support services on campus, including proper course placement, academic advising, learning communities, and tutoring. In addition, funding may also be used for enrichment programs, including cultural celebrations, cultural dances, and food festivals.

Targeting low-income, first-generation students and other at-risk students, these programs have over-enrollments of Indian students compared to the rest of the population. For example, 15% of SSC Upward Bound students, 29% of the students in Educational Talent Search, and 38% of the students in GEAR UP are Native Americans. Once in college, SSC offers special assistance to the students at every opportunity. In an on-campus federal support program, Student Support Services, 32% of the students are American Indians, compared to 23% on campus.

Partnerships

Relationships are a vital part of the lives of American Indians. It would be quite difficult for institutions to manage the enrollment of American Indian students without the cooperation and support of persons close to those students. Beyond the family, this support is often found in tribal leaders and educational representatives.

There is a well-known adage that "if momma ain't happy, ain't nobody happy." In tribal terms, that could be translated to "if the chief ain't happy, ain't nobody happy." It may be difficult for non-Indians to understand or appreciate the reverence paid to tribal leaders. The chiefs of many tribes are held in very high esteem. Tribal council members are often members of clans, which may be extended tribal families. To make tribal partnerships last over time, it is important for colleges to establish meaningful relationships with these types of tribal leaders and elders, whom young people are taught to appreciate and respect.

SSC has utilized numerous partnerships to foster recruitment as well as retention, of American Indian students. The SSC Educational Foundation has enjoyed substantial support from many tribes across the state. At the time of this writing, the chief of the Seminole and chairman of the Citizen Potawatomi Nations of Oklahoma and his accompanying leaders are active members of the SSC Educational Foundation Board of Trustees. The Chickasaw Nation is represented on the foundation by its president of corporate development. The chief of the Sac and Fox has also served on the foundation's board of directors. Tribal governments' engaging with SSC and, conversely, SSC's engaging with tribal governments are keys to successful recruitment and retention of American Indian students.

Moreover, the college has been quite successful in its attempts to graduate Native students once they enroll. In 2013, for example, 25% of all the graduates of SSC were Native American. This success is not by accident. SSC takes seriously the issues related to making students feel welcomed. At every turn, college officials ask themselves how and what they can do better for Native students.

Importance of Family and Time

The role of relationships in the lives of Native American college students cannot be overstated. Saggio (2001) showed that family influences affected both the choice of institutions by students as well as the persistence of those students. At SSC, Native students have brought children and even parents to classes. Many American Indian students have reported loneliness and separation issues as the largest source of their anxiety on campus.

On many campuses, there is a similar cultural discontinuity relative to the issue of time. Most people have heard comments or jokes about "Indian time." On a college campus, as it relates to student success, this cultural insensitivity is not a laughing matter. Time is not important in many Native American cultures in the same ways as in other cultures. To the extent possible, faculty and staff need to be understanding of this issue.

Any college that is not sensitive to working around cultural issues related to family values and time will not retain Native American students. Schmidtke (2009) similarly concluded from a series of previous studies that "if instructors are truly student-centered, they must adapt to the needs of their students and not expect students to be the ones to change" (p. 50).

Discussion

Addressing issues related to the recruitment and retention of American Indian students is at once imperative as well as commendable. From a financial standpoint, increased retention of just a few percentage points can result in hundreds of thousands of dollars in increased revenue. At least equally important, creating a culturally sensitive environment designed to improve the success of at-risk students reflects important values at the very core of the institution.

The law of the land supports a focus on the value of student diversity. Writing for the majority in *Grutter v. Bollinger* (2003), U.S. Supreme Court Justice Sandra Day O'Connor noted that

> student body diversity is a compelling state interest. . . . [It] promotes cross-racial understanding, helps breakdown racial stereotypes, and enables students to better understand persons of different races. These benefits are important and laudable, because classroom discussion is livelier, more spir-

ited, and simply more enlightening and interesting when the students have the greatest possible variety of backgrounds. (539 U.S. at 330–333)

At every level—in every manner possible—SSC has made special and significant efforts designed to increase the success of Native American students. One overarching goal in dealing with American Indians is to let them know that the college recognizes and values their heritage. Every year, SSC celebrates Native American Day with special traditional activities.

Utilizing partnerships with tribes, colleges can demonstrate a true concern and understand the issues facing American Indian students. Tribal leaders play a pivotal role in influencing the postsecondary educational choices of students. In addition, everyone on campus benefits from the concomitant increase of diversity on campus that occurs with the establishment of meaningful partnerships.

Special federal programs, including TRIO and Title III grants, can provide important student support services as well as funds for cultural and educational activities. Utilization of the student support mechanisms prevalent in these programs increases the chances of student success. In the difficult financial climate currently being faced by many institutions, the provision of these types of academic and student support programs would be a daunting challenge.

In the final analysis, the enrollment management of American Indian students comes down to *respect*. Being cognizant and appreciative of time-honored traditions, the importance of ceremonies, and the pride that comes with being an American Indian can pave the way for success of Native students. By pursuing this with passion, colleges can help generations of students to achieve their educational dreams. Like the Comanche warriors, educators should stand their ground for the success of underrepresented, at-risk students.

References

Astin, A. W. (1975). *Preventing students from dropping out.* San Francisco, CA: Jossey-Bass.

Astin, A. W. (1982). *Minorities in American higher education: Recent trends, current prospects, and recommendations.* San Francisco, CA: Jossey-Bass.

Astin, A. W. (1993). *What matters in college? Four critical years revisited.* San Francisco, CA: Jossey-Bass.

Clever, G. (1983). The Native American dean: Two shirts in conflict. *NASPA Journal, 21*(2), 60–63.

Creighton, L. M. (2007). Factors affecting the graduation rates of university students from underrepresented populations. *International Electronic Journal for Leadership in Learning, 11*(7), 1–15.

Cunningham, A. F. (2007). *The path of many journeys: The benefits of higher education for Native people and communities.* Washington, DC: Institute for Higher Education Policy. Retrieved from http://www.aihec.org/our-stories/docs/reports/ThePathOfManyJourneys.pdf

Haney, E. K. (2014). Enoch Kelly Haney sculpture. Retrieved from http://www.kellyhaney.com

Laskey, M., & Hetzel, C. (2011). Investing factors related to retention of at-risk college students. *Learning Assistance Review, 16*(1), 31–43.

O'Keeffe, P. (2013). A sense of belonging: Improving student retention. *College Student Journal, 47*(4), 605–613.

Saggio, J. (2001, November). *Family and its effect on institutional choice and post-freshman retention of American Indian/Alaska Native students at a Bible college.* Paper presented at the annual conference of the Association for the Study of Higher Education, Richmond, VA.

Schmidtke, C. (2009). "That's what really helped me was their teaching": Instructor impact on the retention of American Indian students at a two-year technical college. *Journal of Industrial Teacher Education, 46*(1), 48–80.

Shotton, H. J., Oosahwe, E. S. L., & Cintron, R. (2007). Stories of success: Experiences of American Indian students in a peer-mentoring retention program. *Review of Higher Education, 31*(1), 81–107.

Turner, P., & Thompson, E. (2014). College retention initiatives meeting the needs of millennial freshman students. *College Student Journal, 48*(1), 94–104.

U.S. Census Bureau. (2015). *Quick facts.* Retrieved from http://www.census.gov/quickfacts/table/PST045215/40133,40

PART FOUR

ASIAN AMERICAN AND PACIFIC ISLANDER STUDENT POPULATIONS

10

VOICE OF THE NATIONAL RESEARCHER

Asian American and Pacific Islanders in the Community College

Robert Teranishi

The older I grow, the more I am convinced that there is no education which one can get from books and costly apparatus that is equal to that which can be gotten from contact with great men and women.

—Booker T. Washington

The racial composition of many postsecondary institutions is projected to undergo significant demographic changes in the coming decades (Kena, Aud, Johnson, Wang, Zhang, Rathbun, et al. 2014). These fundamental shifts in the racial composition of higher education require more attention to specific subgroups that have historically been overlooked and underserved (Hurtado, 2007). The Asian American and Pacific Islander (AAPI) undergraduate student population, for example, is projected to increase by 35% over the next decade, which is a larger proportional gain than any other major racial group (Teranishi, 2010). While popular perceptions of AAPI enrollment in higher education have mostly revolved around highly selective universities, *the majority of AAPI students attend less selective and lower resourced institutions.* In fact, it is in the community college sector where AAPI undergraduates have their greatest representation and where the population is projected to increase at its fastest rate over the next decade (National Commission on Asian American and Pacific Islander Research in Education [CARE], 2010).

With the increase in AAPI college participation in coming years—especially in community colleges—there is a need for greater insight into the AAPI community college population and a thoughtful consideration of how the higher education community can respond to the unique needs of these students. In this chapter, data are presented on the demography of the national AAPI population, the ways these demographic factors contribute to the composition of AAPI students attending community colleges, and the ways AAPIs in community colleges are similar to and different from AAPIs in four-year colleges. The chapter then makes recommendations for promising practices and targeted interventions that promote access and success for this population. This chapter is complementary to the following (chapter 11) submitted by Lee Lambert, which discusses the needs and challenges associated with advocacy in the AAPI community relative to college access and success.

The Demography of AAPI Populations

The remarkable change in the AAPI student population in American higher education is reflective of larger demographic changes that are occurring in the national population. Thus, population trends in actual and projected numbers for the AAPI population demonstrate significant changes that require attention by higher education practitioners, policymakers, and researchers. While the AAPI population was relatively small until 1960, when it was less than 1 million, it has doubled in size nearly every decade since then. Growing at an exponential rate, the AAPI population reached over 15 million persons in 2010 (Table 10.1). The growth in the population is anticipated to continue at a significant pace. According to projections to 2050, this population is estimated to reach nearly 40 million persons.

The remarkable growth of the AAPI population has been particularly pronounced following changes to immigration policy in 1965 and refugee policy in 1975 and 1980, which vastly increased the growth, diversity, and complexity of the AAPI population (Teranishi, 2010). Therefore, a

TABLE 10.1
**Asian American and Pacific Islander Population Change, 1890–2010
(in Thousands)**

Year	Number	Percentage (%) Change
1890	109	—
1930	265	143
1970	1,539	481
2010	15,214	889

Source. U.S. Census Bureau, Population Division, 2015.

particularly salient issue for the AAPI community is the extent to which it is unlike any other major racial group in the United States in regard to its heterogeneity. According to research from the National Commission on Asian Americans and Pacific Islanders in Education (2010), for example, the AAPI racial category consists of 48 different ethnic groups that occupy positions along the full range of the socioeconomic spectrum, from the poor and underprivileged to the affluent and highly skilled. AAPIs also vary demographically in regard to language background, immigration history, culture, and religion.

If we focus on median household income, for example, we can see that the average for the AAPI population in the aggregate conceals significant differences between AAPI subgroups. Hmong, Bangladeshis, and Cambodians have household income levels that are approximately $20,000 less than the median household income of all AAPIs. However, Asian Indians have a median household income that is more than $20,000 greater than the median household income for all AAPIs, which is $40,000 more than Hmong, Bangladeshis, and Cambodians (CARE, 2013).

While a significant proportion of immigrants from Asia come to the United States already highly educated, others enter the United States from countries that have provided only limited opportunities for educational and social mobility. *Pacific Islanders*, defined as people whose origins are from Polynesia, Micronesia, or Melanesia, are a diverse pan-ethnic group in themselves, whose histories include such challenges as the struggle for sovereignty. Yet these and other unique circumstances in such populations are often overshadowed by being grouped with Asian Americans. Thus, while the AAPI population represents a single entity in certain contexts, such as for interracial group comparisons, it is equally important to understand the ways in which the demography of the population comprises a complex set of social realities for individuals and communities that fall within this category.

These national demographic trends are representative of the changing demography of our schools and colleges, and these changes in enrollment are projected to continue in the future. Public K–12 enrollment of AAPIs, for example, grew fourfold in the 30-year period between 1979 and 2009, from 650,000 to 2.5 million (Table 10.2). Enrollment projections show that this trend will continue through 2019. While the proportional representation of Whites and Blacks is projected to decrease by 4% each, Hispanics are projected to increase by 36%, AAPIs by 31%, and Native Americans by 13% (U.S. Department of Education, 2011b).

The face of American higher education has also experienced profound changes that are important to note. AAPI college enrollment grew fivefold,

TABLE 10.2
AAPI Public K–12 and Undergraduate Enrollment, 1979–2019

Year	AAPI Public K–12 Enrollment	AAPI Undergraduate Enrollment
1979	650,000	235,000
1989	1,267,000	550,000
1999	1,892,000	913,000
2009	2,523,000	1,332,000
2019	3,140,000	1,698,000

Source. U.S. Department of Education, 2011b.

for instance, between 1979 and 2009 from 235,000 to 1.3 million (U.S. Department of Education, 2011a). And while college enrollment is projected to increase for all racial groups, AAPIs will experience a particularly high proportional increase of 30% between 2009 and 2019. Given these trends, equity and diversity need to be at the heart of how we think about reform in American higher education.

AAPI Enrollment in Community Colleges

A particularly important sector of higher education for the AAPI community is the American community college. AAPI community college enrollment is greater than their enrollment in any other sector of higher education. In 2005, for example, AAPI enrollment in public, two-year colleges was 471,299, while their enrollment in public, four-year colleges was 383,166 (Table 10.3). As a result, 47.3% of the total AAPI enrollment in American higher education was in public, two-year colleges.

The increase in size and proportional representation of AAPIs in community colleges is also a notable trend in American higher education. Between 1985 and 2005, for example, their numerical and proportional representation at community colleges has been increasing faster than is the case at four-year institutions. Just in the decade between 1990 and 2000, AAPI community college enrollment increased by 73.3%, compared to an increase of 42.2% in the public four-year institutions (CARE, 2010). As a result of the rise in AAPI enrollment in community colleges, AAPI students represent more than 7% of community college enrollment nationally, while AAPIs made up less than 5% of the national population in 2007. These trends are projected to continue, with AAPI enrollment at community colleges outpacing their change in enrollment in all other sectors of higher education.

TABLE 10.3
**AAPI Total Enrollment in Public Two-Year and Public Four-Year Institutions,
1985–2005**

	Public Two-Year		Public Four-Year	
	Number	Percent	Number	Percent
1985	184,792	41.7	185,421	41.8
1995	345,303	44.6	310,650	40.1
2005	471,299	47.3	383,166	38.4

Source. U.S. Department of Education, IPEDS, 2015.

Educational Experiences and Outcomes of AAPI Community College Students

The demographic trends of AAPIs in community colleges have a number of implications for understanding this population's needs, challenges, and opportunities. Perhaps most paramount is the importance of community colleges to the most marginalized and vulnerable AAPI subgroups—groups that have historically experienced low college participation rates. Trends in educational attainment for a number of AAPI subgroups are representative of this problem. Consider that 51.1% of Vietnamese, 63.2% of Hmong, 65.5% of Laotian, and 65.8% of Cambodian adults (25 years or older) have not enrolled in or completed any postsecondary education. Similar trends can be found among Pacific Islanders, with 49.3% of Native Hawaiian, 53.0% of Guamanian, 56.8% of Samoan, and 57.9% of Tongan adults who have not enrolled in any form of postsecondary education.

While community colleges can be a key point of entry for many AAPI students, it is also important to recognize the potential challenges associated with their rise in college enrollment. Put another way, AAPI community college students are characteristically different from AAPI students in four-year institutions, although it is in selective four-year institutions that we know most about the AAPI student population. Thus, it is important to consider the characteristics of AAPI community college students and understand their experiences and outcomes relative to the more common perceptions that exist about AAPI college students.

Perhaps the most important difference between AAPI students in community colleges versus those in four-year colleges can be found in their likelihood of resembling a more "traditional student," attending college full-time, enrolling immediately after high school, living on campus, and so on. Analysis of recent data on AAPI community college students shows that 62.9% enrolled as part-time, students, and 31.7% delayed matriculation by two years or more (Kena et al., 2014). With an average age of 27.3 years, AAPI community college students also tended to be older than their AAPI counterparts at four-year institutions. These differences suggest that AAPIs at community colleges, compared to AAPI students at four-year institutions, were more likely to fit the characteristics of "nontraditional" students.

Compared to AAPIs at four-year institutions, AAPI community college students were also more likely to enter college with lower levels of academic preparation in English and mathematics. In 2003, 55.2% of AAPI students entering two-year colleges had never taken a math course beyond Algebra II in high school, as compared to 12.7% of AAPI students entering four-year institutions in that same year (U.S. Department of Education, 2008). With one in five needing remediation in English (Chang, Park, Lin, Poon, & Nakanishi, 2007), AAPI students are also particularly vulnerable to policies and practices that relegate remedial English courses to two-year institutions. These data demonstrate that AAPI students in community colleges carry many risk factors that are correlated with lower rates of persistence and completion among two-year college students. The factors include delayed enrollment, lack of a high school diploma (including GED recipients), part-time enrollment, having dependents other than a spouse, single-parent status, and working full-time while enrolled (35 hours or more).

Differential access to different types of institutions and significant differences in the characteristics of AAPI students attending community colleges and four-year institutions result in a number of implications for the likelihood of degree attainment. Consider that less than one-third of all students who enter community college with the intention of earning a degree accomplish this goal in a six-year period (U.S. Institute of Education Sciences, 2002). Significantly underfunded compared to their public four-year college counterparts, community colleges often lack the resources they need to support their student population, which is heavily composed of those who lack the academic skills needed to succeed in college, those without the resources to finance a college education, working adults, parents, English language learners (ELLs), and first-generation college-goers.

Because some AAPI subgroups are more likely to enroll in community colleges and less selective institutions, there are significant differences in degree attainment rates within the AAPI student population. Consider, for example, that while more than four out of five East Asians (Chinese, Japanese, and Korean) and South Asians (Asian Indian and Pakistani) who entered college earned at least a bachelor's degree, large proportions of other AAPI subgroups are attending college but not earning a degree. Among Southeast Asians, 33.7% of Vietnamese, 42.9% of Cambodians, 46.5% of Laotians, and 47.5% of Hmong adults (25 years or older) reported having attended college but did not earn a degree. Similar to Southeast Asians, Pacific Islanders have a very high proportion of attrition during college. Among Pacific Islanders, 47.0% of Guamanians, 50.0% of Native Hawaiians, 54.0% of Tongans, and 58.1% of Samoans entered college but left without earning a degree. Southeast Asians and Pacific Islanders also had a higher proportion of their college attendees who had an associate degree as their highest level of education, while East Asians and South Asians were more likely to have a bachelor's degree or advanced degree.

Asian American and Native American Pacific Islander–Serving Institutions as Sites for Possibilities

The changing demography of our nation means that our system of higher education must realize a fundamentally different approach to teaching, learning, and student support. With a high concentration of students of color within certain sectors of higher education, one effective policy effort is the federal investment in minority-serving institutions. The Asian American and Native American Pacific Islander–Serving Institution (AANAPISI) Program, for example, initially authorized by the College Cost Reduction and Access Act of 2007, is structured as a competitive grant process for institutions with at least a 10% enrollment of AAPI students, a minimum threshold of low-income students, and lower than average educational and general expenditures per student (similar to requirements for Hispanic-serving institutions). As of 2013, there were 153 institutions eligible to be designated AANAPISIs.

The AANAPISI program, one of the most significant investments ever made for the AAPI college student population by the federal government, is also notable for at least three reasons: First, it acknowledges the unique challenges facing AAPI students in college access and completion. Second, the AANAPISI designation represents a significant commitment of much-needed resources to improving the postsecondary completion rates among AAPI and low-income students. Third, it acknowledges how campus settings can be mutable points of intervention—sites of possibilities for responding to the impediments AAPI students encounter. Research conducted by CARE has examined the extent to which the program is reaching a large concentration of AAPI students, identified the opportunities and resources that are created by the program, and studied the growth potential of the program to reach an even greater concentration of low-income AAPI students.

As discussed earlier, enrollment trends for AAPI students are unique and have implications for policy strategies that target these students. While earlier discussion focused on the size and growth of AAPI enrollment, it is also important to consider the concentration of AAPI undergraduates in a small number of postsecondary institutions. As of 2010, nearly two-thirds of AAPI undergraduate enrollment was concentrated in 200 institutions (CARE, 2011). Among the 153 institutions eligible to be AANAPISIs, as of 2010, the total undergraduate enrollment was 2,857,525, of which 18.8% (536,544) were AAPI students (Figure 10.1). While these 153 institutions represented only 3.4% of all Title IV degree-granting institutions in the U.S. higher education system, they enrolled 41.2% of AAPI undergraduates nationally. Put another way, two-fifths of AAPI undergraduate students[1] in the United States attended an institution eligible to be an AANAPISI, indicating the AANAPISI program has the potential to reach a high proportion of enrolled AAPI students nationally.

A large proportion of AAPI students at AANAPISIs were from low-income backgrounds, were the first in their families to attend college, and struggled to secure the financial resources to support themselves while in school (Yeh, 2004). According to the Congressional Research Service (2009), the first 116 institutions that met the criteria for AANAPISI eligibility enrolled 75% of low-income AAPI undergraduate students. AAPI students attending AANAPISIs were also more likely than their peers to be immigrants; nonnative English speakers; and students who enrolled in ELL programs, which are typically geared toward Spanish speakers (Suzuki, 2002; Teranishi, Nguyen, & Lok, 2013; Yeh, 2004).

While AANAPISIs enroll a disproportionately high number and concentration of AAPI undergraduates, there is a particularly large concentration of community college students served by these institutions. This is because more than half (55.3%) of AANAPISIs are two-year colleges. In terms of

Figure 10.1. Distribution of total enrollment and all AAPI enrollment in AANAPISIs, 2010.

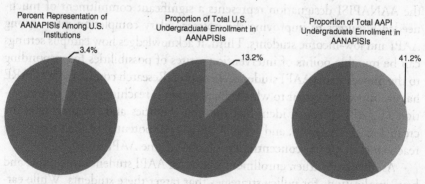

Source. U.S. Department of Education, National Center for Education Statistics (NCES), Integrated Postsecondary Education Data System (IPEDS), 12-month unduplicated headcount, 2015b.

associate degree production, while AANAPISIs represented 3.4% of all Title IV degree-granting institutions and conferred 12.2% of all associate degrees nationally, they represented 47.3% of all associate degrees conferred to AAPI students nationally in 2010 (Figure 10.2).

The backgrounds of students attending AANAPISI campuses present a number of unique challenges for which resources can be targeted. In 2010, CARE analyzed the 2008 American Community Survey (ACS) data and found that the neighborhoods served by the University of Hawai'i at Hilo had an average poverty rate for Pacific Islanders that was 20.1%—nearly twice the national poverty rate of 12.4%. In the neighborhoods served by South Seattle Community College, 57.8% of Asian Americans and 70.8% of Pacific Islanders had a high school diploma or less.

The 2010 CARE report also found that large proportions of AAPI students are arriving on campuses underprepared for college-level work, often as a result of growing up in poverty, attending low-performing schools, and being the first in their families to attend college. At De Anza Community College, for example, most of the AAPI students are not prepared for college-level work; AAPI students account for more than half of students enrolled in remedial English and other basic skills classes. More than 80% of the students at Guam Community College were eligible for financial aid, and 58% of the students were older than the traditional college age (18–22 years old). The AANAPISI program not only represents a significant commitment to the AAPI community but also provides much-needed resources to respond to specific needs that affect college access and success for AAPI students.

Figure 10.2. Distribution of associate degrees conferred by AANAPISIs to all students and AAPI students, 2010.

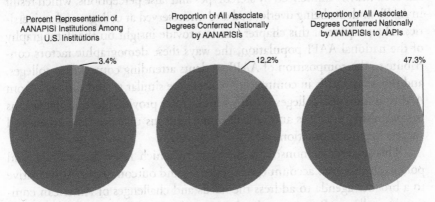

| Percent Representation of AANAPISI Institutions Among U.S. Institutions | Proportion of All Associate Degrees Conferred Nationally by AANAPISIs | Proportion of All Associate Degrees Conferred Nationally by AANAPISIs to AAPIs |
| 3.4% | 12.2% | 47.3% |

Source. U.S. Department of Education, National Center for Education Statistics (NCES), Integrated Postsecondary Education Data System (IPEDS), full-year degree production, 2015a.

AANAPISIs engage in a range of initiatives aimed at increasing access to and success in college for AAPI students. While each one of the AANAPISIs is using the funding in unique ways, several commonalities exist among the programs. In the area of student services, AANAPISI funding is being used to develop student learning communities, first-year experience programs, academic and personal counselors and advisers, and tutoring programs. These programs improve the quality of students' experiences during college, improve persistence, and connect students with services that they may have not otherwise utilized.

Funding is also being used for curricular and academic program development, which includes improving the academic quality of the education offered, increasing the quantity and variety of courses being offered to students, and increasing student participation in certain academic programs. AANAPISI funding is being used to provide students with increased levels of access to leadership development and mentorship opportunities, which is aimed at increasing the academic and career success of the students involved, both during college as well as post-graduation. Other uses of the funding include the development of new research about the AAPI population; staff development opportunities to help administrators, faculty, and staff better understand the complexities of the AAPI population; and the utilization of funding for infrastructure.

Conclusion

There is a dearth of knowledge regarding the demography of AAPI students, their educational trajectories, and their postsecondary outcomes. Rather, a considerable amount of what is known about the AAPI student population has been heavily influenced by stereotypes and false perceptions, which result in AAPI students being overlooked and underserved at colleges and universities. The purpose of this chapter was to provide insight on the demography of the national AAPI population, the ways these demographic factors contribute to the composition of AAPI students attending community colleges, and the ways AAPIs in community colleges are similar to and different from AAPIs in four-year colleges. Finally, this chapter provided recommendations for promising practices and targeted interventions that promote access and success for this population.

This chapter demonstrates the ways in which research, practice, and policy can take into account the experiences and outcomes of AAPIs relative to a broader agenda to address the needs and challenges of American community colleges. Paramount in the research on AAPI community college students is the need to disaggregate data for the AAPI student population. Are regional recruitment efforts reaching the most marginalized and vulnerable subgroups in the AAPI community, for instance? Do certain support services need to be developed or enhanced for them? Is there additional information you need to have in order to respond more effectively to the unique needs and challenges of your current AAPI student body? Our ability to increase the proportion of Americans with postsecondary knowledge, skills, and credentials can be achieved only through a fundamental change in how we support the participation of all Americans, including AAPI students in community colleges.

Note

1. Among Title IV undergraduate degree-granting, public institutions.

References

Chang, M., Park, J. J., Lin, M., Poon, O., & Nakanishi, D. (2007). *Beyond myths: The growth and diversity of Asian American college freshmen, 1971–2005.* Los Angeles, CA: Higher Education Research Institute, University of California.

Congressional Research Service. (2009). *Memorandum regarding the number of institutions potentially eligible to receive grants under the Assistance to Asian American and Native American and Pacific Islander-Serving Institutions program.* Washington, DC: Author.

Hurtado, S. (2007). Linking diversity with the educational and civic missions of higher education. *Review of Higher Education, 30*(2), 185–196.

Kena, G., Aud, S., Johnson, F., Wang, X., Zhang, J., Rathbun, A., . . . & Kristapovich, P. (2014). *The condition of education 2014* (NCES 2014-083). Washington, DC: U.S. Department of Education, National Center for Education Statistics.

National Commission on Asian American and Pacific Islander Research in Education. (2010). *Federal higher education policy priorities and the Asian American and Pacific Islander community.* New York, NY: Author.

National Commission on Asian American and Pacific Islander Research in Education. (2011). *The relevance of Asian Americans and Pacific Islanders in the college completion agenda.* New York, NY: Author.

Suzuki, B. H. (2002). Revisiting the model minority stereotype: Implications for student affairs practice and higher education. *New Directions for Student Services, 97,* 21–32.

Teranishi, R. T. (2010). *Asians in the ivory tower: Dilemmas of racial inequality in American higher education.* New York, NY: Teachers College Press.

Teranishi, R. T., Nguyen, D., & Lok, L. (2013). *iCount: A data quality movement for Asian Americans and Pacific Islanders in higher education.* Los Angeles, CA:

Educational Testing Service and the National Commission on Asian American and Pacific Islander Research in Education.

U.S. Department of Education. (2011a). *Integrated postsecondary education data system fall enrollment survey* (IPEDS-FE). Washington, DC: Author.

U.S. Department of Education. (2011b). *Projections of education statistics to 2019: Thirty-eighth edition.* Washington, DC: Author.

U.S. Institute of Education Sciences. (2002). *Descriptive summary of 1995–96 BPS: Six years later* (NCES 2003–151). Washington, DC: Author.

U.S. Bureau of the Census, Population Division. (2015). *Historical data. Population Estimates.* U.S. Department of Commerce. Washington, DC. Retrieved from https://www.census.gov/popest/data/historical/index.html

U.S. Department of Education. (2007). *Persistence and attainment of 2003–04 beginning postsecondary students: After three years.* Institute of Education Sciences; National Center for Education Statistics.

U.S. Department of Education. (2014). *Integrated postsecondary education data system number and percent of AAPI total enrollment in public two-year and public four-year institutions, 1985–2005 (IPEDS).* National Center for Education Statistics. Washington, DC: Author.

U.S. Department of Education, National Center for Education Statistics. (2015a). *Integrated postsecondary education data system full-year degree production (IPEDS).* National Center for Education Statistics. Washington, DC: Author.

U.S. Department of Education, National Center for Education Statistics (2015b). *Integrated postsecondary education data system number 12-month unduplicated headcount (IPEDS).* National Center for Education Statistics. Washington, DC: Author.

Yeh, T. (2004). Issues of college persistence between Asian and Asian Pacific American students. *Journal of College Student Retention, 6*(1), 81–96.

II

VOICE OF THE NATIONAL LEADER

Where Are All the Asian American Auto Mechanics? Thoughts on Diversity, Globalism, and Middle-Skill Jobs

Lee Lambert

Every great dream begins with a dreamer.

—Harriet Tubman

I was born in Seoul, South Korea. From 1974 to 1977, I lived in a neighborhood south of the city. At that time, Banpo consisted of low-slung apartment complexes, farmland, and not much else. It was poor, just like the rest of South Korea. One paved road ran through the area. Indoor plumbing was rare; we used an outhouse. Korea gets very cold in the winter, and it was not uncommon to hear that someone had died of carbon monoxide poisoning due to a malfunctioning kerosene heater.

In 2007, as president of Shoreline Community College, I was invited by then–Washington governor Christine Gregoire to attend a trade mission in Seoul, South Korea. While there, I went back looking for Banpo. At first, I couldn't find it, but in the process, I discovered so much more.

When I flew into South Korea, I didn't arrive at old Kimpo Airport but at Incheon International, one of the finest in the world. I arrived at night and could not really see Seoul. The next morning, I had meetings in south Seoul. Growing up, you could see my neighborhood from south Seoul because the city did not have a real skyline. That was not the case anymore. I couldn't see Banpo. Seoul had a modern skyline that obstructed my view. Banpo, once a row of apartment complexes, turned out to be bustling with commercial and residential development. Nearby were the headquarters of Hyundai and Kia. The area is home to some of the highest-priced real estate in the world. Twenty-seven bridges span the Han River that cuts through Seoul. Yet, while I was growing up, there were only two.

The transformation of South Korea in just 30 years is an example of what is happening throughout Asia. Once one of the poorest nations on Earth, South Korea now has the world's 11th largest economy (International Monetary Fund, 2016). As you may know, China and India are advancing economically. The lives of billions of people are being changed profoundly. This incredible advance, as I realized zipping through wired, sky-scraped, glittering Seoul, is being engineered, managed, and inspired by Asian leaders. Let me emphasize: Asian *leaders*. Presidents, CEOs, movers, shakers, decision-makers. But wait: Doesn't that conflict with conventional wisdom? Isn't "Asian leader" something of an oxymoron?

The "Model Minority" Myth

A framed poster adorns a wall in the office of one of my colleagues. The poster features a drawing of a young Asian male. In one hand, he holds an open book, likely a textbook. He appears confident as he looks slightly skyward, toward a celestial light that illuminates his features and could very well be bestowing cosmic insight and knowledge. Above the drawing appear the words, "When in need of academic guidance ask . . ." Below the photo: "WWAD—What Would an Asian Do?"

The poster is a not-too-subtle reminder of a pervasive stereotype, of course. My colleague, a Filipina American, is doing excellent work attempting to combat the notion of Asian Americans as the monolithic "model minority"—serious, studious, successful. Everyone knows that Asian Americans do well in school and excel in science and mathematics. They're scientists and engineers.

They are not leaders, however. They provide support and work behind the scenes but, despite their many admirable characteristics, lack that ineffable ability to take charge. You want them in your chemistry study group, but they can't be expected to captain the cheer squad, be elected student body president, or run the company or school. My return to Seoul and personal experiences confirmed the absurdity of what is perhaps the most pernicious aspect of the myth: It discounts individual human potential and undercuts the need for self-actualization, to become the person you can and should be. In higher education, the data reflect this narrative. Among higher education institutions, Asian Americans and Pacific Islanders (AAPIs) make up than less than 2% of presidents and chancellors (Adams, 2011).

That the world of the Asian American is complex and nuanced is true in Arizona, and it is appropriate that I, as chancellor of Pima Community College (PCC), share a few data points, as Tucson, in the southern part of the state, is home to PCC. Our state's data reflect the reality that a one-size-fits-all label does not do justice to the experiences of the diverse tapestry of our state's Asian Americans, in regard to education and other areas.

- U.S. Census information from 2000 indicates that in Arizona, while 70% of Pakistani and more than 70% of Asian Indians have a college degree or more, 10% of Cambodian, Laotian, and Vietnamese Americans in the state had no formal schooling (Nakagawa, 2008, p. 44).
- "The State of Asian American and Pacific Islanders in Arizona," a 2008 report developed by the Asian Pacific Arizona Initiative (APAZI) and Arizona State University, notes that regarding college majors among 2003–2004 Arizona AAPI students in higher education, 41.9% are "undeclared," a slightly higher percentage than for Whites. So much for the notion that our state's Asian Pacific Islanders (APIs) are laser-focused on the STEM fields (Nakagawa, 2008).
- Significantly, the APAZI report also notes that while "empirical evidence suggests that Asian American adolescents have higher levels of depressive symptoms than to their white counterparts," they are less likely to "receive services for emotional health problems due to the model-minority myth" (A. C. -C. Chen, 2008, p. 28).
- At PCC, the diversity of the AAPI population can be summed by juxtaposing these realities: The 2010 AAPI cohort had our school's highest graduation and transfer-out rates, and our current Refugee Education Program is serving students from Bhutan, one of the poorest nations in the world (PCC, 2014).

A National Leader's Perspective

I am well aware of the persistence of the model minority myth and its potential to cause a variety of harms. (And for the record, my mother is a Korean who moved to the United States after marrying my father, who is from North Carolina; they met while he was stationed in Korea while serving in the army.) As chancellor of PCC, I can vouch for the commitment of our faculty, administrators, staff, and Governing Board to create an institutional climate that values diverse cultures, recognizes the ties that bind us all, and treats everyone as individuals. As a national leader, the perspective from which this chapter springs, it is my responsibility to identify and focus on key issues and derive comprehensive solutions that reflect the values shared by community colleges; integrate with our mission; and can lead to success for the widest range of students, our investors.

Thus, it is my job to appreciate the specific, unique concerns of AAPIs and other minority groups and, wherever possible, ameliorate them, with the best possible outcome being discerning commonalities in order to find ways to make things better for *everyone*. Let me offer a personal experience as an example. I attended law school at Seattle University. In one of my first-year classes, the instructor told each of the students seated in his class to look to the left and to the right. He then informed us—matter-of-factly, and, really, a little too gleefully—that one of the students we had glanced at would flunk his class. The instructor's method of illustrating his course's 50% failure rate left me a bit stricken. In my family, my mom's expectation for me was to succeed at the highest level academically, with no excuses, and if things went bad, I would have only myself to blame.

What part of this expectation stemmed from my mom's upbringing in Korea—her culture—and what part was due to my mom being my mom— her personality—I will leave for others to ponder. The point is that while the instructor's laissez-faire, tough-love approach may have been especially diffi- cult for me, as an AAPI, to swallow, it was a terrible approach for *any* student, of *any* race or ethnic group, to labor under. It is my responsibility as PCC chancellor and national leader to create a culture that rejects higher education's easy out—that, somehow, giving students the freedom to fail strengthens their moral fiber—and replaces it with one committed to student success and inclu- siveness. It is my job to create structures and processes that reflect those values, which are a hallmark of community colleges and should be a hallmark of all educational institutions, even—and perhaps especially—law schools.

Diversity in Context

In the spring 2014 semester, 822 Asian students were enrolled at PCC. They constitute 3.4% of our unduplicated headcount. The number of Asian stu- dents reflects our community—2.5% of Pima County residents are Asian. Similarly, 67 students at PCC are Native Hawaiian or Pacific Islander, 0.3% of our headcount and in line with the 0.1% of the Pima County population that identifies as belonging to that ethnic group (Reece & Vasilieva, 2014).

What if the percentages were different? What if instead of 3.4% of our headcount, Asians accounted for 34%? Should the college's commitment to the success of Asian students be significantly altered? To an extent. PCC is cognizant of its enrollment and would allocate resources as effectively and efficiently as possible. What if the percentage were a mere .34%—would that impact the college's approach? Yes. Our commitment to reflecting the community means reaching out to underrepresented populations. We would analyze and improve our recruitment efforts.

However, a point about data needs to be made here. While aware of the realities of its operating environment, a community college must adopt approaches that are based less on demographics than on values. Values are the foundation of an organization, the unshakable core principles on which the mission of the organization rests. Without values, the decision-making resulting from data analysis becomes unmoored and will not lead to success.

Diversity is one of the six core values of PCC. It may be obvious, but it bears stating clearly that the number of students of any minority group should inform, but should not drive, our efforts to help those students succeed. If you substituted any racial-ethnic group for "Asian" in the previous paragraph, our commitment to them would still be the same.

Clearly, what is needed is a values-driven model of diversity that leaves no one at a community college behind. It must go beyond making sure that Asian American (or African American or Hispanic American) heritage month is celebrated on the campus. It must go beyond supporting the Native American club. We need an organizational approach that recognizes the differences in experiences and outlook of Navajo and Laotian students, Chinese and Tohono O'odham students, cisgender and transgender students, hearing and deaf students. It must be institutionalized and obvious. Enrollment management must recruit and retain students who represent all sectors of the community. Human Resources must work toward hiring and retaining employees that, likewise, reflect their constituents and can serve as role models and mentors. Students in our poetry classes should be exposed to the work of Li Bai, the great Chinese poet of the eighth century, as well as Walt Whitman, Langston Hughes, and Octavio Paz. There should be zero tolerance of bias-based behaviors and attitudes. Our mission, goals, policies, and curriculum should integrate into a culture of inclusive excellence. But creating that environment will fulfill only part of our mission.

On Globalism and "Meaningful Collisions"

During the first 18 years of my life, I lived in nine different places, spanning four countries and three continents. I knew what it was to be the biracial "new kid." I was, as Eric Liu (1998) writes in *The Accidental Asian*, "keenly aware of the unflattering mythologies that attach to Asian Americans: that we are indelibly foreign, exotic, math and science geeks, numbers people rather than people people, followers and not leaders, physically frail but devious and sneaky, unknowable and potentially treacherous" (p. 50). When I told my classmates I was born in Seoul, they'd respond, "So, you're Korean." No, I thought, I'm an American.

Like Liu (who became a speechwriter for President Clinton), I was determined to chip away at the expectations of those around me. I was sensitive to the feelings of those around me, as one must be when a newcomer in a group; a circumstance that also made me comfortable with uncertainty, paradox, and, indirectly, strategic thinking, a skill essential for thriving in high school and one which I honed by playing games. (My dad stressed strategy games; do not underestimate the real-life value of Stratego, Battleship, and chess.) I was outgoing. I played football and ran track. I attended a progressive liberal arts college. I went to law school. My passion for economic and educational equity led me to community colleges, and my fervent belief in the power of middle-skills jobs to transform individual lives and reinvigorate economic development has made me a champion of career and technical education (more about that later).

Most important, my background, upbringing, and subsequent experiences also have instilled in me an appreciation of the power of meeting, talking to, and sharing a meal with people who are not like me. Obviously it is important for Asian Americans attending community college, as it is for all hyphenated Americans, to learn about their culture, to see themselves reflected in the institution, and to feel valued. It is also important to create an institution that creates "meaningful collisions" among all these hyphenates. Students must be encouraged to take part in service-learning so they can be mentored by African Americans. They need to attend classes taught by Hispanic Americans, tutor poor White Americans, and raise funds with Native Americans.

They also need to be taught to break bread regularly with students who are not American. My experiences have led me to realize that the greatest gift we can give our students is appreciation of a global perspective. The reality of the twenty-first century is that our homegrown students will grow up in a world that will value transnational leadership skills, fluency in multiple languages, and respect for and understanding of other cultures. For community colleges, one of the best ways to impart those skills is by bringing diverse students into close proximity with each other. In the context of this chapter, it means bringing Asian American students into contact with Asian students. Community colleges should emphasize developing study-abroad opportunities. It also means that community colleges should intensify their global outreach and recruitment efforts. We need to bring students from around the world to community colleges, for the benefit of everyone.

Where Are All the Asian American Auto Mechanics?

Now let us turn to a related, if slightly different, topic. Another colleague of mine has a daughter whose friend Sandy is Chinese American. Sandy's goal is to become a pharmacist. As high school valedictorian, she has received several scholarships. But her parents are of very modest means—they both work at restaurants—and the burden of paying tuition at a four-year university is significant. Clearly, Sandy could benefit from attending PCC for the first two years of her postsecondary studies. PCC's tuition is modest, our instructors first-rate, and our transfer to in-state universities seamless. But for Sandy's parents, PCC was out of the question; they wanted only "the best" for their daughter, which in Tucson means attending the University of Arizona for four years. Sandy and her family are taking out loans to cover much of the cost of her education.

It is difficult to argue with the choice made by Sandy, a superior student with dedicated parents. Plus, Sandy's sights are set on a specific, rewarding career. But few students, Asian or not, are as gifted as Sandy. As I stated earlier, 42% of Asian students enter higher education in Arizona undecided about their major. For those Asian students who graduate with a bachelor's degree, it's likely they will end up with jobs unrelated to their field of study, as 73% of all U.S. students do, according to a 2013 study by the Federal Reserve Bank of New York (Plumer, 2013).

Here I must come clean. I have been a longtime advocate and proponent of middle-skills jobs. I am a former chair of the American Association of Community Colleges' Committee on Program Initiatives and Workforce Training. I have served as board chair of the National Coalition of Certification Centers, an important organization that addresses the need for strong industry partnerships with educational institutions in order to develop industry-recognized portable, validated certifications that have strong validation and assessment standards. I also am a founding member of the Manufacturing Institute's Education Council, which assists in developing national strategies to expand and enhance our manufacturing workforce.

Thus, I am well acquainted with the current economic landscape. Each day in the United States about 10,000 workers are retiring; in the heating–cooling–air conditioning field, for example, the average age of a technician is 55 (Kessler, 2014). And the much-debated skills gap is real—80% of the members of the National Association of Manufacturers report difficulty in finding qualified employees (Morrison et al., 2011). An obvious supply-demand issue exists for jobs that require two or fewer years of training but not a bachelor's degree—middle-skills jobs. By 2017, 2.5 million new middle-skills jobs are likely to be added to the workforce, accounting for

40% of all job growth (Webster, 2014). These jobs are driven by rapid technological advances in industry, pay anywhere from $12 to $35 an hour and encompass industries ranging from health care (think radiology technicians and medical secretaries) to construction (electricians, carpenters) to energy (power line installers) to manufacturing (precision sheet metal fabrication, aviation technology) (Webster, 2014). Uniquely positioned to provide training, community colleges are the ideal launching pad for these types of jobs.

Now let me share some data, from a 2014 U.S. Bureau of Labor Statistics report, regarding employment by ethnicity. In 2014, Asians age 16 and older represented 5.7% of the employed workforce. Here is the percentage of Asians employed in specific, selected industries and occupations:

- Construction, 2.0%
- Mining, quarrying, and oil and gas, 1.6%
- Machinery manufacturing, 4.2%
- Utilities, 2.9%
- Automotive repair and maintenance, 3.2%
- Commercial and industrial machinery and equipment repair and maintenance, 1.4%

Asians are underrepresented in several key sectors of the middle-skills economy.. The challenge for community colleges is to educate the Asian American community about middle-skills education opportunities and the role community colleges can play in helping the community's members find rewarding, meaningful careers. Clearly, community colleges should work with community partners to uncover outreach opportunities. For example, Tucson has a vibrant Chinese cultural center and strong networks of Filipino and Korean churches. We need to work with these entities to break through whatever preconceived notions regarding the "status" of various trades and occupations their constituents may hold. For example, gone are the days when HVAC technicians spent most of their time climbing through ceiling crawl spaces. Climate control of modern buildings requires reading sophisticated computerized monitoring tools and quickly diagnosing problems remotely. (In fact, the skills needed for the job are becoming more aligned with those of information technology.)

But the reality is that this bias, while it may or may not be more obvious among the Asian American community, is not limited to this community. Again, I will leave it to others to discern what role Asian culture plays in their holding the trades in low esteem. We need to educate everyone, shaping our efforts to our knowledge of the intricacies of each community, while developing across-the-board strategies to evangelize the possibilities inherent in career and technical education, so that students of every ethnic and racial group may benefit.

Concluding Thoughts: What Can Community Colleges Do?

Let's return to the poster described earlier and undertake a redesign so that it can serve as an ideal for which community colleges can strive, rather than an ironic, semi-facetious depiction of a stereotype. There would be dozens of students in the poster. Several would be Asian American, but all races and ethnicities would be represented, along with students from outside the United States. For every male, there would be a female. Some would dress business casual; others would be wearing work clothes and hard hats.

Some would hold textbooks, but others would hold instruction manuals, and others would carry multimeters—sophisticated *electronic measuring instruments* that measure *voltage, current,* and *resistance* and are used throughout industry. They're calculators that require a strong background in college algebra, and their mastery opens the doors of employment in a wide array of industries. Still others would be holding wrenches, for knowledge of torque, the precise way to tighten nuts and bolts, is a skill valued by industries ranging from energy (where torque ensures windmills' blades are connected properly) to medicine (so that screws used to implant surgical devices are properly tightened).

Perhaps most important, they wouldn't be looking upward, to receive knowledge from a distant source—they would be talking to each other. (There would be no texting in this idealized poster.) The participants would be engaged in meaningful conversations, sharing knowledge, learning about new cultures, appreciating differences, and recognizing the underlying ties that make us all Americans and all human. The text accompanying the image would not be WWAD, but WCCCD—what can community colleges do? If we emphasize student success and inclusiveness, the answer is plenty, for all Americans.

References

Adams, S. (2011, May 11). Why aren't there more Asian-American leaders? *Forbes.* Retrieved from http://www.forbes.com/sites/susanadams/2011/05/11/why-arent-there-more-asian-american-leaders/#32ed999d7dc2

Chen, A. C.-C. (2008). The mental and behavioral health of AAPI youth. In *The state of Asian Americans and Pacific Islanders in Arizona*, pp. 28 & 30. Retrieved from http://apas.clas.asu.edu/pdfs/State_of_AAPI_in_AZ_2008.pdf

International Monetary Fund. (2016, April). *World economic outlook*. Retrieved from http://knoema.com/IMFWEO2016Apr/imf-world-economic-outlook-weo-april-2016

Kessler, G. (2014, July 20). Do 10,000 baby boomers retire every day? *Washington Post*. Retrieved from http://www.washingtonpost.com/blogs/fact-checker/wp/2014/07/24/do-10000-baby-boomers-retire-every-day/

Liu, E. (1998). *The accidental Asian: Notes of a native speaker*. New York, NY: Vintage Books.

Morrison, T., Stover DeRocco, E., Maciejewski, B., McNelly, J., Giff, C., & Carrick, G. (2011). *Boiling point: The skills gap in manufacturing*. New York, NY: Manufacturing Institute. Retrieved from http://www.themanufacturinginstitute.org/~/media/A07730B2A798437D98501E798C2E13AA.ashx

Nakagawa, K. (2008). Moving beyond the model minority myth. In *The State of Asian Americans and Pacific Islanders in Arizona*, p. 40. A report presented by the APAZI Coalition, ASU Asian American Pacific Studies Program, and ASU for Arizona Office of Public Affairs. Retrieved from http://apas.clas.asu.edu/pdfs/State_of_AAPI_in_AZ_2008.pdf

Pima Community College. (2014). *Graduation rates 2013–14*. Retrieved from https://www.pima.edu/about-pima/reports/federal-reporting/docs/ipeds-graduation-rates1.pdf

Plumer, B. (2013, May 20). Only 27 percent of college grads have a job related to their major. *Washington Post Wonkblog*. Retrieved from http://www.washingtonpost.com/blogs/wonkblog/wp/2013/05/20/only-27-percent-of-college-grads-have-a-job-related-to-their-major/

Reece, D., & Vasilieva, M. (2014, September). *Spring 2014 student characteristics report*. Retrieved from https://www.pima.edu/about-pima/reports/student-reports/docs-student-characteristics/docs-spring/sp14-ethnicity.pdf

U.S. Bureau of Labor Statistics. (2014). Employed persons by detailed industry, sex, race, and Hispanic or Latino ethnicity. In *Labor force statistics from the current population survey*, p. 1.6. Retrieved from http://www.bls.gov/cps/cpsaat18.pdf

Webster, M. (2014, September 30). Where the jobs are: The new blue collar. *USA Today*. Retrieved from http://www.usatoday.com/story/news/nation/2014/09/30/job-economy-middle-skill-growth-wage-blue-collar/14797413/

12

CUTTING-EDGE MODELS FOR BEST PRACTICE

Negotiating Multiple Identities: De Anza College's IMPACT AAPI Program

Brian Murphy and Rowena M. Tomaneng

A teacher affects eternity, he can never tell where his influence stops.

—Henry B. Adams

D e Anza is one of 112 public community colleges in California and serves the San Jose region of Northern California. Established in 1967, De Anza has grown into one of the largest colleges in California, serving over 23,000 students. Recognized for its academic excellence and high transfer rates, De Anza has undergone a deep transition as its student body has come to reflect the broader demographic transition of Silicon Valley into one of the most diverse regions of the United States. De Anza has long had an equity agenda at its core, to serve all students and prepare them at the highest level. How can the college work effectively and successfully with students coming from the most marginalized communities in the region, many of whom come to the college without college-level academic skills? If our formal mission declares a commitment to students of all backgrounds, how will we succeed in making our promises real?

De Anza's work with Asian American and Pacific Islander (AAPI) students is located in this larger agenda, to recognize the challenges faced by the wide range of students who come to us and aim at the success of all of them. The college's strategic plan is rooted in a demographic analysis of the region and aims to increase the enrollment and success of students from the least-served communities. Among those communities are the varied and growing Asian American communities of the region. In their ethnic, linguistic, cultural, and class diversity, our Asian students defy any single label, much less the stereo-types associated with any "model minority." Often immigrants, often poor, often isolated in their high schools and from each other, many of our Asian American students are burdened by the conventional—dare we say racist—assumptions that they are all alike and all successful. We have thousands of students who struggle, and it matters to embrace their diversity and their spec-ificity. The college's success with AAPI students reflects this beginning assump-tion: that we are working with students of many talents and capacities but not always beginning with the conventional advantages others think they possess.

De Anza's Students

Who are our AAPI students? De Anza College's service area is home to one of the highest concentrations of AAPIs in the United States, and our demo-graphics reflect this fact. Approximately 45% of De Anza students self-report as Asian, Filipino, or Native American Pacific Islander (see Table 12.1). Chinese American, Vietnamese, and Filipino students comprise the largest AAPI subgroups (see Table 12.2). Additionally, first-generation status for fall 2012 was 31%. To qualify as first-generation, a student has parents with high school experience or less and no college experience. Unlike the national breakdown of 60% female and 40% male, De Anza students are divided roughly equally between the genders: 49% of students are female and 51% of students are male (see Table 12.3).

Although course completion for AAPI students at De Anza is higher than it is for any other ethnic group—when all groups are lumped together into one generic category—this ignores significant gaps in academic achievement between different AAPI subgroups and contributes to the model minority myth that all Asian students excel at academics. When we disaggregate the data on course success, several AAPI subgroups, such as Filipinos, Southeast Asians, and Pacific Islanders, score significantly lower. This disparity in stu-dent success among AAPI subgroups also reflects different socioeconomic standing among AAPI groups, and these students became the focus of our Asian American and Native American Pacific Islander–serving institution (AANAPISI) project. As is often the case, our work demonstrated a range of effective practices that have proved effective beyond our initial target groups but were especially effective with the most disadvantaged students.

High-Impact Practices and De Anza's IMPACT AAPI Program

The historic establishment of AANAPISIs by Congress in 2007 brought the educational needs of AAPI students into the fold of minority-serving

TABLE 12.1
Ethnicity of All Students, 2012–2013 (Reflecting the Sum of Three Quarters' Enrollment)

Ethnicity	Students	Percent (%)
African American	1,671	4
Asian	14,494	38
Decline to State	2,651	7
Filipino	2,192	6
Latino/a	7,725	20
Native American	240	1
Pacific Islander	209	1
White	8,714	23
Total	37,896	100

Source. De Anza College Institutional Research Office, 2014. Reprinted with permission.

TABLE 12.2
AAPI Subgroups for 2012–2013

Subgroup	Students	Percent (%)
Asian — Cambodian	148	1
Asian — Chinese	5,533	33
Asian — Indian	2,335	14
Asian — Japanese	693	4
Asian — Korean	1,193	7
Asian — Laotian	48	0
Asian — Vietnamese	3,278	19
Asian Other	1,266	8
Filipino	2,192	13
Pacific Islander	209	1
Total	16,895	100

Note. Ethnic groups established by first ethnic group chosen.
Source. De Anza Institutional Research Office, 2014. Reprinted with permission. Retrieved from www.deanza.edu/ir

institutions (MSIs). The inclusion of AAPI communities within the MSI network was also a response to studies that argued the "model minority" stereotype ascribed to Asian students obscured the educational needs of AAPI subgroups (College Board and National Commission on Asian American and Pacific

TABLE 12.3
Gender of Students, 2012–2013

Gender	Students	Percent (%)
Female	18,603	49
Male	19,293	51
Total	37,896	100

Source. De Anza College Institutional Research Office, 2014. Reprinted with permission.

Islander Research in Education [CARE], 2008). AANAPISIs were established by Congress in 2007 as part of the College Cost Reduction and Access Act and expanded in 2008 under the Higher Education Opportunity Act. The program is funded in part through a mandatory portion of the federal budget and in part through annual congressional appropriations. Specifically, the AANAPISI grant program seeks both to address the needs of low-income and underserved AAPI college students and to build the capacity of postsecondary institutions that serve them (Asian American and Pacific Islander Association of Colleges and Universities [APIACU], 2014).

In 2008, De Anza College received one of the six inaugural two-year AANAPISI grants to serve low-income Filipino, Southeast Asian, and Pacific Islander students. In 2011 De Anza received a second grant with a five-year cycle (De Anza College, 2014). Both grants were designed to meet the aims of the federal AANAPISI grant program through strategic campus partnerships, primarily between instructional departments and student services. The direct aim of these partnerships was to improve academic achievement by increasing access, college readiness, success, and persistence for underserved AAPI students, which at De Anza were identified as the following: Filipinos, Pacific Islanders (Guamanians, Hawaiians, Samoans, and others), and Southeast Asians (Vietnamese, Cambodians, Laotians).

De Anza's IMPACT (Initiatives to Maximize Positive Academic Achievement and Cultural Thriving) AAPI students illustrate the heterogeneity of AAPI populations that Teranishi (2010) has researched across U.S. schools. Our students identify as Cambodian, Chamorro, Fijian, Filipino, Hawaiian, Indian, Indonesian, Samoan, Vietnamese, but almost as critical they also reflect diversity in their immigration histories, language backgrounds, educational attainment, and economic status. The IMPACT AAPI project began with an understanding that this diversity was a critical asset and that our students would bring cultural capacities and knowledge that could frame our pedagogical approach.

The Asset Model

We knew from our work before the AAPI grant that many of our students have a strong awareness of their ethnic and cultural identities and that they have deep intuitive knowledge of the social processes of immigration and race that has framed their family experience—even though that knowledge may never have been given an academic framework or even acknowledged as a form of knowledge. But our faculty knew that this knowledge has deep significance for our students, and the IMPACT AAPI project began with a commitment that we would begin with the assets our students brought rather than with their formal deficits.

What does this mean, and how does it frame our pedagogy? In the IMPACT AAPI courses and programs, our students begin with themselves; they share stories that contrast their lives in America to the lives of their parents and family members who grew up in Southeast Asia and the various Pacific Islands. The Philippines, Vietnam, and Samoa, for example, are often experienced or imagined as poverty-ridden while America is imagined as a place of dreams and opportunity. Identifying as children of immigrants, IMPACT AAPI students recognize that the privileges they have in America are a result of their parents' hard work and struggle, and they have an understanding of marginality and cultural isolation based on race and immigrant status. At the heart of our work was our own learning that when our students began to name their experience, to frame it and reflect on it, they were developing critical learning skills and powerful insights into both themselves and the contexts in which they lived. These insights were valuable in how they would more effectively navigate their education.

How do IMPACT AAPI learning communities create an environment to facilitate student learning and student academic success? There are six elements: (1) the development of effective learning communities with linked courses; (2) a pedagogy of self-reflection and personal narrative; (3) wraparound student services integrated into our learning communities; (4) the creation of a learning community among the faculty and staff; (5) the opportunity for community and civic engagement for students; and (6) the social organization of courses into sustaining support groups, or "Pamilya."

1. IMPACT AAPI has relied on the support of the college's Learning in Communities (LinC) program for the design of its curricular pathways in English and math. A LinC learning community uses a variety of approaches that link or cluster classes during a school term around an interdisciplinary theme and enroll a common cohort of students. This represents an intentional restructuring of students' time, credit, and learning experiences to build community and foster more explicit

connections among students, teachers, and disciplines. In this context it is more likely, the faculty report, that students will come to trust each other, to listen effectively, and to work collaboratively across deep cultural divides.

2. Multicultural thinking is also encouraged and developed to promote inclusive perspectives, and collaborative learning and experiential learning methods ground the pedagogy. Beginning with narrative and reflection, our courses aim to locate our students' experiences in a broader framework of analysis and critique.

3. IMPACT AAPI students have dedicated counselors who work with our learning communities and work collaboratively with our instructional faculty to assess each student's progress and challenges. This personalized counseling element of the program develops continuity between students and counselors and integrates the experience of classroom faculty and counselors.

4. LinC offers IMPACT AAPI faculty an effective professional development opportunity annually with a two-day LinC Summer Institute that facilitates faculty development and offers training in methods for teaching integrated learning communities that increase the likelihood of student success, with a focus on developmental to college-level courses. The institute includes sharing of best practices related to the teaching and design of learning communities, cohort learning, and other interdisciplinary learning models. IMPACT AAPI faculty and counselors enjoy, then, a deep community of practice themselves.

5. Many of our IMPACT AAPI courses and programs are simultaneously linked to the work of the college's Institute for Community and Civic Engagement, and many of the IMPACT AAPI courses require or offer opportunities for students to do project-based learning in a community or civic setting. IMPACT AAPI benefits from the college-wide ethos of engagement, through which our students are encouraged to exercise their civic rights and obligations. Indeed, one of the IMPACT AAPI programs, the Asian Pacific American Leadership Institute, predates our grant and has produced legions of Asian American organizers and even elected officials.

6. Finally, the social organization of our courses reflects a cultural understanding that many of our most challenged students have rich and sustaining experience of family and neighborhood solidarity and mutual aid. Based on the experience of Latino/a Empowerment at De Anza (LEAD), IMPACT AAPI built structures of mutual support into classes, using the Tagalog term for family, *Pamilya*. In this model students are expected to reach out to others who struggle, help find solutions, assist in searching out student or social services, and alert each other when others are in trouble.

Curricular Pathways and Learning Communities

Since 2008, IMPACT AAPI has developed two curricular pathways using the LinC model: LinC Readiness and Success in College-Level English and CREM: Readiness and Success in College-Level English and Math. The LinC Readiness and Success in College-Level English offers a five-class sequence for students who place at two levels below college-level English through transfer-level English that fulfills multiple general education requirements as well as transfer requirements (Table 12.4).

CREM: Readiness and Success in College-Level English and Math is a three-course sequence for students who place one level below college-level English and two levels below college-level math. This sequence includes embedded counseling support (Table 12.5):

How Are We Doing?

In 2014, CARE and the Asian Pacific Islander American Scholarship Fund (APIASF) published *Measuring the Impact of MSI-Funded Programs*

TABLE 12.4
Sample Pathway for Readiness and Success in College-Level English

Quarter	Class	Students Targeted
Winter	**LART 200** Developing Reading and Writing Connections	Students who place at two levels below college-level English
Spring	**LART 211** Integrated Reading and Writing	Students who place at one level below college-level English
Summer	**APALI Youth Leadership Academy** ICS 22: Contemporary Issues in Asian America + ICS 4: Race, Ethnicity, Inequality	Students who want to fulfill GE requirements in Area D Behavioral Science (ICS 4) and Area D History and Society (ICS 22)
Fall	**EWRT 1A + ICS 24** EWRT 1A: Composition and Reading + ICS 24: Asian American Literature	Students who want to fulfill GE requirements in Area A English Composition (EWRT 1A) and Area C Humanities (ICS 24)
Winter	**EWRT 2 + SPCH 10** EWRT 2: Critical Reading, Writing, Thinking + SPCH 10: Oral Communication	Students who want to fulfill both GE (Area A) and transfer (Area 1) requirements in Critical Thinking (EWRT 2) and Oral Communication (SPCH 10)

Source. DeAnza College, 2013. IMPACT AAPI: Curricular pathways. Reprinted with permission.

TABLE 12.5

Sample Pathway for Readiness and Success in English and Math

Quarter	Learning Communities	Students Targeted
Fall	**READ 211 + MATH 210** READ 211: Developmental Reading + MATH 210: Pre-algebra	Students placed at one level below college-level reading and three levels below college-level math
Winter	**EWRT 211 + MATH 212** EWRT 211: Preparatory Reading and Writing Skills + MATH 212: Beginning Algebra	Students placed at one level below college-level writing and two levels below college-level math
Spring	**EWRT 1A + MATH 114** EWRT 1A: Composition and Reading + MATH 114: Intermediate Algebra	Students who want to fulfill the GE requirement in Area A English (EWRT 1A) and the degree-applicable math requirement (Math 114)

Source. De Anza College, 2013. Reprinted with permission.

on Student Success: Findings from the Evaluation of AANAPISIs. This study highlighted the achievements of De Anza's IMPACT AAPI program. The Executive Summary argued that the key findings in the analysis of De Anza's IMPACT AAPI learning communities were as follows:

- Students in the IMPACT AAPI learning community were more likely than the comparison group to transition from developmental to college-level English.
- Compared to the comparison group, students in the IMPACT AAPI learning community passed their college-level English course and accomplished the transition in less time.
- Students in the IMPACT AAPI learning communities were more likely than the comparison group to earn associate degrees. (CARE & APIASF, 2014, p. 3)

The bottom line for De Anza is that the success rate for students enrolled in IMPACT AAPI courses is 92%, meaning that 92% of the students successfully complete the course and proceed to the next level. This is among the highest success rate of any program working with any group of students. The AANAPISI research report attributed IMPACT AAPI's successful outcomes to the program's use of wraparound student services, culturally relevant curriculum, and civically engaged curriculum (CARE & APIASF, 2014).

Conclusion

Our own work demonstrates that a culturally relevant curriculum is a critical element for increasing student success and academic performance among students of color. Educational research has shown the negative impact on academic performance of students of color due to cultural difference and the privileging of White, English-speaking culture (Ladson-Billings & Tate, 1995; Valenzuela, 2005; Yosso, 2005). IMPACT AAPI intentionally infuses AAPI studies into its curricular pathways. More specifically, IMPACT AAPI learning communities include course offerings with the following characteristics:

- Respect for the diversity of AAPI communities.
- Curriculum that recognizes the importance of AAPI cultural traditions and histories.
- Assignments that connect course readings to students' personal, familial, and community experiences.
- Use of the concept of *Pamilya* to build peer support networks within and outside of the classroom.

At the heart of this model is a necessary cultural shift on the part of college faculty and staff: to begin with the assets and capacities of our widely diverse AAPI students and not with what they do not yet possess. No one at De Anza is confused: our students will need to demonstrate mastery over all the university skills required to be successful when they transfer from De Anza. But to get there takes more than a listing of what they don't yet know or don't yet have; it requires an understanding that they have already demonstrated enormous skill and capacity to have brought themselves to us and trust in the community we build with them. When we trust them, and they trust each other, they will learn quickly and well. The numbers validate the claim, but our lived experience validates the numbers.

References

Asian American and Pacific Islander Association of Colleges and Universities. (2014). History of AANAPSIs. Retrieved from http://www.apiacu.org/about/history-of-aanapisis/

College Board & National Commission on Asian American and Pacific Islander Research in Education. (2008). *Asian American and Pacific Islanders: Facts, not fiction: Setting the record straight.* New York, NY: Asian/Pacific/American Institute at New York University and Steinhardt Institute for Higher Education Policy at New York University. Retrieved from https://secure-media.collegeboard.org/

digitalServices/pdf/professionals/asian-americans-and-pacific-islanders-facts-not-fiction.pdf

De Anza College. (2013). *IMPACT AAPI: Curricular pathways*. Retrieved from https://www.deanza.edu/impact-aapi/curriculum.html

De Anza College. (2014). *IMPACT AAPI: Program overview*. Retrieved from http://www.deanza.edu/impact-aapi/

De Anza College Institutional Research Office. (2014). *IMPACT AAPI: Ethnicity of all students*. Retrieved from http://www.deanza.edu/ir/

Ladson-Billings, G., & Tate, W. (1995). Toward a critical race theory of education. *Teachers College Record, 97*(1), 47–68.

National Commission on Asian American and Pacific Islander Research in Education & Asian Pacific Islander American Scholarship Fund. (2014). *Measuring the impact of MSI-funded programs on student success: Findings from the evaluation of AANAPISIs*. New York, NY: Partnership for Equity in Education Research.

Teranishi, R. T. (2010). *Asians in the ivory tower: Dilemmas of racial inequality in American higher education*. Multicultural Education Series. New York, NY: Teachers College Press.

Valenzuela, A. (2005). Subtractive schooling, caring relations, and social capital in the schooling of U.S.-Mexican youth. From an unidentified anthology. In L. Weis and M. Fine (Eds.), *Beyond silenced voices: Class, race, and gender in United States schools*. Albany, NY: State University of New York Press.

Yosso, T. J. (2005). Whose culture has capital? A critical race theory discussion of community cultural wealth. *Race Ethnicity and Education, 8*(1), 69–91.

PART FIVE

CAUCASIAN STUDENTS IN POVERTY

13

VOICE OF THE NATIONAL RESEARCHER

Invisible Poverty: Caucasian Student Poverty and the College Experience

Christopher M. Mullin

Wisdom is not a product of schooling, but of the lifelong attempt to acquire it.

—Albert Einstein

Close your eyes and imagine a student living in poverty. How would you describe that person? To most people, poverty has a certain "look." And more often than not it is not the face of a White person that people imagine. For example, Clawson (2002) studied the content within economics textbooks to understand how poverty was being portrayed and found that Black populations are overwhelmingly represented. This finding aligns with the perspective of Shipp, McCormick, and Rocco (2013), who suggested that the social construct of poverty has developed to equate poverty with persons of color. Perceptions of poverty, including race-based generalizations, carry over to inform higher education policy conversation.

In 2011, during the Great Recession, corresponding policy conversations relating to costs of the Pell Grant program and student eligibility changes for the program that impacted at-risk students prompted me to examine the "face" of poverty within a higher education policy context—the extent to which the percent of the population receiving a Pell Grant that was White. I conducted the research and included it in a policy brief published by the American Association of Community Colleges (AACC) (Baime & Mullin,

2011). The study showed that poverty does not apply only to persons of color, by any stretch. This chapter builds on some of what we found.

The purpose of this chapter is to provide a balance to the poverty dialogue by giving form to White poverty. The focus applies particularly to the participation of and outcomes for poor White students attending community colleges and the private and public labor-market returns.

A Portrait of the Impoverished White Population

Prior to a discussion of poor White students in higher education, it is informative to understand the extent of White poverty in the United States. To this end, the following section provides key data points to illustrate the extent of the U.S. White population living in poverty.

Poverty Rates and Counts

When quantifying any measure, two primary approaches are employed. The first is the relative proportion of the population—the percent of a given population. The second is the total amount—or magnitude—of the population.

Poverty Rates

The proportion of U.S. population living in poverty in 2012 was 15%, which was 2.5% higher than in 2007—the year before the Great Recession (DeNavas-Walt, Proctor, & Smith, 2013). The poverty rate varies by race and ethnicity:

- The poverty rate for non-Hispanic Whites was 9.7%,
- The poverty rate for Blacks was 27.2%,
- The poverty rate for Hispanics was 25.6%, and
- The poverty rate for Asians was 11.7% (DeNavas-Walt, Proctor, & Smith, 2013, p. 14).

Clearly the White (non-Hispanic) population had the lowest poverty rate. It may therefore be concluded that poverty is a more pressing issue for persons of color and may further be a contributing factor as to why the "face" of poverty is not White.

Poverty Counts

Beyond representative percentages, there are real people, quantified by actual counts of individuals, who are economically challenged. So, while the percent of the population in poverty was 15%, the total number of people in poverty was 46.5 million in 2012 (DeNavas-Walt, Proctor, & Smith, 2013).

When examined through the lens of the total population, the largest number of people living in poverty in the United States was White (Figure 13.1).

The practice of putting a non-White face on poverty suggests that efforts and attention to this—invisible—group may be limited. The unmasking of White poverty is important, for "[t]he belief that poverty is solely a Black or Brown issue fragments the society along racial lines," according to Shipp, McCormick, and Rocco (2013). They continued, "This fragmentation dilutes the possibility for class solidarity that is needed to push for health, housing, education, and employment reforms."

Thresholds to Determine Poverty

The extent to which the current poverty rate calculation accurately represents poverty continues to be debated. Alternative metrics, including a consumption measure that looks at how much individuals spend—such as the Supplemental Poverty Measure (SPM)—have also been considered, for example (Short, 2013). However, the income-based perspective on poverty continues to hold its position, with slight modifications that include the determination of poverty at various thresholds beyond the 100% poverty threshold, such as at 150% or 200% of poverty.

What has to a lesser extent been examined is the number of people falling within each mutually exclusive poverty threshold category—from 0% to 50% of poverty, 51% to 100% of poverty, 101% to 150% of poverty, and 151% to 200% of poverty. As illustrated in Figure 13.2, the White

Figure 13.1. People in poverty, by race/ethnicity, 2012.

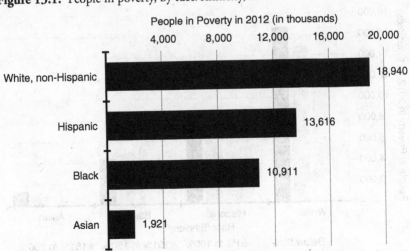

Source. DeNavas-Walt, Proctor, & Smith, 2013. Adapted from data presented in Table 3.

population with an income that was 50% of the poverty level or less totaled 8.5 million in 2012. An additional 10.5 million had incomes between 51% and 100% of the poverty level. Taken together, a total of 19 million Whites lived in poverty (100% or below) in 2012.

A closer look at Figure 13.2 shows that the distribution of poverty for both the Asian and White populations increases across the four categories of poverty below the 200% of poverty threshold. Alternatively, the Hispanic and Black populations exhibit a distribution that appears to center around the 100% of poverty level, as the number of people in poverty between 150% and 200% are comparatively fewer than the number of people between 101% and 150% of poverty. In total, 50.5 million White people in the United States in 2012 had an income equal to or less than 200% of poverty, as compared to 29 million Hispanic, 20 million Black, and 4.5 million Asians. This large number of poor Whites justifies their inclusion in an explicit conversation about low-income students.

Concentration of Poverty

Poverty extends across the United States, with some areas having higher concentrations than others. More specifically, while it is true that poverty remains largely concentrated in Appalachia, the Mississippi Delta, Indian reservations, the Lower Rio Grande River Valley, and the "Black Belt" extending from Arkansas to North Carolina, not all poverty is experienced solely in

Figure 13.2. People in poverty, by four poverty thresholds and race/ethnicity, 2012.

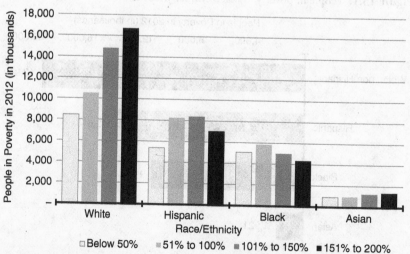

Source. DeNavas-Walt, Proctor, & Smith, 2013. Adapted from data presented in Table 5.

these areas; nearly 50% of those in poverty live in districts with low poverty rates (Lichter & Parisi, 2008). The other 50% of those living in poverty reside in areas that are not characterized by low poverty rates. This does not mean that poor and nonpoor are neighbors, rather that there is economic segregation within comparatively wealthier areas.

The degree of segregation is important as it illustrates the exposure of economic and social opportunities. Segregation limits identity development available to people of more affluent areas, extending from the exposure to jobs with higher returns on investments to schools with a strong academic culture. Simply put, people adapt to the circumstance in which they live. The theory of adaptive preference suggests

> that in choosing what they will do, how they will spend their time or resources or what kind of life they will lead, people are affected by or take into account, for example, what they can afford, the likely responses of others to their choice, and the values and practices which shape them and the communities in which they live. They must do this more or less self-consciously—in some cases with little awareness of the ways in which these factors have circumscribed their choice. They may experience their decision as a free choice, but it is one which has been adapted to the *limited options set by their circumstances*. (Bridges, 2006, pp. 15–16; emphasis added)

As a student who went to college on the Pell Grant, a student grant aid program that will be discussed shortly, and a former K–12 teacher in both poor and nonpoor communities of Spanish Harlem, New York, and Boca Raton, Florida, I understand the limitations of circumstance. These experiences led me to wonder:

> As a child, did you have a comfortable bed to sleep in or did you sleep in a bathtub because bullets could not penetrate its cast iron frame? As an adolescent, did someone expose you to possibilities or reinforce limitations? Did you attend a high school with a college-going culture or did your high school continually fail adequately yearly progress? If you answered yes to the latter part of these questions, or others like them, you understand the limitations of circumstance. (Mullin, 2013, pp. 26–27)

It is, however, uplifting to note that the innovative spirit exists in peoples of all educational attainment levels. The Kaufman Index of Entrepreneurial Activity has consistently found a higher entrepreneurial index for people whose educational attainment level was less than high school (0.52%) as compared to individuals with a bachelor's degree (0.28%; Fairlie, 2013). While this is good news for those from poverty who are less likely to complete high school, let alone college, it is also the case that median earnings for those with less than a high school diploma are substantially less than those with higher levels of educational attainment (Mullin, Baime, & Honeyman, 2015).

Community colleges serve as a place-based site for students to enhance their standing in society by capitalizing on their entrepreneurial spirit via the open-access philosophy and the offering of courses to promote small business development and entrepreneurs. Unpublished data from the Association of Small Business Development Centers indicated that one-fifth of all small business development centers are located on community college campuses. The nexus of low-income White students and the community college is examined in the next section.

The Community College and Impoverished White Students

In this section I examine the prevalence of impoverished White students in college, beginning with a broad focus on their participation in college. The section will then focus on this population in the community college access and outcomes, interventions to address poverty, and private and public returns that have not been realized from low-income White students attending community colleges.

College Access and Outcomes

Community colleges serve as access points to higher education for students of all academic abilities, demographic backgrounds, and economic standing. Increasingly, their mission is being rebalanced to include not only access to, but also success in college.

College Access

In the 2011–2012 academic year, community colleges enrolled 8 million students (AACC, 2013a). Of those students, 3.9 million had incomes at 150% of poverty or less. And while community colleges enroll the plurality of students from all races and ethnicities, 44% of all students attending community colleges and living in poverty were White (Figure 13.3).

College Outcomes

A student's financial standing has long been acknowledged as a risk factor negatively impacting college completion. The data presented in Table 13.1 lend further support to this well-known maxim; the lower the income, the less likely a person is to earn a college degree or certificate.

Figure 13.3. Percentage of the community college student body with incomes equal to or below the 150% of poverty threshold, by select races/ethnicities, 2011–2012.

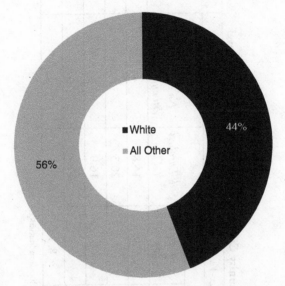

Source. Author's analysis of National Postsecondary Student Aid Study (National Center for Education Statistics, n.d.).

Specifically, 18.9% of White students attending community colleges at or below the poverty level earned a degree or certificate after six years, as compared to 41% of White students with incomes greater than the 200% poverty level threshold. A positive sign, however, is the commitment of these students, as one-fifth are still enrolled after six years. This signifies that they do not just give up but persist at a rate higher than their wealthier peers.

Interventions for Impoverished White Students

Community colleges employ two approaches to mitigate financial barriers to college. The first is philosophical and expressed as a commitment to lowering out-of-pocket costs to students in the form of low tuition and fee rates. The second is extended by the federal and state governments that provide need-based student financial aid. Both of these interventions are discussed later, with special attention to how they affect poor White students at community colleges.

Low-Cost Access

The low tuition philosophy has been a hallmark of the community college movement. In the 2013–2014 academic year, community college tuition

TABLE 13.1

Six-Year Outcomes for White Students Starting at Community Colleges in 2003–2004, by Poverty Level

Income as Percent of Poverty Level	Six-Year Outcomes					
	Earned a Credential			Still Enrolled (%)	No Degree, Left Without Return (%)	Total (%)
	Attained Bachelor's Degree (%)	Attained Associate Degree (%)	Attained Certificate (%)			
Total	13.5	16.1	9.0	16.8	44.5	100
At or Below Poverty Level	5.2	13.7	*	20.3	52.6	100
101%–150%	*	14.2	*	16.0	45.1	100
151%–200%	14.1	14.9	9.6	14.0	47.4	100
201% or above	15.7	17.0	8.3	16.6	42.4	100

Source. Author's analysis of National Postsecondary Student Aid Study (National Center for Education Statistics, n.d.).
Note. * denotes an unstable estimate.

and fees were $3,264 as compared to $8,893 at public four-year colleges and universities (College Board, 2013). Decreasing state support currently makes this commitment difficult, yet there are justifications for the maintenance of a low-tuition philosophy: (a) during their development, public four-year colleges were free in some places; (b) students have costs in addition to tuition and fees; (c) price serves as a barrier to college participation; (d) low cost supports the social ideals of equal opportunity; and (e) money can be saved by students and the state by starting at a community college (Mullin, Baime, & Honeyman, 2015). The low-price alternative has not been found to be better; rather, attempts to shift away from the policy are based in the belief that other options were better or the fiscal revenues were not available to support the policy (Lombardi, 1976). Suffice it to say, the low-cost model continues to serve as a hallmark of the community college system and the primary intervention to price serving as a barrier to participation that colleges may implement.

The Pell Grant

The primary noninstitutional intervention for low-income students attending community colleges, without regard to race or ethnicity, is the Pell Grant. In 1972, the federal government decided to help students afford college by developing a national grant program for students based on their financial need. It was believed that such a program would remove, for many, the financial barrier to college participation (Gladiuex & Wolanin, 1976).

Over time, community colleges have educated an increasing number of community college students receiving the Pell Grant. In 2011–2012, community colleges enrolled 3.35 million students receiving Pell Grants (AACC, 2013b). This represented 37% of all Pell Grant recipients attending all institutions of higher education.

In terms of the community college student body, 37% of the student body received a Pell Grant in 2011–2012. Among White students, 31% received a Pell Grant. However, given that the Pell Grant covers less than the total cost of education—which includes tuition and fees, books and supplies, transportation, and a couple of other allowed expenses depending on the student's circumstance—the maximum award may not be enough to cover the student costs. Table 13.2 details the percentage of White students participating in various student aid programs. As would be expected, those students with incomes below the poverty level (100% of poverty) participated in student aid programs.

The disappointing truth is that more community college students are eligible for the Pell Grant than receive it. This disconnect has been a focus of a couple of high-profile reports, and actions to rectify the gap between the availability and the access to financial supports are underway (King, 2004).

TABLE 13.2
Participation in the Pell Grant and Other Student Aid Programs, by White Students Attending Community Colleges in
2011–2012 Academic Year

Income Percent of Poverty Level	No Pell Grant Received (%)	Aid Package With Pell Grants						Total (%)
		Pell Grant Only (%)	Pell and Campus-Based Only (%)	Pell and Direct Subsidized and Unsubsidized Loans Only (%)	Pell, Campus-Based and Direct Sub. and Unsub. Loans (%)	Pell and Other, No Direct Sub. and Unsub. Loans (%)	Pell, Other, and Direct Sub. and Unsub. Loans (%)	
Total	68.7	9.9	0.8	6.4	0.7	9.3	4.2	100
0%	36.8	17.8	*	13.2	*	19.1	8.8	100
1%–100%	38.5	19.1	1.9	13.6	1.8	17.5	7.6	100
101%–150%	43.0	20.9	1.7	10.4	1.0	16.4	6.6	100
151%–200%	55.8	14.9	*	8.3	*	13.4	5.9	100
201% or above	90.6	2.6	*	2.0	*	3.1	1.6	100

Source. Author's analysis of National Postsecondary Student Aid Study (National Center for Education Statistics, n.d.).
Note. * denotes an unstable estimate.

TABLE 13.3

Changes in Earnings and Estimated Taxes Paid Associated with Each Change in Educational Attainment for Whites: 2009

Highest Level of Educational Attainment	Earnings			Taxes Paid		
	Annual wages	*Increase in annual wages*	*Percentage increase in Earnings*	*Annual taxes paid*	*Increase in taxes Paid*	*Percentage increase in taxes paid*
Less than a high school diploma	$20,457			$3,956.70		
High-school graduate	$31,429	$10,972	54%	$6,601.95	$2,645.25	67%
Some college/associate degree	$35,634	$4,205	13%	$7,890.39	$1,288.44	20%
Bachelor's degree	$57,762	$22,128	62%	$13,481.26	$5,590.87	71%

Source. U.S. Census Bureau (2014), Baum, Ma, & Payea (2010).

Note. Annual taxes paid were estimated by determining taxes as a percentage of earnings for data presented in Figure 1.1 in Baume, Ma, & Payea (2010). The rates were then applied to annual earnings in 2009 for Whites reported by the U.S. Census Bureau (2014). These data present estimates; tax rates may have changed. The Some College category includes those who earned postsecondary certificates.

Public and Private Returns Missed

On average, as educational attainment increases, both the private returns (wages) and public returns (taxes paid) increase. These increases occur at each level of educational attainment completed (Table 13.3).

If the 99,800 White students attending community colleges and living at or below the poverty level in 2003–2004 who did not earn a college credential (extrapolated from data in Table 13.1) were to earn an associate degree, the cumulative effect would be an additional $419 million in wages and $129 million in taxes paid. This is the best-case scenario.

Yet, expecting every student to complete a credential is not a practical reality, as (a) prestigious institutions that select their student body with admissions requirements do not have a 100% graduation rate, and (b) some community college students do not wish to earn a credential. Given these caveats, if 90% of students were to have completed an associate degree, the private returns would be $378 million and the public returns in the form of taxes paid would be $116 million. These values reflect the returns for just one cohort of students in just one year (2009). Taken over a work life, the labor-market impact, not to mention the non-labor-market impact, is substantial.

Moving Forward

Community colleges serve nearly every square inch of the country. As such, the potential to address and change economic segregation and the limitations of poverty—for both Whites and all other populations—lies with these colleges. By acknowledging the presence of poor White students, the nation may better address the financial barriers of all students while more accurately portraying the faces of poverty.

References

American Association of Community Colleges. (2013a). *2013 community college fast facts*. Washington, DC: Author. Retrieved from http://www.aacc.nche.edu/AboutCC/Documents/Archive/FactSheet2013.pdf

American Association of Community Colleges. (2013b). *Pell facts*. Washington, DC: Author. Retrieved from http://www.aacc.nche.edu/ADVOCACY/PELLAC-TION/Pages/pellfacts.aspx

Baime, D. S., & Mullin, C. M. (2011, July). *Promoting educational opportunity: The Pell Grant program at community colleges* (Policy Brief 2011-03PBL). Washington, DC: American Association of Community Colleges.

Baum, S. Ma, J. Payea, K. (2010). Education pays 2010: The benefits of higher education for individuals and society. CollegeBoard Advocacy & Policy Center: Trends in Higher Education Series. Retrieved at: https://trends.collegeboard.org/sites/default/files/education-pays-2010-full-report.pdf

Bridges, D. (2006). Adaptive preference, justice, and identity in the context of widening participation in higher education. *Ethics and Education, 1*(1), 15–28.

Clawson, R. A. (2002). Poor people, Black faces: The portrayal of poverty in economics textbooks. *Journal of Black Studies, 32*(3), 352–361.

College Board. (2013, October). *Trends in college pricing 2013.* Washington, DC: Author.

DeNavas-Walt, C., Proctor, B. D., & Smith, J. C. (2013). *Income, poverty, and health insurance coverage in the United States: 2012* (Current Population Reports, P60-245). Washington, DC: U.S. Government Printing Office, U.S. Census Bureau.

Fairlie, R. W. (2013, April). Kauffman Index of Entrepreneurial Activity: 1996–2012. Kansas City, MO: Ewing Marion Kauffman Foundation.

Gladieux, L. E., & Wolanin, T. R. (1976). *Congress and the colleges: The national politics of higher education.* Lexington, MA: Lexington Books.

King, J. E. (2004). *Missed opportunities: Students who do not apply for financial aid.* Washington, DC: American Council on Education.

Lichter, D. T., & Parisi, D. (2008). *Concentrated rural poverty and the geography of exclusion* (The Carsey School of Public Policy at the Scholars' Repository. Paper 55). Durham, NH: Carsey Institute.

Lombardi, J. (1976, October). *No or low-tuition: A lost cause* (Topical Paper No. 58). Los Angeles, CA: University of California Los Angeles, ERIC Clearinghouse for Junior Colleges.

Mullin, C. M. (2013, June). The Pell Grant: A signal of value. In *Reflections on Pell: Championing social justice through 40 years of educational opportunity* (pp. 26–27). Washington, DC: Pell Institute for the Study of Opportunity in Higher Education.

Mullin, C. M., Baime, D. S., & Honeyman, D. S. (2015). *Community college finance: A guide for institutional leaders.* San Francisco, CA: Jossey-Bass.

National Center for Education Statistics. (n.d.). *Powerstats* [Data files]. Washington, DC: U.S. Department of Education, Institute for Education Sciences.

Shipp, S., McCormick, L., & Rocco, M. (2013, August 8). Op-Ed: White poverty must be good poverty. *Faculty forum.* New York, NY: Roosevelt House, Public Policy Institute at Hunter College. Retrieved from http://www.roosevelthouse.hunter.cuny.edu/?forum-post=op-ed-white-poverty-must-be-good-poverty

Short, K. (2013, December). *The research: Supplemental poverty measure: 2012* (Current Population Reports, P60-247). Washington, DC: U.S. Government Printing Office, U.S. Census Bureau.

U.S. Bureau of the Census. (2014). Annual earnings in *2009 for whites. U.S. Department of Commerce.* Washington, DC: Author.

14

VOICE OF THE NATIONAL LEADER

The Role of Community Colleges in Helping People
Move From Poverty to Prosperity

G. Edward Hughes

I raise up my voice—not so I can shout but so that those without a voice can be heard. . . .
We cannot succeed when half of us are held back.

—Malala Yousafzai

In 1985 I arrived in Hazard, Kentucky, as president of a small, rural community college. Hazard is in the heart of the Kentucky Appalachian Mountains, a region that contains some of the poorest counties in America. Its decades-long dwindling population boasts a family-oriented culture tied to the mountain geography and the historic "boom and bust" economy of coal. Predominantly White in racial composition, the region once was home to one of the largest concentrations of African Americans in the commonwealth of Kentucky in the coal towns of nearby Benham and Lynch. This is the region where President Lyndon Johnson was so moved during his 1964 visit to some poor families living in extremely difficult conditions in Inez, Kentucky, that he returned to Washington, DC, and launched the War on Poverty (Eller, 2008).

Full of confidence in my leadership abilities, some of the region's leaders asked me if I was in culture shock. They were surprised to learn that I was not completely unaware of the challenges that lay ahead. I had come to Hazard from a small, rural community college in New York's North Country serving Franklin and Essex Counties. Franklin County is the home of Lake Placid, the winter and summer playground of the wealthy. Essex County was described by Governor Mario Cuomo in his 1984 speech to the Democratic

Convention as the home of "the abject poor of Essex County, New York." Also predominantly White, the region was known for its reliance on the cyclic tourism industry as well as logging and timber industries. The silent and invisible culture was poverty.

Within two weeks of my start, a faculty member came to see me with a story. She had just met a student, Sherry (not her real name), who was the valedictorian of a local high school and whose dream was to become a science teacher and return to her high school as a teacher. I was puzzled by the faculty member's distressed expression; we were going to register the top student of a local high school, which was a big deal. So I asked her what was wrong. "Sherry is not coming to the college because she is the oldest of seven kids and she does not want to take money *away* from the other kids and her family *'just to go to college.'* She is going to get a job and might come to college later in life."

Sherry's decision dumbfounded me. I was a product of a White, middle-class upbringing with two parents who were teachers and surrounded by a community that valued education and provided opportunities for positive growth for kids. While distressing, her personal decision also energized me to learn more about the daily struggles faced by Sherry and many of the students at the college. My educational journey into poverty began with Harry Caudill's (1962) *Night Comes to the Cumberlands: A Biography of a Depressed Area*, the book that powerfully described the culture of the coal fields, a culture that created perpetual generational poverty in Appalachia.

My personal mentors were regional leaders like Mike Mullins at the Hindman Settlement School and University of Kentucky researcher and author Ron Eller, whose career has focused almost exclusively on the history of at-risk populations in the South. But my most impactful teacher was Bruce Ayers, a lifelong resident of Cumberland, Kentucky, who enjoyed a 50-year career at Southeast Community and Technical College as a student, teacher, administrator, and for his last 15 years, president. Ayers brought the issue of poverty and its effects on people to a personal level. "Ed," he'd say, "our people need our colleges to be different, do different things that other colleges don't do. We have to do everything possible to help them, make them feel wanted, and cared for. We are their only hope in many cases." That statement is true today in America for an increasing number of students from poverty. What needs to change is the urgency with which community colleges must act to truly be a pathway out of poverty.

The Impoverished White American Experience

Poverty cuts across all population groups in America. As described earlier in this section, the largest number of Americans living in or near poverty is

White, and many are women and children. Poverty comes in various forms and is felt by over 45 million Americans each day (Coley & Baker, 2013). For the purpose of this discussion, I will use the term *poverty* to include two primary types of poverty, situational and generational.

Situational poverty is an existence that many refer to as "living on the edge of poverty" or "the working poor." In America, millions are living on the edge of poverty. One fewer paycheck or a delayed financial aid disbursement, job loss, family illness, or any crisis is likely to plunge the individual in to a poverty state. Most of America's poor are single female–headed families with children, and when the crisis occurs, the individual's family takes the plunge too. From these families come hundreds of thousands of students to community colleges, each looking for more permanent solutions that can result in a stable, safe, and secure life.

Generational poverty creates a unique life perspective that can lead to an individual's feelings of hopelessness and despair. For individuals who view the world through a lens crafted by generational poverty, college is an unattainable goal, something that other people do, and besides, "I'm not smart enough anyway."

According to the ETS Center for Research on Human Capital and Education (Coley & Baker, 2013), income is *the* factor in determining the future educational success of a student. "Yet today, income has surpassed race/ethnicity as the great divider. Income-related achievement gaps (Black-White) have continued to grow as the gap between the richest and poorest American families has surged" (Coley & Baker, 2013, p. 8). Sean Reardon of Stanford University, quoted in the *New York Times*, said, "We have moved from a society in the 1950s and 1960s, in which race was more consequential than family income, to one today in which family income appears more determinative of educational success than race" (Tavernise, 2012).

Many researchers have described poverty in terms of racial and ethnic characteristics, and, indeed, there are differences faced by persons of color in poverty than by their White counterparts. Clearly, poverty cuts across all racial and ethnic lines, but as Beegle (2007) writes, "Research studies on poverty often ignore the White people in poverty" (p. 24). She further describes the unique situations of White people in poverty that include the following:

1. While poverty among minorities is frequently associated with "unjust and inequitable conditions," Whites are frequently blamed for their poverty because they made bad choices and have personal deficiencies.

2. Being White leads other people to assume that they had privileged lives once and can return to those lives, irrespective of their birth into

generational poverty, if they just make better choices and take advantage of everything that is available.

3. Whites in poverty are "the one group we can publicly humiliate." "White trash" parties, posters, hats, cookbooks, and jokes are rampant. (Beegle, 2007, p. 56)

Over the past century, popular literature, entertainment, and the media have perpetuated stereotypes based on the previously noted inaccurate perceptions. The *Lil' Abner* comic strips, *Lum and Abner* radio broadcasts, and television's *The Beverly Hillbillies* depicted poor Whites in less-than-flattering circumstances. And today, those stereotypes are reinforced through reality shows like *Duck Dynasty* and *Here Comes Honey Boo Boo*. Unfortunately, many of today's students from poverty carry with them self-concepts created and reinforced by a lifetime of misleading public and private messages.

Research on the personal effects of poverty provides the following composite picture of the impoverished American on his or her way to the local community college:

- They are born with little prenatal care and lack a consistent medical home (including dental, mental health) throughout early life into adulthood. They are less likely to be insured for their health-care needs (Coley & Baker, 2013).
- Their parents are less likely to receive early intervention support during the first two years of life when brain development is crucial (Kristof & WuDunn, 2014).
- Their parent(s) often work at jobs that pay poverty-level wages or who, involuntarily, work less than full-time. These jobs go hand in hand with few benefits, unstable hours, and little opportunity for advancement (Matthews, 2014).
- They are less likely to receive high-quality child care and arrive at kindergarten well behind students from non-poverty backgrounds. And they experience greater declines in learning during long periods away from school (often referred to as the "summer slide") owing the lack of engaged family educational support than do students from upper income families (Coley & Baker, 2013).
- They experience food insecurity and parental job insecurity, which fosters a present-oriented approach to life and hinders the formation of a future that is significantly better and one that is "deserved" (Beegle, 2007).

- They feel socially isolated and immobile (Levine & Nidiffer, 1996) and report feeling that they simply do not belong outside their families and communities (Beegle, 2000).
- They often communicate using an oral style. This orality emphasizes connections to people and the environment and utilizes sensory input and individual relationships for learning (Ong, 2002; Beegle, 2007).
- They experience negative consequences of being poor that include restricted school activities due to unaffordable "participation" fees, lack of bank accounts due to their inability to secure proper IDs (leading to bad or no credit), and use of payday lenders. They lack transportation options, especially personal vehicles requiring insurance. And they lack access to adequate housing because they do not have previous stable housing or access to homeownership credit programs (Coley & Baker, 2013).
- They spend inordinate amounts of time during their impoverished lives traveling among a myriad of social agencies in the community to obtain the assistance needed to survive. Beegle (2007) reports that during her time in poverty she "often spent 90% of my time going from agency to agency to get $25 from each one to add up to the $150 needed to get my lights turned back on" (p. 61).
- Those in generational poverty struggle to deal with the harsh realities of daily life. They are left feeling like they have no control of their existence. They become resigned to responding to what life brings and abandon planning for a different future.
- Their experiences in school are often negative, and education simply adds more negative stress to their lives. School becomes just another example of a place where they do not belong or feel welcome (Beegle, 2007; Sigle-Rushton & McLanahan, 2004).
- They are often single women with children who work multiple low-wage jobs and have little consistent family support. If they are male, they often feel humiliated by not being able to be the "breadwinner" (Beegle, 2007).
- They have been humiliated publicly in the media and popular entertainment, embarrassed by being the butt of jokes. They have experienced a lifetime of being labeled "White trash."

It is from this background and with these characteristics that students of poverty come to the community college doorstep. They arrive with a different communication style and language from a culture that is not well understood by the very professionals they anxiously and *cautiously* look to for support. They arrive feeling that they may not belong, that they are probably not smart enough, and that they have few tangible resources or skills with which to succeed. They are often embarrassed and blame themselves for making bad choices; they often question whether starting college is the latest "bad decision." They are operating in the bottom levels of Maslow's Hierarchy of Needs, stuck in survival mode. They desire love and belonging, yet they are not likely to be able to articulate well those concepts. They are, in essence, venturing into an unknown world. They are the modern-day nineteenth-century immigrants to America, and the community colleges are their Ellis Island.

Often unrecognized in all of the research and dialog is the fact that poverty fosters survival skills from which individuals can begin their journey out of poverty if they are understood and supported by others. Community college professionals must understand and appreciate the cultures from which White students from poverty come. Equally important, they must navigate the difference in communication and language styles of students of White poverty. And they must build on the survival skills of these students as they tout their college's prowess of being where Americans in despair find hope and build a future. They are not "White trash"; instead they are students with great promise.

Community Colleges: The Modern-Day Educational Ellis Island?

What does all of this teach us about poverty and how community colleges must adapt to meet students and families in or near poverty? What can we do as professionals and community colleges to truly become the egalitarian, inclusive institutions of which our marketing campaigns boast?

If community colleges are to be the modern-day Ellis Island for this country's education immigrants, they must focus on income insecurity and the impact it has on students from poverty. A college's inclusion plan must address the effects of poverty on students as much, if not more so, than any other issue (e.g., race, ethnicity, gender, etc.) as poverty cuts across all segments of the community from which the college derives its student body. The greater the extent to which a college can use the research on poverty and help its professionals begin to internalize the lives of their poverty-oriented students, the greater the chance for improved student success.

As leaders, presidents and senior administrators need to become immersed in the reality of poverty and its devastating effects on students, their families, and their communities. It is often stated that "perception is reality," and in the case of poverty, we need to admit that as professionals we are woefully ignorant of the totality of the experiences individuals from poverty face daily.

College leaders need to understand that their colleagues and employees mostly came from middle- and upper-income families. Tankersley (2014) reported that "study after study shows that students from wealthier families are increasingly more likely to graduate from college than students from low-income families with 1 of 8 nationally earning an associate degree within three years." Therefore, relatively few individuals from poverty attain the educational credentials to become community college professionals, which means their colleges are not filled with employees from whom they can learn about poverty from a personal perspective. While colleges have diversity and inclusion plans and hire employees from diverse backgrounds, very few consider the need to seek persons from a poverty background in their hiring practices.

Failure to seek qualified candidates from poverty backgrounds as a component of inclusion will lead to a continuation of ineffective programs and services that can benefit students. Community college programs and practices born out of a non-poverty worldview lead some professionals to visualize the future of their students, establish strategies for helping students "overcome" their circumstances, and treat students from poverty from the wrong perspective. In his book *War on the Poor: The Underclass and Antipoverty Policy*, Herbert Gans (1995) provides a fundamental basis for understanding why many community colleges inadequately serve students from poverty. His premise is that professionals keep asking people in poverty to act like those who have lived a life in the middle class when they do not have the resources, including experiences, expectations, and worldview, to do so.

Immersion in the poverty experience (White and non-White) must include all of the institution's stakeholders, including boards of trustees, foundation boards, full- and part-time faculty, staff, community partners, and students. When colleges purposefully engage in the topic of poverty, they will discover that many of their policies, practices, and procedures have been developed from a middle- or upper-income class perspective. By involving students from poverty in the activities, their unique perspectives will provide clarity about the college policies, practices, and procedures that are significant barriers to student success. Strategies that will eliminate or reduce institutional barriers and increase the student success will be revealed.

There are ample resources available to colleges as they learn about their students from poverty. Ruby Payne's Bridges Out of Poverty, the Working Poor Families Project, Center for Law and Social Policy (CLASP) Benefit Access Initiative, and Beegle's Communication Across Barriers offer a rich set of resources for any college. This collective body of work reveals a consistent set of factors and barriers that impede efforts of students from poverty to experience success. Beegle (2007) suggests the barriers fall into two categories, *systemic* and *internalized*. She writes that

> many barriers emanate from the structure of our social system. Many of these barriers are the result of the way institutions are currently organized, and stem from the values and perspectives that people in poverty adopt from the daily conditions they experience. These structures put people from generational poverty in many challenging positions where they see no levels of support or avenues of opportunity. In most cases, the fact that many of the barriers have systemic roots is invisible, even to people in poverty. (p. 55)

Systemic barriers include the fragmentation of agencies and college services, both in terms of physical location and service silos. Students in poverty spend an enormous amount of time traveling to a variety of community and state agencies and college departments seeking assistance. They report having no control over their lives because they have no time except to work, seek assistance for a variety of life issues, and attend school. Initiatives like the CLASP Benefits Access Initiative are pilot testing strategies that link state agencies to community colleges so that college professionals can assist students with accessing public benefits from campus. The focus is to reduce the barrier of travel to a state agency (often agencies in different locations) and to help students obtain the public benefits that will enable them to stay in and complete college.

As one of the seven pilot colleges in CLASP's national study, Gateway Community and Technical College has partnered with the Kentucky Cabinet for Family and Children to assist students from poverty. Public kiosks are now in multiple locations on each campus, and faculty and staff have been trained to help students apply for benefits like child care vouchers, food stamps, medical cards, transportation vouchers, and housing assistance. Advisers are trained to ask appropriate questions that can lead to a conversation about assistance that is available. Over 700 students have been served to date.

Community colleges themselves have policies, practices, and procedures that are systemic barriers to students from poverty. Often they are created from a middle-class perspective, one in which sufficient personal resources are available, concepts of work and achievement are valued and supported, and planning for the future is the norm. These are not characteristics normally found in poor families.

For example, one policy on most college campuses that often becomes a barrier is class attendance. Many attendance policies still equate learning with seat time and limit absences to one or two (often with a note from a physician). What are students from poverty who are working one or two low-wage jobs and caring for a family member (usually children) to do when faced with a sick child, lack of a backup caregiver, and employers who can easily replace a tardy or absent worker? Most, if not all, will make the decision to care for the child some way, get to work, and then deal with the college class the next time they are able to attend. Their first time they may be creative, but when they arrive at class a few minutes late with their child in tow, they may be met by a second policy: "No admittance once class begins." Or a third policy: "No children in class, no exceptions." Or a fourth policy: "Bring in a note from the doctor." Is there any wonder why students may feel that the institution does not care about them when, despite extremely conflicting demands, they came to class?

Attendance-related policies would be different if they were based on an understanding of students from poverty. One would anticipate policies that take into account the characteristics of people in poverty described by Beegle (2007): They are in survival mode, rely on relationships, and deal with the world in the present. They make decisions based on feelings or survival (self and family) and do not deal with the future ramifications of the decision. Instead of a rigid classroom attendance policy, a "learning engagement" policy might be fashioned around competency-based learning, with multiple learning modes and delivery mechanisms offered. Instead of a rigid "no children in class" policy, emergency child care services might be created with a community partner, or child care might be provided on campus. And instead of a practice of excluding a student who comes in late, faculty should be encouraged and trained to plan for latecomers with activities designed to catch a student up, a buddy learner system, or other creative ways to engage the student.

Internalized barriers may be more challenging for colleges. Students from families in poverty have often internalized the negative perceptions experienced all around them. They are led to believe that poverty is a result of "bad choices" or some negative personal characteristics like laziness, low morals, or bad company. This internalized perception is exacerbated by the belief that America is the land of equal opportunity and all people need to do is "lift themselves up by their bootstraps." White people in poverty especially experience the disconnection with their non-impoverished White counterparts. They report that their "Whiteness" leads people to assume that they once were privileged, but owing to poor choices and personal deficiencies, they have fallen into poverty. And since they were once privileged, they can work harder and should be able to "make it" (Beegle, 2007).

Internalized barriers include but are not limited to the following (Payne, DeVol, & Dreussi Smith, 2006; Beegle, 2007):

- Internalizing blame through experiences that teach them that they are not as good as everyone else and consequently should feel enormous shame. This is especially true for Whites who view other Whites, even those in the lower middle class, as affluent.
- Internalizing covert messages from their experiences that they are different and inferior. Examples of these messages include waiting in long lines for services, a take-your-number-and-wait culture, nonverbal negative reactions from others, and a general lack of respect shown to them in many situations.
- A belief in a very limited future that does not include future-oriented goals.
- A low expectation of what education can do, including a view that education and schooling is just another stress of life that might not be worth it.
- A pervasive self-view that "I'm not good enough, this is where I was born to be, and I should not consider becoming better than others in my neighborhood."

Community colleges must address the systemic and internalized barriers intentionally and in a comprehensive manner and not be engaged in "feel-good" practices that only provide surface-level solutions and temporary fixes. Simply training employees to repeatedly tell students from poverty that they should not feel they are not good enough, or that the lines they stand in don't mean they are inferior, or that education is the pathway to a new future, will not be sufficient. Nor will establishing a one-stop service center or adding kiosks for public benefits or even changing some attendance policies be enough to alter the life path for students from poverty. It will take a comprehensive and consistent approach arrived at through an inclusive institutional process that involves all stakeholders.

What More Can Community Colleges Do?

First, community college personnel must learn about poverty. The literature on poverty is rife with examples of best practices about conducting a poverty competency assessment that leads to an institutional action plan. Educating stakeholders about poverty and its impact on the success of students must be the first action step, and that step must come from the institution's top leader. The statistics about poverty are sobering and easily available at the local, state, and national levels. However, it is the stories of the college's own students and employees that make poverty personal and impact future behaviors. While it may be a logistical challenge in larger institutions, the use of structured poverty simulations involving as many college employees as possible is an important tool for personalizing poverty. At Gateway, all full-time employees are engaged in a poverty simulation that utilizes students in the college's Ready to Work and Learn program as facilitators and mentors. It has proved to be a powerful experience that has led to some personal changes in behavior and attitudes toward students from poverty. The most often reported reaction to the simulation is that it is exhausting to be poor, a result of struggling against never-ending barriers to obtaining and maintaining assistance, schooling, and employment.

Second, the institutional action plan created from a poverty culture assessment must focus on developing and maintaining relationships with students from poverty through the use of the language and communication styles of the poverty culture. Community college personnel must put aside middle-class values and communication styles that will create another negative schooling experience for students. The work of Walter Ong (2002) regarding the characteristics of an "oral-culture of learning and communications styles" is instructive. Ong was one of the first authors to connect the style of learning and communications to people in poverty. A reading of his work will identify seven characteristics that can help professionals understand how to communicate in an *oral culture* manner, as opposed to in a *print culture manner,* which aligns better with middle- and upper-income populations. Individuals using oral communication style obtain much information through relationships and storytelling; accordingly, personal relationships are highly valued. They are spontaneous and go with the flow, are comfortable expressing emotions, use nonverbal cues, and are physical in their interactions. They are present oriented and often repeat stories as a means of understanding a situation and moving information into long-term memory.

Community college professionals typically use a print-oriented communications style that in recent years has been expanded through the use of technology. Print culture is future oriented, information heavy, print dependent, logical, and analytical. It is not relational. In essence, colleges are foreign territories to many students from poverty simply because the communication culture from which they come is totally different from that found at the community college. As Beegle related in her own story, "I am now 'bilingual,' I speak the language of generational poverty (oral culture), and I speak middle-class (print-culture) language" (Beegle, 2007, p. 12).

Third, community colleges must build on the enormous strengths of students from poverty and begin to focus on them as "students of great promise." People from poverty have unique strengths and characteristics developed from learning to survive. What they need are consistent personal relationships with caring professionals who meet them where they are and help them see that they have a future. There is ample evidence in the literature that points to the success mentoring programs can have on improving the success rates of students. These programs are especially critical for students from poverty who have little personal experience and often little or no family support with which to navigate uncharted educational waters. These programs include the use of trained professional, volunteer, and peer mentors. The caution here is that the mentoring programs must be adapted to use the oral-culture style of communication as a starting point toward helping the student become "bilingual."

Fourth, community colleges must review policies, practices, and procedures and reshape them to fit the lives of students from poverty and the working poor. As noted previously, well-intentioned policies and procedures crafted with a middle-class, print-oriented lens can create significant barriers for student from poverty. Critics who suggest that this approach will "dumb down" the academy should be reminded that the success of students is at the core of virtually every community college mission in America. With at least 15% of American families living in or near in poverty (U.S. Census Bureau, 2014), neglecting these students is in direct conflict with the reason that colleges exist. Given that community colleges market themselves as places of hope and opportunity for all, they must change their operations to improve the success of students from poverty.

Fifth, community colleges need to redefine their role related to people in poverty. Community colleges generally excel at developing relationships with community agencies to support the needs of students and employees, but they often neglect the specific needs of students from poverty. Where possible, providing public benefit service support on campus can greatly reduce the time students from poverty spend navigating multiple agencies in order to survive. Crucial wraparound services need to be in place to help students stabilize difficult situations, build connections to resources, learn new skills and language, take action toward greater self-reliance, manage day-to-day living more effectively, and build financial and nonfinancial assets, including education, for the future. Strategic partnerships that create coalitions designed to provide a community "safety net" for persons in poverty will ultimately benefit the community college's students and their families. The community college must be a core member and in some cases the community convener of such coalitions. Effective partnerships with community agencies and organizations to provide these services can be game changers for students.

Sixth, colleges should provide meaningful work experiences on campus or in community agencies, especially for students from poverty. Work-and-learn programs not only provide income but also help students regain a sense of dignity and purpose while building more connections. Programs like Kentucky's Work and Learn, Ready to Work, apprenticeship programs, and others have been shown to be effective pathways out of poverty. Strategic implementation of a college's federal work/study program that is redesigned to provide holistic support for students from poverty should be considered. Colleges should consider partnering with companies to establish work centers on campuses for students. The important issue here is that students from poverty need income now, while they are learning, through a carefully structured program that demonstrates that "they belong" and are "good enough." Those two messages, when internalized, can lead to a realization that education can be a path out of poverty and into greater self-sufficiency.

Seventh, hiring employees with a poverty background to be teachers, counselors, and administrators will diversify the workforce. We have long understood that in terms of race, gender, and ethnicity, hiring a diverse workforce provides a fundamental element necessary to the implementation of a diverse institutional culture. Community colleges need to add persons from a poverty background as part of their inclusion plan. Students from poverty will readily learn that there are "people like them" at the college. They will tell their families and neighbors, with personal stories, that the college is a good place with good people who can personally identify with them. They will tell of incidents that demonstrate the college is making their lives easier and better. They will describe a place where hope and opportunity exist.

Eighth, community college leaders must become more visible in their advocacy for the needs of students from poverty. The leaders of community colleges, a key sector of American higher education, should assume a prominent role to advocate for public policy changes that have become systemic barriers to student success. Federal and state policies that cut off public benefits to students in good standing effectively reduce student success and crush hope. Abramsky (2013) and Coley & Baker (2013) offer a comprehensive review of approaches to change public policy in order to move more people from poverty into and through college and other training programs. Leaders in higher education must advocate for significant changes in state and federal work-and-learn programs (i.e., Temporary Assistance for Needy Families and Federal Work Study Program) to allow for more investment in funding and prioritizing opportunities for students from poverty (Altstadt, 2014).

So whatever happened to Sherry, the valedictorian from eastern Kentucky described at the beginning of this chapter? When I learned of her decision to stay home and help "provide" for her family, I went to the chairman of the foundation and stated that I wanted to begin a scholarship program for any valedictorian or salutatorian from the high schools in the service area that would guarantee them 100% tuition and books through the completion of their associate degree. I related Sherry's story, and we agreed on the spot that Sherry would be the first in the scholarship program. The faculty member with whom Sherry had a relationship informed her of the scholarship offer. Sherry completed her associate degree and transferred to a regional university, where she earned a bachelor's degree in education and a secondary teaching certificate. She returned to her high school and has enjoyed a nearly two-decade career giving back to her community as a teacher. She set a new level of education expectation within her family, as many of her siblings attended and completed college. She became a model for others in her community, which helped increase the number of students from her high school who now plan for the future with a college education in mind.

As community colleges respond to the 2012 report of the American Association of Community Colleges' 21st-Century Commission on the Future of Community Colleges, *Reclaiming the American Dream*, they must not neglect the students from poverty. America's community colleges are in a unique position to shine the light on the needs of these students. Community college leaders must provide national, state, and local leadership to open a public dialog about poverty as a fundamental component of the inclusion and completion agendas. It may be one of the most important national dialogs that will determine America's future. As John F. Kennedy asked, "If not us, who? If not now, when?"

References

Abramsky, S. (2013). *American way of poverty: How the other half still lives.* New York, NY: Nation Books.

Altstadt, D. (2014). *Earn to learn: How states can reimagine and reinvest in work-study to help low-income adults pay for college, enhance their academic studies and prepare for post-college careers.* Washington, DC: Working Poor Families Project.

American Association of Community Colleges. (2012, April). *Reclaiming the American Dream: A report from the 21st-Century Commission on the Future of Community Colleges.* Washington, DC: Author. Retrieved from http://www.aacc.nche.edu/aboutcc/21stcenturyreport_old/index.html

Beegle, D. (2000). Interrupting generational poverty: Factors influencing successful completion of the bachelor's degree. PhD diss., Portland State University, Portland, OR.

Beegle, D. M. (2007). *See poverty . . . Be the difference! Discovering the missing pieces for helping people move out of poverty.* Tigard, OR: Communication Across Barriers.

Caudill, H. M. (1962). *Night comes to the Cumberlands: A biography of a depressed area.* Boston: Little, Brown.

Center for Law and Social Policy. (2014). New census data tell us that poverty fell in 2014: Children and young adults still face the greatest risks. Retrieved from www.clasp.org

Coley, R. J., & Baker, B. (2013). *Poverty and education: Finding the way forward.* Washington, DC: ETS Center for Research on Human Capital and Education.

Eller, R. D. (2008). *Uneven ground: Appalachia since 1949.* Lexington, KY: University Press of Kentucky.

Gans, H. J. (1995). *The war against the poor: The underclass and antipoverty policy.* New York, NY: Basic Books.

Kristof, N., & WuDunn, S. (2014, September 12). The way to beat poverty. *New York Times.*

Levine, A. and Nidiffer, J. (1996). *Beating the odds: How the poor get to college.* San Francisco, CA: Jossey Bass.

Matthews, H. (2014). *2013 poverty data: A glimpse of good news for children, but we can do better.* Retrieved from www.clasp.org

Ong, W. J. (2002). *Orality and literacy: The technologizing of the word.* 2nd ed. New York, NY: Routledge. (Original work published 1982.)

Payne, R. K., DeVol, P., & Dreussi Smith, T. (2006). *Bridges out of poverty: Strategies for professionals and communities workbook.* Highlands, TX: aha Process.

Sigle-Rushton, W., & McLanahan, S. (2004). Father absence and child well-being. In D. Moynihan, T. Speeding, & L. Rainwater (Eds.), *The future of the family* (pp. 116–155). New York, NY: Russell Sage Foundation.

Tankersley, J. (2014, December 15). The college trap that keeps people poor. *Washington Post.* Retrieved from http://www.washingtonpost.com/sf/business/2014/12/15/the-college-trap-that-keeps-people-poor/

Tavernise, S. (2012, February 9). Education gap grows between rich and poor studies say. *New York Times.* Retrieved from http://www.nytimes.com/2012/02/10/education/education-gap-grows-between-rich-and-poor-studies-show.html?_r=0

U.S. Census Bureau. (2014). *Poverty 2013 highlights.* Washington, DC: Social, Economic, and Housing Statistics Division: Poverty.

15

CUTTING-EDGE MODELS FOR BEST PRACTICE

Caucasian Student Populations in Poverty: Voices of Reluctant Advocates

Russell Lowery-Hart and Cara Crowley

> *There is no education like adversity.*
> —Benjamin Disraeli

In October 2011, Amarillo College held a data summit for all faculty and staff. Our data did not paint a pretty picture of student success. Our retention rates were lower than we imagined, and our completion rates were barely in double digits. We and our colleagues had never really reviewed data in such a systematic manner. We knew we needed to improve. Our community needed us to improve. Most important, our students needed us to improve the statistical representations of their success. As good, strong "academics," we knew what these distressing numbers really meant—we needed more academic support and more effective academic interventions to help students. We began by collecting more data, through surveys and focus groups, to identify the greatest barriers to student completion. We made assumptions about what barriers would be identified—fully expecting tutoring hours, instructional practices, and scheduling to be the greatest barriers to our students' success. We were wrong.

While the "academic" supports were vitally important, our students identified the top 10 barriers to their completion—and none of them were based in academics—none. Each of the greatest 10 barriers to completion was "life" related rather than "academic" in structure. The five biggest barriers for our students were food, housing, transportation, child care, and health care.

215

When we initially evaluated our student success data, we were so focused on academic success that we failed to realize the more powerful and debilitating barrier. Poverty is the single greatest barrier to student success facing higher education. Caucasian students are living on the front lines of the poverty battle, and higher education must actively and intentionally engage the issue of poverty. Through simplistic data analysis, basic poverty training for faculty and staff, and unique partnerships with the community, higher education can do more than mitigate poverty—we can eradicate it.

Developing the Voices of Reluctant Advocates

Perspective as an Administrator

As administrators, we were not trained to advocate for people from poverty, our conference proceedings did not focus on poverty, and our institutional missions did not include poverty mitigation. Yet, increasing demographic shifts along with increasing legislative funding pressures for completion will require higher education administrators to become active and vocal poverty advocates within our institutions and communities.

Our local, state, and national data indicated that our populations were increasingly poorer and less likely to attain a college certificate or degree. For our Amarillo, Texas, community (and we are certain for your communities as well) the fastest-growing population is children born into poverty. For our community, over 38% of our children are living in poverty, 67% of our students in the local school district are eligible for free and reduced lunch, and over 50% of Amarillo College students themselves were trapped in the war zone of poverty (United Way of Amarillo and Canyon, 2014).

Most administrators enter higher education with a commitment to students and a desire to make a difference. Yet, few of us would declare that we entered higher education to advocate for people from poverty. While we may be emerging as reluctant advocates, our communities and country demand we step forward and shoulder this responsibility.

At Amarillo College, our emerging philosophical alignment with "No Excuses University" gave us a road map forward as advocates for people from poverty. Through the Turn Around Schools organization with Damen Lopez, Amarillo College became the first higher education partner to embrace "no excuses" (Lopez, 2009).

At the foundation, *No Excuses* means we believe all students hold potential for college and career success. We embrace our responsibility for the "whole" student by setting high expectations for students and then assisting them in reaching these expectations. We aspire to treat each student as an individual with unique challenges and needs.

The Amarillo College No Excuses philosophy analyzes and evaluates reasons for students' successes and struggles and does not allow them to become our excuse for lack of success. As a member of the Amarillo College family, employees embrace the six C's of a No Excuses professional.

- *Committed:* We are committed to being the right person for each student by expecting students' best efforts and then guiding them to excellence. We are committed to being the right person for each other by supporting efforts to improve student success from our colleagues across the institution.
- *Courageous:* We will have the courage to confront the status quo when it impedes student success. We will have courage to ensure our important work is not deterred by those who tell us our dreams for students are unrealistic or impossible.
- *Collaborative:* We support and trust each other in our work toward student completion.
- *Creative:* We are innovative and embrace new ways to better serve our students. We are not satisfied with continuing the "AC way" if our data show we can do better.
- *Character centered:* We will do the right thing for our students and each other.
- *Completion focused:* College completion and career readiness drive our efforts, no matter our job descriptions or reporting structures—we are all on the college completion team.

Our students often get one shot at success—they depend on us. Amarillo College employees strive to be the right person for each student who crosses our paths.

Perspective as a Professor

In 2012, Amarillo College launched its No Excuses University philosophy. With the inception of the philosophy change on campus, faculty refocused their attention and efforts to talk with students and learn who they are as people, their passions, and their types of backgrounds. A number of faculty made comments showing how this renewed focus changed their lives. One faculty member in particular commented that she learned that the majority of her students were first-generation, attended Amarillo College part-time because they worked 30-plus hours per week, were single parents or had a child as a teenager, and were struggling to find a balance among family, college, and the simple need to financially survive. By simply speaking with her students, she learned she often used lingo or terminology unfamiliar to them. She learned she was often wrong by thinking the students were lazy and did not want to read the lessons or complete homework assignments.

No Excuses University opened the door for Amarillo College faculty to recognize and understand that our preconceived notions of what our students are like do not match the reality of who our students are as a collective body. Faculty came to the realization we were living through a narrow view of college, believing our students and their college experience were similar to our college experience.

As Amarillo College engrained the No Excuses University philosophy into our courses, programs, and initiatives, faculty began noticing our students (like college students across America) are different today than they were 10 years ago, much less 5 years ago. Amarillo College's student demographic shift, just in the last 5 years, reflects an increase in enrollment by certain ethnicities and continual decline by certain groups. According to Amarillo College's (2014) data book, between 2009 and 2013, the college has seen a dramatic increase in enrollment of Hispanic students (27% to 36%), yet a decrease in Caucasian student enrollment (63% to 54%). Furthermore, the male enrollment is declining annually (41% to 39%). Yet the most significant difference in college students today is the increase in financial need, whether that need takes the form of a Pell award or other financial aid, such as student loans, grants, and/or scholarships (14% increase).

What we as faculty have learned over the last two years is that students do rise to the challenge and want academic rigor, but they need flexibility with their schedules. We learned that students want their college professors to simply talk with them, learn from them as they are learning from us. We learned that faculty are meant to advocate for these bright and capable students who bear more on their shoulders than we can imagine. We learned that these students inspire us daily. But in order to learn all these things about our students, we had to learn that we were the ones needing to change. We were the ones putting preconceived notions on our students. We learned that change comes from within. Change comes from seeing, hearing, speaking, and adapting willingly to a student's needs. We learned that No Excuses University is more than a philosophy; it's an entrenched part of our daily culture at Amarillo College.

Perspective as an Institution

With poverty as a clear issue for our students, the college, and the community, we searched for a way forward. Our journey started with basic training. Through the work of Communication Across Barriers with Donna Beegle, all faculty and staff built a foundation of common understanding:

- Poverty is like living in a war zone.
- Poverty affects one's worldview and expectations.
- Poverty teaches those living in its war zone that surviving today is the sole focus instead of planning for tomorrow.
- Poverty creates an isolating experience.
- Poverty is demeaning, painful, and life changing.
- Poverty has its own language.
- Poverty teaches incredible problem-solving skills.

Our faculty and staff completed the initial training. It was transformative. Our minds were broadened. Our hearts were softened. Our resolve was solidified.

However, the greatest lesson from our initial training was not about poverty, but about our institution. We were willing to help, even if we didn't initially see poverty as a part of our institutional mission. We cared. Yet, caring and awareness of poverty were not enough.

The day after our initial training with Donna Beegle, seven different Amarillo College faculty and staff were calling community agencies to advocate for eight different homeless students. Through the investigative work of one agency, Amarillo College learned that all seven of our faculty, thinking they were advocating for "their" eight students, were soliciting community help for the exact same student. Awareness of poverty was not the end of the institutional journey, but the beginning. We had a community agency and seven college employees working for a single student. As an institution, we realized poverty awareness would be helpful only if we had a systemic approach through which our faculty and staff could act on that awareness.

With the No Excuses philosophical foundation that we are responsible for the whole student, and with data showing poverty as the greatest threat to student success, we became advocates for students from poverty. Students were hurting, and no academic intervention was addressing the core issue causing their pain. We had to act.

We were ready to advocate for our students, but we needed a broader understanding of the barriers they were facing living in the war zone of poverty before we could build a systemic response. Our institution had to build a system that would educate the students we have, not the ones we wish we had.

Barriers for Students Living in the War Zone of Poverty

According to the 2014 U.S. Census report *Dynamics of Economic Well-Being: Poverty 2009–2011*, 31.6% of the U.S. population lives in poverty for at least two months annually, an increase of 4.5% from the 2005–2007 study. Additionally, poverty status for Caucasian individuals increases annually by at least .25%. The average Caucasian person stays in poverty for six months annually. Despite this determination, the number of chronically poor Caucasians is on the rise. *Chronically poor* describes an individual who has been in poverty all 12 months of the calendar year. Per the U.S. Census report, Caucasian individuals considered chronically poor have increased from 33.1% (2004–2008 panel) to 38.3% in the 2009–2011 study. This reflects a 5.2% increase in Caucasian individuals considered chronically poor.

Following the national trend, Amarillo College's community of Amarillo, Texas, has seen an increase in chronically poor among its Caucasian population. Per a 2013 Texas Department of State Health Services profile, nearly 20% of Amarillo's community is living in poverty. But more telling is that over 25% of students in the Amarillo Independent School District live in poverty, and 66% are considered economically disadvantaged. It is these students and individuals who are future Amarillo College students. But how do individuals who live in poverty or are economically disadvantaged realize their dreams of a college education? Students must look to the federal government for financial aid.

Per the College Board (2013), the need for financial aid is an increasing trend in higher education; however, the majority of students borrow federal funds via loans to support their educational attainment. When comparing financial aid recipients at public two-year colleges for the 2011–2012 academic year with those for the 2012–2013 academic year, Pell Grant recipients increased 2.6%; direct subsidized student loans rose a dramatic 7.4%; and direct unsubsidized student loans expanded by 1.4%. Yet Parent Loans for Undergraduate Students (PLUS) decreased from 1.1% to 0.7%.

Amarillo College distributes nearly $16 million in federal financial aid; yet less than 35% of these funds are Pell Grant awards. Amarillo College students fund their college dreams with student loans. During the 2012–2013 academic year, Amarillo College students borrowed an astonishing $10 million to support their educational dreams. Unfortunately, the reality for Amarillo College students, particularly Caucasian students, is that borrowing federal funds is often the only available resource for supporting college costs.

In a National Center for Education Statistics (2008) study, Caucasian students borrowed student loans at a greater rate than minority students, in part because Caucasian students receive Pell Grants at a lower rate and lower dollar amount than minority students. Between fall 2013 and fall 2014, Amarillo College's enrollment of Caucasian students decreased by 20%. Yet the college only had a 1% decrease (31% versus 30%) in Caucasian students receiving Pell awards (Amarillo College, 2014). Because of the dramatic decrease in enrollment of Caucasian students and the increased need of these students for financial aid, Amarillo College has created a poverty task force to study how Amarillo College's policies, procedures, and processes are affecting our students and how we can eliminate institutional barriers preventing student success.

Understanding Poverty

In order to build a responsive system targeting the biggest barriers to creating poverty, Amarillo College leveraged the work of Donna Beegle in truly understanding poverty.

Situational Versus Generational Poverty

A foundational understanding of poverty required Amarillo College to understand the difference between situational and generational poverty. In order to help our students, we have to understand where they are, not where we wish they were. Most social stereotypes of poverty and our guiding myths about poverty are based in a situational understanding.

Situational poverty is usually associated with those coming from a stable, middle-class condition who face a crisis in poverty. These individuals are surrounded by role models and possibilities. Most of the time, situational poverty arises from a sudden event affecting income, like a divorce or death. Yet individuals living in situational poverty still have their networks, work history, and life experiences to help pull them out of poverty. The life outlook for someone in situational poverty is "I pulled myself out of poverty. If I did it, anyone can—you just have to make better choices, work harder, and make sacrifices" (Beegle, 2007, p. 27).

Generational poverty brings a more destructive and debilitating perspective. Those living in generational poverty have never owned land or property. Most family members work in unskilled, low-paying jobs. Family literacy is low and mobility is high as children move from school to school and miss out on education. Most in generational poverty often do not know anyone who has benefitted from education, has "moved up," or has been respected in a job. The focus is on making it through the day. The life outlook for someone in generational poverty is "Life happens to me and I don't have any control over it" (Beegle, 2007, p. 28).

Most of our higher education employees' understanding about poverty is through a middle-class lens. Yet many of our students come to higher education with a generational poverty lens. Students from situational poverty approach the higher education experience with an understanding of and confidence in working the system to their benefit. Students surviving generational poverty approach higher education with fear, lack of understanding, and a perspective that they do not belong. Our systems reward those from situational poverty and fail to understand or support those from generations of poverty.

Oral Versus Written Cultures

In his groundbreaking work *Orality and Literacy: The Technologizing of the World*, Walter Ong (1982) reported a difference in communication based on income status. Donna Beegle (2007) built a training approach based on Ong's findings. People in generational poverty overwhelmingly communicate in oral styles, while those from middle-class backgrounds communicate in print forms.

Oral communication characteristics are important to understand because our systems are set up to devalue them. Students who are more comfortable in an oral culture seek information through relationships rather than through the printed word. They use stories to share and gain information and rely heavily on nonverbal cues.

Print culture students follow information in a linear thought process and communicate in turn-taking. Reading is the main form of knowledge. Print culture students rely less on nonverbals and more on precise language.

Higher education systems, from application and registration to course and program completion, almost exclusively honor print cultures. Many students from generational poverty are smart, capable problem-solvers but are viewed as less capable because they are not fluent in "middle-class language" cultures (Beegle, 2007).

Immediacy Versus Long-Term Planning

Students from generational poverty are focused on surviving today. The concept of long-term planning is for those with the luxury of time and resources. The life experiences of people in generational poverty are defined by low expectations, lack of support, misunderstandings, and limited possibilities for success (Beegle, 2007). Thus, those living in poverty are focused on meeting the immediate needs before them. Planning for a semester, a year, or a long-term career is not a part of the "normal" poverty experience. Yet most of higher education rewards are built on delayed gratification and forward thinking.

Poverty Limits Talent Development

In *See Poverty . . . Be the Difference*, Donna Beegle (2007) addresses the systematic and internalized barriers institutions create when working with individuals living in poverty. Beegle writes, "People in poverty face many barriers that impede their efforts to experience success and create life-changing opportunities" (p. 55). In order to remove the barriers poverty places on individuals, higher education institutions must be willing to recognize and understand the limitations poverty places on entire families, neighborhoods, and communities.

Amarillo College understands the limitations poverty has placed on our community and thereby our students. We recognize that our students living in poverty struggle with limited educational opportunities. We understand our students grapple with daily hardships from not understanding the meanings of words and statements (the use of middle-class language), disbelief surrounding their own abilities and capabilities, to fearing that failure is inevitable. Amarillo College's No Excuses University philosophy has opened the doors for faculty, staff, and students to engage in meaningful dialogue, programs, and support services to ensure student success for all. Amarillo College's environment does not shame individuals living in poverty. Instead we acknowledge the struggles of our students living in poverty and work to assist them with overcoming their barriers.

Amarillo College works daily to ensure no student fears enrolling in college or failing. We work to ensure student success by connecting students with available resources across our campus and throughout our community. Amarillo College is committed to student success—no excuses. Amarillo College daily seeks to overcome the stigma surrounding poverty. We strive to assist students living in poverty with creating a new outlook on life—an outlook that *removes fear* and replaces it with hope, belief in oneself, and a focus on the future.

Institutionally Created Barriers to Success for Students Living in Poverty

In 2012, Amarillo College made a huge leap forward in addressing student success for students living in poverty when we hired a social worker full-time to address the highest at-risk students. Each year the social worker leads the Amarillo College community (students, faculty, and staff) to identify the top 10 barriers to student success. Amarillo College's top 10 barriers for 2014–2015, ranked in order by highest need, include assistance with affordable housing, utilities, transportation to and from school, food, clothing, child care, substance abuse, medical/dental, counseling, and legal issues. And though there is an extensive process to identify the individual needs of the student, the intended outcome gives Amarillo College a defined approach to addressing poverty by working across campus and through the local community to aid students with much-needed resources.

Today, Amarillo College has developed a systematic approach to addressing student poverty on campus by working across the campus. We have a committee that focuses on addressing policies, procedures, and innovative approaches to overcoming poverty barriers for our students. An example of this systematic approach is reflected in Amarillo College's method for addressing hungry students. Three out of our five campuses have a 100% donation-supported food pantry that offers food, toiletries, and household items free to students. The other two campuses are planning to open their food pantries during the next year.

However, opening a food pantry was just an initial approach. Today, Amarillo College has developed a process connecting students who visit the food pantry more than twice per month with Amarillo College's social worker. By having open dialogue on campus about poverty and our students, Amarillo College is ensuring students are connected with local and state resources available to aid them with basic needs.

In 2008, Amarillo College was designated a Hispanic-serving institution (HSI) by the U.S. Department of Education. Coinciding with this new designation, Amarillo College began college-wide discussions on ways to increase success for first-generation college students. With approximately 65% of students declaring themselves first-generation, Amarillo College needed to find new approaches for student success. Today, Amarillo College continues to find meaningful ways to connect students to support services but recognizes first-generation is not a trait of only minority students. In fall 2014, 52% of Amarillo College's students were Caucasian, and the majority declared themselves first-generation college students.

Our students face significant barriers to success in higher education. Some of those barriers are actually created by higher education itself. Many institutions do not see poverty as an issue demanding action. Most higher education missions focus on changing lives, educating students, meeting industry needs, and serving the community. These missions rarely address poverty directly, nor should they.

Fulfilling these missions requires institutions to address poverty directly. However, as the issue of poverty rises, many institutions respond in the same way Amarillo College initially responded: "Addressing poverty isn't our mission; educating students is." We create institutional barriers because we fail to understand the full intent of the missions that drive our work. In order to educate our students, meet workforce demands, and serve the community, we must recognize that the demographic shifts of college students make poverty central to mission fulfillment.

Institutional processes are written in "middle-class" language and are full of confusing acronyms. This "middle-class" language limits access to college on the basis of experiences and cultural cues rather than on the basis of abilities and desire for an education.

Additionally, many institutions—and Amarillo College was no exception—respond to student needs through siloes. Each division within an institution may have unique ways of responding to student needs. Yet these efforts lack institutional support, have limited accountability and effectiveness, and often contradict efforts and practices in other parts of the college. Thus, a lack of a systemic approach to the issue of poverty creates the biggest barrier of all for students seeking success.

Building a Systemic Approach to Reducing Poverty and Increasing Completion

The groundbreaking work of Donna Beegle helped us realize that responding to student needs with goodwill and caring will not be enough. Institutions must build systems that leverage caring behaviors with institutional support.

Institutionalizing and Systemizing Relationships

Relationships are the key to successful interventions for students living in the war zone of poverty. Because many students from generational poverty lack the language, experience, and confidence to navigate higher education processes, having a person serve as an advocate is critical.

The Beegle model for winning the war of poverty is to connect students to a navigator. These individuals, both internal and external to institutions, connect students to their network of people. Navigators share their own college experiences and leverage their understanding of the higher education processes and classroom expectations. When students have the benefit of this one voice—a single advocate—their success rates increase impressively.

For example, using Beegle's Neighbor/Navigator Community Collaborative model, Amarillo College developed a case management system for our most at-risk students that systemized advocacy and supportive institutional relationships for students. The pilot program connected more than 400 first-time-in-college and Pell-eligible students to a navigator. Each navigator volunteered to hold a minimum of five meetings with his or her assigned student at strategic times through the semester. Each navigator was trained to use the campus resources and understand institutional practices. Previous to this pilot, the target student group had a 47% retention rate, fall to fall. After the first year of the pilot, these same students—connected to a navigator and plugged into the system of support—showed a 92% retention rate fall to fall. If an institution wants to ensure that students living in the war zone of poverty taste success, intentional relational advocacy is the key. Students will not access the resources created for them without a person they trust connecting them to those resources.

Leveraging Community Resources and Partnerships

Helen Keller said "The world is moved along, not only by the mighty shoves of its heroes, but also by the aggregate of tiny pushes of each honest worker" (Wallis, 1983, p. 240). Amarillo College believes in the tiny pushes of its faculty, administrators, and staff who all work together in the name of student success. Amarillo College's No Excuses University initiative centers on humanity for all—students, faculty, administrators, and staff. Only as a collective team can we enrich the lives of our community and change the lives of our students.

Amarillo College supports a systematic social services program both within its own campuses and within our larger communities in Amarillo, Dumas, and Hereford. Amarillo College's social services program supports six major components: social services, a food pantry, the Money Management Center, the Career and Employment Services Center, mentoring (coaches/ champions), and an early alert system. These six components bring together the Amarillo College community, area nonprofits, business and industry, and Texas agencies to offer our students a comprehensive student support services program. Each of these components was initially funded by private foundation grants and community donor funds.

Amarillo College's social services program includes a full-time social worker and two interns majoring in social work. The internship in our Social Services Department is part of a coordinated effort between Amarillo College and our local university, West Texas A&M University. Amarillo College began the social services component by hiring a full-time social worker to provide intensive case management to our highest risk students. After we identified our top 10 student needs, we then worked across our campus and community to address each of these needs. The top 10 list is revised annually. Students are referred to our Social Services Department in a variety of ways: Retention Alert system, advisers, faculty/staff, and self-referral. Once a referral is received, we connect students to services, including housing, food, child care, utility, and/or transportation assistance; money management guidance; career and employment services; and counseling. Whether the social service need can be supported via Amarillo College or an outside community partner, the aim of this program is to assist our students and help them achieve their educational goals.

During 2013 and 2014, our Social Services Department provided assistance to nearly 600 students. The single greatest need met was assistance with tuition, fees, and/or books. Transportation and housing were also key needs met by Amarillo College and our community partners. The proof is in the data, and Amarillo College's social services program is successful. By addressing students' basic needs, students can and will continue with their educational goals. In 2013, students who received assistance from our Social Services Department have a successful course completion rate of 84.4% (82.5% in 2014). In comparison, Amarillo College's college-wide course completion rate is 78.6%.

Amarillo College's food pantry initiative began in 2012 when several faculty members recognized an unmet need for our students. By working together and in support of leadership, they opened a 100% donation-based food pantry available for students at our Washington Street campus. Today, two of our other four campuses have food pantries for students and staff. The remaining two campuses anticipate opening food pantries. All food pantries are 100% donation-based, and no institutional funds are used to purchase food or household items. But in order to ensure we are closing the loop, students who access food pantries more than twice per month are referred to Amarillo College's Social Services Department. Our social worker then connects the students with community agencies who can provide food assistance to the students on a larger scale.

Amarillo College's Money Management and Career and Employment Services Center provide students with a variety of programs, including financial literacy seminars, résumé and job-building skills workshops, career advising, and coordination of job fairs with area businesses and corporations. This center also houses full-time workforce specialists from Workforce Solutions Panhandle to provide our students with job search and employment services, labor market information, career planning and training, and aid, including subsidized or free child care.

Our No Excuses University mentoring component pairs recent high-school graduates (champions) with Amarillo College faculty and staff (coaches) who work together as students navigate their college experiences. Amarillo College selects recent high school graduates who are participating in the Achievement Through Commitment Education (ACE) program. This program is a scholarship program available to graduating students from three area high schools. The ACE program guarantees payment for tuition, fees, and books for up to 130 semester hours at Amarillo College and West Texas A&M University. The typical ACE student is low-income, needs higher levels of academic support, and is a first-generation student. By focusing on the ACE students with our mentoring project, Amarillo College is connecting at-risk students to needed academic support and interventions before these students drop out of college. The fall-to-fall persistence rate for students in the mentoring project averages 20 percentage points higher than Amarillo College's college-wide persistence

rate. In addition, the graduation and/or transfer rate for mentoring participants' averages 10 to 15 percentage points higher.

In fall 2012, Amarillo College initiated an early alert system on campus.
Amarillo College's Retention Alert allows faculty to send electronic alerts to key
student support staff. Alerts are sent to advisers for academic intervention when
a student has low grades, has excessive absences, or needs additional academic
support. Alerts can also be sent to our Social Services Department to connect
students with community partnership resources, including transportation,
housing, food, and mental health. The final alert allows faculty to inform
Amarillo College's vice president of student affairs about any student behavioral
issues or concerns. Amarillo College plans to expand the early alert system in
our quest to continue connecting students to needed support services.

As our No Excuses University initiative flourishes, Amarillo College
continues its commitment to leveraging partnerships, both internally and
externally, and community resources. Our faculty and staff's commitment to our
students and support for their educational goals endures and thrives each semester. The excitement and support of our community is reflected not only by their
financial commitment but also by their call for community action to increase
student success and eradicate poverty in the Texas Panhandle. The relentless support of each group allows Amarillo College to truly be a No Excuses University.

Concluding Remarks

As administrators and faculty, we never expected to become advocates for
students from poverty. We never expected our work as advocates to emerge
as the most rewarding work of our professional careers.

Because of the systemic approach to poverty, we are affecting the success
of all students, but particularly our Caucasian students. Our systems are
changing the lives of our students and affecting entire neighborhoods and
communities.

Poverty may be the biggest barrier our students face. As such, institutions
must evaluate our systems and student needs through a new lens—*no excuses*.

References

Amarillo College. (2014). *AC institutional research databook*. Retrieved from https://
    iresearch.actx.edu/html/databook/databook.htm
Beegle, D. M. (2007). *See poverty . . . Be the difference! Discovering the missing pieces
    for helping people move out of poverty*. Tigard, OR: Communications Across Bar-
    riers.

College Board. (2013). *Trends in higher education.* Retrieved from https://trends
.collegeboard.org/student-aid/figures-tables/percentage-distribution-federal-aid-
funds-sector-2012-13

Lopez, D. (2009). *No Excuses University: How six exceptional systems are revolution-
izing our schools.* Argyle, TX: TurnAround Schools Publications.

National Center for Education Statistics. (2008). *Trends in undergraduate borrowing
II: Federal student loans in 1995–96, 1999–2000, and 2003–04.* Retrieved from
https://nces.ed.gov/pubsearch/pubsinfo.asp?pubid=2008179rev

Ong, W. J. (1982). *Orality and literacy: The technologizing of the word.* London, England: Methuen.

Texas Department of State Health Services. (2013). *Health facts profile. Pottery County,
2013.* Retrieved from http://healthdata.dshs.texas.gov/HealthFactsProfiles

United Way of Amarillo and Canyon. (2014). *2014 community status report.* Retrieved
from http://www.unitedwayama.org/resources/communityimpact/appendix%20
a%20-%20full%20-%202014-06-04.pdf

U.S. Census. (2014). *Dynamics of economic well-being: Poverty 2009–2011.* Retrieved
from http://www.census.gov/prod/2014pubs/p70-137.pdf

Wallis, C. L. (1983). *The treasure chest.* San Francisco, CA: HarperSanFrancisco.
Retrieved from http://www.bartleby.com/73/2029.html

PART SIX

CONCLUSIONS AND RECOMMENDATIONS

16

REDESIGNING STUDENTS' EDUCATIONAL EXPERIENCES

Angela Long

It seems to me that education has a two-fold function to perform in the life of man and society: the one is utility and the other is culture.

—Martin Luther King Jr.

The expression "American Dream" was coined by James Truslow Adams and appeared in print in his book *The Epic of America* (Adams, 1931, p. 251). Adams defined the *American Dream* as being "that dream of a land in which life should be better and richer and fuller for everyone, with opportunity for each according to ability." Today, the Merriam-Webster Online Dictionary (n.d.) defines the term as "a social ideal that stresses egalitarianism and especially material prosperity." Synonyms of egalitarian include "equality" and "sameness."

Seasoned teachers are fully aware that all learners are not the same. In describing the differences in student learning, they often use erudite catch-phrases such as "multiple intelligences," "cognitive differences," "psychological types," or "learning styles" to explain why students learn in different ways. But, curiously, even as educators publicly endorse diversity, their everyday teaching practices still tend to be heavily biased in favor of uniformity rather than diversity. Those who promote diversity prefer Merriam-Webster's definition of the *American Dream*—"equality" ("sameness")—rather than the definition originally given to this term by James Truslow Adams—"opportunity according to ability."

The demographics of the United States of America have changed significantly since Adams coined a term that became an American ethos. Anglo

White college professors of the 1930s taught Anglo White students, nearly all of whom were reared in upper-middle-class families. And because the children of well-to-do parents were the only ones who could afford to attend college during the Great Depression era, the college classrooms of that generation were indeed reflective of the egalitarian social ideal of sameness. But when Public Law 89-236 (popularly known as the Immigration and Naturalization Act of 1965) became effective on June 30, 1968, the face of America began to swiftly change. By 2015 the "melting pot" of Adams' generation had begun to take on the blurred appearance of a "salad bowl."

Indeed, the population of the United States doubled in size between 1950 and 2010, growing from 150 million residents to 300 million. But America's growth rate is on the verge of expanding even faster. Statisticians at the U.S. Census Bureau (2014) and Pew Charitable Trusts (2014), to name just a few, expect America's populace to exceed 440 million residents by the year 2060. Several public and private researchers are also predicting that the American Hispanic demographic will overtake Anglo Whites as America's majority demographic sometime between 2045 and 2050. Also, these researchers think Asian Americans will become the third largest demographic group by then, with the fourth largest racial group consisting of immigrants from Middle Eastern nations. And even though immigration from African nations will boost America's Black population, researchers expect the African American demographic to drop from its traditional second place position down to fifth place. Native Americans and Pacific Islanders are likely to be the sixth largest ethnic group when the 2050 U.S. Decennial Census is published.

If current immigration laws and trends remain unaltered, up to 89% of the projected 117 million increase in population between now and 2060 will consist of foreign-born immigrants and their children. Perhaps the most startling of all demographic predictions is this one: Pew Charitable Trusts (2014) statistically reckons that 93% of America's working-age population will come from immigrants and their children in the year 2050.

Beyond these demographic projections, three other bits of information need to be brought to the reader's attention before a summary of the thematic core of this book:

1. "Since 1995, 82% of new white enrollments have gone to the 468 most selective colleges, while 72% of new Hispanic enrollment and 68% of new African-American enrollment have gone to the two-year open-access schools" (Carnevale and Strohl, 2013, p. 9).

2. The U.S. Census data garnered from the 2013 American Community Survey reveals that 61.8 million U.S. residents spoke a language other than English (U.S. Census Bureau, 2014).

3. The states of Tennessee and Oregon recently adopted legislation that made their community colleges tuition-free, and some of the politicians seeking their party's presidential nomination for 2016 publicly pledged to make community colleges in all 50 states tuition-free.

For policymakers at community colleges, this set of data should not be seen as the proverbial "writing on the wall" but rather as a road map for guiding their long-term planning. Because high school diplomas no longer impress employers, the 100 million or so people added to America's 2050 census will need a college education to compete in the workplace. Furthermore, if 62 million of America's resident population were speaking a language other than English at home in 2013, that number is certain to significantly escalate by the year 2050. And because standardized tests favor students who possess a large English vocabulary, the bulk of that immigrant population will likely enroll in community colleges, just as they do today. Tuition-free community colleges are certain to be even more appealing to immigrants as a launching point for their postsecondary educations.

But here is the poignant question that community college presidents will soon be forced to answer: Because recent survey data collected by the U.S. Department of Education's National Center for Education Statistics (NCES) (Aud, Wilkinson-Flicker, Kristapovich, Rathbun, Wang, & Zhang, 2013) show that nearly three out of every four minority students who begin their postsecondary educations at a community college become college dropouts by the end of their freshman year, and the bulk of community colleges presently are experiencing difficulties in keeping students of color enrolled, *how are college policymakers going to solve this ongoing problem before 2050, when two-thirds of their student bodies will consist of diverse students with various cultural heritages?* Perhaps the more germane question is this: Will the bulk of community colleges consider the advice given by educators who have devised teaching methodologies that have resolved the inequitable disparities that exist between White students and students of color in their respective persistence and attainment rates—expert educators such as those found in this book?

Educational Racism

Sociologists say racism manifests itself in three differing yet closely related forms. Those three forms are termed *individual* (or interpersonal) racism, *institutional* (or systemic) racism, and *cultural* racism. Each of these three forms of racism can demean the learning abilities of students of color by causing them to internalize feelings of indignation, anger, powerlessness, and even loss of self-esteem. In recent years, numerous books and scientific journals dealing with racism have been published by various publishers, including Stylus Publishing. The bulk of that corpus of literature is couched in highly technical language. But here are examples of the three basic forms of racism that everyone can understand:

- **Individual** (or interpersonal) racism can manifest itself in overt confrontational behaviors such as verbal abuse, name-calling, offensive jokes, comments that perpetuate negative stereotypes, and violent hate crimes directed at a person or group based on skin color, ethnicity, or national origin. However, individual racism also can manifest itself in forms that are neither consciously malicious nor threatening, such as ignoring or avoiding contact with members of a racist's target group.
- **Cultural** racism involves the production and ongoing reproduction of a society's value system that privileges people of one culture over people of other cultures. The dominant feature of cultural racism is that it views conformity to a single culture as both normal and desirable. An example of cultural racism is seen in advertising or television programs that principally represent only racially White actors.
- **Institutional** (or systemic) racism involves the use of laws, rules, or practices, by both private and public entities, that have the effect of providing benefits to one group that are not given to other groups. Institutional racism is manifested in negative ways, such as refusing to provide services to a particular group, or through the cultural expectations of institutions that normalize the values of the original founders to the detriment of underrepresented groups.

Students who are subjected to both overt and covert racist behaviors tend to have poor academic results and poor study performance. As a consequence of these two things, students who are victims of perceived racism usually have high rates of class absenteeism. Nearly all community colleges are intolerant of racist behaviors on their campuses and have adopted anti-racism policies and grievance procedures to deal with problems of those kinds. People who commit overt racist acts on college campuses are reported to legal authorities and prosecuted under existing legal statutes.

Although overt forms of racism occur and must be combatted on college campuses, the purpose of this section is to address the subtler forms of bias stemming from cultural and institutional racism occurring in the community college classroom and to draw attention to the ways such bias has pervaded the very makeup of our education structure.

Pause for a moment to consider the import of these words written by Jamillah Moore and Edward Bush in chapter 2:

> African American male students on predominantly White campuses perceive that the institutional environment is adversarial, citing greater feelings of unfair treatment, a devaluing of their academic capabilities, and increasing discriminatory or racist practices. (p. 33, this volume)

Furthermore, they write,

> We posit that African American student disengagement, as evident in their under-usage of college services, is symptomatic of a larger disease, which is that African American students perceive the institution as being unsupportive, discriminatory, and not structured to operate in their best interest. These notions are rooted not only in the historical treatment of African Americans in this country but also in the students' own experiences in primary and secondary schools as well as the treatment they receive in a larger societal context. (p. 36, this volume)

If many Blacks who attend community colleges indeed perceive themselves as being subjected to a system of bias—forms of cultural and institutional racism that diminish their abilities to learn—then this question must be posed, as well as answered: Do Hispanic, Native American, and Asian American and Pacific Islander students similarly perceive the community college environment as being potentially biased and adversarial? Furthermore, are generationally impoverished students experiencing related feelings of not belonging?

Despite the fact that these questions have major implications, there's a dearth of national data about the pervasiveness of racial and other bias and their impact on student disengagement. Until relevant survey questions are posed in either the Community College Survey of Student Engagement (CCSSE) or NCES six-year longitudinal surveys, policymakers have no choice but to rely on anecdotal evidence from small-scale studies and reports.

Because national data are sorely lacking, it becomes incumbent on individual community colleges to establish tools to measure their own students' growth and needs for engagement and belonging. Indeed, institutions are responsible for analyzing the structural causes of societal inequality and the often implicit cultural values that work against underrepresented groups on campus. As Bush and Moore claim, "Students [of color] perceive the institution as . . . *not structured* to operate in their best interest" (p. 36, this volume, emphasis added). And

> many barriers emanate from the structure of our social system. Many of these barriers are the result of the way institutions are currently organized, and stem from the values and perspectives that people in poverty adopt from the daily conditions they experience. . . . In most cases, the fact that many of the barriers have *systemic roots* is invisible, even to people in poverty. (Beegle, 2007, cited in chapter 14)

From both a poverty and racial perspective, is this systemic "root" partly responsible for explaining why so many students of color and the impoverished are not performing at the same rate as their middle- and upper-class White classmates?

In response, I invite the reader to ponder a new definition of *racism* that often covertly appears in college classrooms as a barrier to student persistence. This universal definition (which explains the title and purpose of this book) is as follows:

> Educational racism: A cultural bias manifested either overtly or covertly by a system of education and/or educators that benefits or punishes/inhibits students based on their culture, race, ethnicity, ideologies, and/or socioeconomic status.

Manifestations of Educational Racism

Educators at the postsecondary level take offense at the slightest suggestion that they are biased in any way against people of differing races and cultures, and rightfully so. Most see themselves as ardent supporters of the social ideal called *egalitarianism*, having devoted their professional lives to helping students of all backgrounds become successful. Such efforts are to be applauded and not summarily dismissed. Even so, the American system of education contains sundry systemic biases that have become inherit and embedded into the very fabric of higher education. This systemic bias (i.e., educational racism) shows itself within the community college as a systemic network of rules, expectations, and cultural norms based on a model of education that caters to a middle- and upper-class White mind-set in America. Educators who function within this domain often are unaware that they are practicing bias in the classroom because of their own cultural norms and expectations. Some educators, perhaps unintentionally and often unconsciously, express biases toward select student groups because of the cultural differences in the ways these students define success, communicate, or think about upward mobility as compared to the White, middle-class majority. As a result, these student groups often find themselves in a learning environment that appears foreign, hostile, and/or difficult to navigate.

Distinct forms of educational racism within this setting involve both known and unknown instructor bias that stereotypes a student's abilities according to his or her cultural upbringing and manners, employing methods of instruction and reward systems that are geared toward one homogenous style of learning, adhering to a philosophy of instruction that seeks to weed students out of the system, measuring student intelligence via a standardized paper/pencil approach only, and teaching that the pursuit of material wealth and "climbing the ladder" are the same goal and dream for everyone. For example, American educators often emphasize that the true measure of success is accomplished through increased status of employment and attainment of wealth (i.e., the American Dream). However, not all cultures or individuals strive to place work before family, money before happiness, and status before simplicity. Though working hard and attaining wealth is admirable among most groups, not all individuals choose to find their success in a business/corporate/professional lifestyle but instead may choose to invest their time and energies in community and family pursuits that are of equal importance. To encourage diversity of thought and alternative career opportunities, students should be inspired to rationally determine their own set of life goals that will help guide them to personal success.

Educational Racism in the Classroom

Most community college policies and practices are designed to advance students from one stage to the next. Yet, these very same practices have the potential to inhibit student success when students are expected to innately know how to navigate the system without possessing the necessary skill set or awareness to do so. According to Ed Hughes,

> Community colleges themselves have policies, practices, and procedures that are systemic barriers to students from poverty. Often they are created from a middle-class perspective, one in which sufficient personal resources are available, concepts of work and achievement are valued and supported, and planning for the future is the norm. These are not characteristics normally found in poor families. (p. 207, this volume)

Within higher education, there are myriad practices that foster division among students of differing cultural backgrounds and lower socioeconomic levels. Many of these practices may appear obvious to those who have worked extensively with students of diverse cultures. The following simple examples are meant to illustrate just a few of countless educational racism practices in the community college. (Note: The following examples *do not* negate the importance of setting high and rigorous standards in the college classroom but rather give a glimpse of practices that may deter underrepresented students from persisting in higher education.)

One systemic practice may be observed through an emphasis on standardized tests and written language as a means for determining intelligence and student likelihood for success. Colleges often assume a student's potential by means of assessment through written test scores on college exams and placement scores. Similarly, most forms of communication in the college environment cater to the print culture of the middle and upper classes. If students struggle within this capacity because of language deficiencies (English language learners), cultural upbringing (oral language versus written language), or lack of education, they are more likely to feel inferior, out of place, and "in over their heads." Unquestionably, written forms of communication are foundational to the college environment, and written skills must be taught. However, an entering student's abilities should not be assessed via written means alone, but rather, with the combined understanding of a student's multiple intelligences and upbringing in order to equip him or her to navigate the college's written culture.

Another systemic practice may be seen in how instructors punish students for failing to meet the cultural norms of punctuality and attendance. Middle- and upper-class expectations demand that students be on time attend class regularly, and be attentive to class lectures without interruption. While these expectations are perfectly understandable and appear ideal, not all students are able to carry out such demands because of outside circumstances and challenges. According to chapter 8 of this book, the average American Indian student commutes 30 to 100 miles a day to attend class. Utterback writes

> On many campuses, there is a similar cultural discontinuity relative to the issue of time. Most people have heard comments or jokes about "Indian time." On a college campus, as it relates to student success, this cultural insensitivity is not a laughing matter. (p. 147, this volume)

He asserts that to the extent possible, faculty and staff members are obligated to understand their students' needs in regard to time realizing that outside factors (commuting distance, family demands, etc.) have the potential to negatively impact students' attendance. Indeed, poor Whites, Hispanics, and African Americans have all been stereotyped in like regard. Therefore, what should the response of educators be? According to Hughes, "Instead of a rigid classroom attendance policy, a 'learning engagement' policy might be fashioned around competency-based learning, with multiple learning modes and delivery mechanisms offered" (p. 208, this volume).

White middle-class cultural perspectives especially influence teacher-to-student interactions. Within the classroom, it is natural for instructors to favor students who appear to like and respect them over students who refrain from showing personal engagement. Indeed, those students who demonstrate a strong work ethic and personal desire to achieve high grades usually earn the respect of their college professors. But grades are only one means college instructors use to ascertain who wants to succeed and who doesn't. Students who are consistently non-participatory during class lectures or refrain from taking the lead in class activities rarely go unnoticed by their classroom instructors, although in some cultures such behaviors are the norm, not the exception. Most American community college instructors who spend long, tedious hours preparing class activities and lecture materials do not favor students who show no interest in participating or becoming engaged in the classroom. On the other hand, students who give the appearance of being fully engrossed in an instructor's lecture and class activities are usually viewed warmly by that instructor irrespective of the lesson's engagement factor.

Instructor bias can positively or negatively impact a student's academic performance. Negative instructor bias is directly correlated to lower teacher expectations. For example, a 2016 John Hopkins study revealed that White (or non-Black) teachers are more likely to doubt the educational prospects of their Black students. According to the research, "when a White (or other non-Black) teacher and a Black teacher evaluate the same Black student, the White teacher is 30 percent less likely to believe that the student will graduate from a four-year college—and 40 percent less likely to believe the student will graduate from high school" (Rosen, 2016). The authors of the study concluded that teacher expectations are systematically biased and "differences in teachers' assessments may be random in that they reflect mistakes or different information arising from idiosyncratic interactions with a given student" (Gershenson, Holt, & Papageorge, 2016, p. 212).

So, where does "educational racism" come into play? Here is one way: White students from middle to higher socioeconomic backgrounds may be more inclined to ask questions in their classes and fulfill the intended behavioral "expectations" of their instructors than either minority students or White students of generational poverty. Community college instructors tend to perceive student queries as overt signs of the student's personal interest in the course materials being taught. Furthermore, the methods by which students convey their interest in a subject and express their views in a classroom setting become indicative of how they will be treated by the instructor. Students who do not express themselves in a manner deemed "appropriate" can be viewed negatively and as "out of line" in the classroom. The authors of chapter 2 stated: "Our experience has shown us the majority of discipline complaints from non–African American faculty are issues of cultural disconnection masked in the form of student behavioral issues" (p. 35, this volume). Thus, when students are perceived as "loud," "late," "out of turn," or "not paying attention," community college faculty may respond in a negative manner, misreading the root of the student's behavior and, in turn, lowering their expectations of the student.

Alternatively, when students are perceived as "friendly" and "attentive" by their community college instructors, they reciprocate that friendly behavior. Therefore, in the eyes of Black, poor White, Hispanic, Native American, Asian and Pacific Islander students who withdraw from the presence of the instructor and exhibit attitudes of feeling misjudged (i.e., visceral emotions of feeling "out of place," "unwanted," and "misunderstood"), White community college instructors and staff can exhibit signs of educational racism without having any conscious awareness they are doing so.

Interestingly, there are many Black students, Asian and Pacific Islander students, Native American students, and Hispanic students who attend the same classes but who appear to be unaffected or untouched by educational racism as part of their classroom environment. Why do they not show signs of the perceived racial bias that their fellow classmates seemingly endure? Or, if it is strongly sensed, then what prompts these very same students to persist despite the biases felt in the classroom? Several plausible answers to that question are sprinkled throughout this book. But here is one of the simplest to grasp of all of the various answers: Students of this kind know how to successfully navigate through the college-level system of education.

There are three telltale traits that lead us to this notion. First, the students of color who fare well in college usually come from families wherein their parents graduated from college and achieved respectable social status in their communities as well as middle-class or higher economic standing. Second, the well-to-do parents of this group of minority students stress to their children the importance of building résumés that reflect numerous extracurricular activities—student government, community service projects, and so on—that are likely to be seen as impressive to university admissions personnel. And third, the parents of these students also teach their children how to successfully navigate through and communicate in institutions of higher learning, which are often based on "White" teaching protocols and course offerings.

On the other hand, the bulk of community college dropouts, whether students of color or poor Whites, generally share two or more of the following traits: (a) they are either the first or among the first in their families to enroll in college studies; (b) they see extracurricular activities as being mostly a waste of time; (c) their parents and grandparents are poor, as are their friends and the parents of their friends; (d) they perceive that racial prejudice is the "norm" among all peoples; and (e) no one has ever explained to them how to successfully maneuver through the traditional system of higher education.

Would underrepresented students be experiencing higher attainment rates if they had been taught how to "navigate the system"? Simply put, of course they would! Yet the process of navigating through the college's rules and customs for students of color and the impoverished could be significantly improved if college administrators and faculty possessed a clearer understanding of students' diverse cultures and of the reason so many of those students perceive "educational racism" on the college campus.

Overcoming Educational Racism

The purpose of this book is to offer solutions and discuss the commonalities that are shared among all human beings. After all, uniting people never occurs by emphasizing the differences that divide them but rather by putting a spotlight on those things they hold in common. As such, all humans (irrespective of race, ethnicity, or socioeconomic status) share these common six traits:

1. All humans want their physical and emotional needs to be met.
2. All humans want their lives to be meaningful.
3. All humans want to live happy lives.
4. All humans want to be free of fear, injury, and sickness.
5. All humans want and need to be loved.
6. All humans want to be treated with both fairness and respect by others.

Psychologists affirm these desires as deriving from the following fundamental concepts: (a) love, (b) faith/trust, and (c) personal meaning. Human beings who feel either unloved or rejected by others are not consistently happy people. And because human beings are social creatures, they possess an instinctive need to communicate their thoughts with others. As such, when one person refuses to communicate with another, that act of silence is often perceived as a form of overt rejection.

With this fundamental principle kept in mind, when students perceive their college environments as void of love, faith/trust, and personal meaning, many of them leave, never to return. Personal meaning becomes meaningless within the context of mistrust. Furthermore, when students fail to perceive the basic emotions they share with their instructors and other college personnel, they are inclined to likewise perceive their campus environment as a hostile or threatening place. Soon thereafter, they begin to withdraw from social interactions with their instructors and their counselors. Eventually, they become indifferent toward those people, sometimes even feeling hostile toward them. This "fight or flight" reaction is common and may explain why so many students of color and the impoverished drop out of the system and/or display combative behavior in the classroom environment.

In response, what must be done to reverse the effects of educational racism, as well as to overcome students' negative perceptions in the classroom? While there are no simple answers, the 20 contributors to this book have excelled in offering an array of differing methodologies and techniques for enhancing student degree attainment rates and eradicating the barriers to student persistence, including an educational racism mind-set. These recommendations and methodologies contain numerous tactical strategies to be employed on any community college campus by placing the student in the primary role of "producer" rather than "consumer." Although each recommendation has the potential to make a huge difference in the lives of many students, it must be noted that a redesigning of the system is in order if we are to reverse the educational racism practices found in higher education.

Six common factors for retaining students emerged from the pages of this book. Each provides the reader with concrete methods for overcoming educational racism practices and for helping students navigate through the system of higher education:

1. The Financial Factor
2. The Friendship Factor
3. The Faculty Factor
4. The Freedom-to-Learn-From-Failure Factor
5. The Functional Factor
6. The Fondness Factor

(See the appendix for a thorough listing of each factor with related strategies for implementation).

Some of these strategies and approaches are geared toward a particular demographic group; others apply generally to all students, regardless of race, ethnicity, or social/financial status. Each factor has been designed to train faculty and staff on how to become culturally aware of students' needs, as well as provide underrepresented students with the exact tools needed to navigate the college environment.

The analytical framework needed to ameliorate the wrongful perception of "educational racism" must be built by both students and faculty alike. The first plank to be laid in that framework is this: *There is no fear in love.* When students feel truly accepted and cared for by their institutions and faculty, they derive a sense of trust and safety within those relationships and environment. In turn, students will find the freedom to pursue academic excellence as they discover high levels of genuine support, care, and authenticity from their instructors and other college personnel.

Concluding Recommendations

At the outset of this book, recommendations were given by the 21st-Century Commission on the Future of Community Colleges. These recommendations suggested that community colleges "redesign" the educational experiences of their respective student populations, "reinvent" their institutional roles, and "reset" the system of higher education to reverse the high attrition rates of its student populations. This book has begun the process of providing responses to these recommendations in an effort to increase the attainment and persistence rates of underrepresented students, as well as eradicate overtones of educational racism in the community college. In this writer's opinion, as preparation for this coming shift, all community colleges should complete these five tasks before the year 2020:

1. **Establish a Clear and Directive Education Mission Statement for the Future:** Community college administrators are encouraged to collectively sit down with their respective policymakers and exercise foresight regarding the state of education to come. With the potential for free community college to become reality and increased enrollment of varied and diverse student populations flooding campuses, what is the future mission of the community college? Furthermore, how will community colleges address their role in training individuals for technical trades when machines begin to replace human beings in various sectors of the marketplace?
2. **Collate Data and Proactively Assess Minority Student Populations:** Community college institutions must be not only proactive in disaggregating student data but also committed to making data-driven decisions. More researchers are needed to assess the needs of minority and impoverished students' postsecondary education experiences and labor market outcomes. Specific consideration must be given to analyzing the needs of Asian and Pacific Islander, Native American, and Caucasian students in poverty, as they are the most overlooked and under-researched populations in the system; and thus, their needs are the least addressed.
3. **Implement the Six Fundamental Factors for Improving Student Retention:** The 20 experts highlighted in this book have offered

clear-cut strategies and recommendations for improving the retention and persistence rates of minority and impoverished student populations. The six factors that have emerged from the findings of this book, listed previously and described in detail in the appendix, are based on experience and research.

4. **Hire More Diverse Faculty:** At the beginning of the 2013 academic year, only 18% of community college faculty consisted of men and women of color or underrepresented ethnic groups. Yet nearly half of all students attending community colleges are students of color. These numbers are expected to increase. Community college administrators are encouraged to train minority and impoverished students to seek professions in the domain of education, even proactively recruiting outstanding applicants from these diverse backgrounds.

5. **Increase Funding Options as Needed for Select Groups:** While money is not the panacea to solve each of these issues, it is important to understand the gaps that exist in certain communities because of a lack of funding. Even if federal legislation is enacted to make community colleges free for all students, select minority and underrepresented groups (e.g., the Native American population) will continue to be lacking the financial resources needed to bring them to parity with other demographic groups; and without those necessary resources, their instructors will continue to be faced with obstacles that hinder these students from maximizing their secondary and postsecondary education experiences.

A Closing Thought

One of the most famous civil rights speeches in American history is commonly referred to as the "I Have a Dream" speech, penned by Dr. Martin Luther King Jr., wherein he famously said, "I have a dream that my four little children will one day live in a nation where they will not be judged by the color of their skin but by the content of their character."

But far less well-known are the words penned by this same man when he was a student at Morehouse College. In 1947 he wrote an article titled "The Purpose of Education," which his school newspaper, the *Maroon Tiger*, deemed worthy of publication. The following are a few paragraphs from that article:

> Most of the "brethren" think that education should equip them with proper instruments of exploitation so that they can forever trample over the masses. Still others think that education should furnish them with the noble ends rather than the means to an end. It seems to me that education

has a two-fold function to perform in the life of man and in society: the one is utility and the other is culture.

The complete education gives one not only power of concentration, but worthy objectives upon which to concentrate. The broad education will, therefore, transmit to one not only the accumulated knowledge of the race but also the accumulated experience of social living.

If we are not careful, our colleges will produce a group of close-minded, unscientific, illogical propagandists, consumed with immoral acts. Be careful, "brethren"! Be careful, teachers! (King, 1947)

If Martin Luther King Jr. were alive today, I believe he would adjudge each and every one of the chapters contained in *Overcoming Educational Racism in the Community College* as having met the "utility" and the "culture" functions of what he called "The Purpose of Education." And to all the scholars who contributed to the making of this book, I say to them, "Well done educators! Your work has begun a great change."

References

Adams, J. T. (1931). *The epic of America.* Boston, MA: Little Brown.

American dream. (n.d.). Merriam Webster Online, Retrieved from http://www .easybib.com/reference/guide/apa/dictionary

Aud, S., Wilkinson-Flicker, S., Kristapovich, P., Rathbun, A., Wang, X., & Zhang, J. (2013). *The condition of education 2013.* Washington, DC: U.S. Department of Education, Institute of Education Sciences and National Center for Education Statistics. Retrieved from http://nces.ed.gov/pubs2013/2013037.pdf

Carnevale, A., & Strohl, J. (2013, July 31). *Separate and unequal: How higher education reinforces the intergenerational reproduction of White racial privilege.* Washington, DC: Georgetown University Public Policy Institute, Center on Education and the Workforce. Retrieved from https://cew.georgetown.edu/ wp-content/uploads/2014/11/SeparateUnequal.FR_.pdf

Gershenson, S., Holt, S., & Papageorge, N. (2016). Who believes in me? The effect of student-teacher demographic match on teacher expectations. *Economics of Education Review 52*, 209–224. Retrieved from http://www.sciencedirect.com/ science/article/pii/S0272775715300959

King, M. L., Jr. (1947). The purpose of education. *Maroon Tiger.* Retrieved from http://www.drmartinlutherkingjr.com/thepurposeofeducation.htm

Pew Charitable Trusts. (2014, December 18). *Changing patterns in U.S. immigration and population.* Retrieved from http://www.pewtrusts.org/en/research-and-analysis/ issue-briefs/2014/12/changing-patterns-in-us-immigration-and-population

U.S. Census Bureau. (2014). *Quick facts, United States.* Retrieved from http:// quickfacts.census.gov/qfd/states/00000.html

SIX FUNDAMENTAL FACTORS FOR IMPROVING STUDENT RETENTION

Angela Long

The importance of minority and impoverished students experiencing a positive first encounter with college personnel cannot be overstated. Simply put, positive encounters almost always produce positive results. On the other hand, negative encounters tend to bring forth wariness (at best) or ill will (at worst). Underrepresented students who lack adequate access to any of their needed student services—academic counseling, financial advising, and so forth—often are left with the impression that their college environment is both an uncaring and an impersonal place. Even small acts of kindness and attention demonstrated by college personnel during the registration process can go a long way in demonstrating outward signs of friendship and acceptance. As a result, if a student's first encounter with a college adviser or faculty member is perceived as friendly by that student, the seed for future trust is planted at that very moment in time.

The several contributors to this book rank among America's leading educational researchers, analysts, and problem-solvers on the topic of attrition and attainment among postsecondary students of color and students of generational poverty. All of them approached the problem of poor student persistence rates by focusing on their own racial demographic. Even so, six distinct retention themes appeared time and again within all of their analyses. These six factors have repeatedly proved to be efficacious in the enhancement of minority and impoverished student persistence rates.

The Financial Factor

Students from poverty need income now, while they are learning, through a carefully structured program that demonstrates that "they belong" and are "good enough."

—G. Edward Hughes, President, Gateway Community Technical College (p. 212, this voume)

Research has revealed that college students who lack funding to pay for their tuition and living expenses, regardless of whether they are nontraditional or traditional students, are at risk of dropping out of college. Similarly, there are many students, both minority and in poverty, who dream of obtaining a college education but dismiss that dream as pure fancy because they view themselves as indigent. No matter one's racial background, finances and financial challenges are often enumerated as one of the primary rationales for student departure. Despite their dire needs for financial aid, many students (especially Native American and Hispanic) fear that they will incur too much debt if they rely on loans to fund their higher education. According to Coley and Baker (2013), income is *the* factor in determining the future educational success of a student. Too often low-income students encounter difficult trade-offs when identifying the financial aid that will allow them to access and persist to degree completion. Generally speaking, underrepresented students have not been exposed to financial literacy training. Most of them have little awareness of the several steps needed to apply for financial aid and charitable grants. If underrepresented students begin their college experience without having first been exposed to any type of financial literacy training, they tend to become discouraged quickly, causing them to drop out of college within a few months after being matriculated. And because many of these students are in "survival" mode, it is imperative that community colleges address the financial needs of these students right away. The primary goal of the Financial Factor is to illuminate the pathway that enables underfunded students to gain understanding and knowledge of financial aid opportunities at the very outset of their college experience and to prepare them for the sundry costs of college. The following intervention strategies have been proven efficacious by numerous community colleges for integrating underrepresented students into the college environment:

- **Provide Assistance in the Application Process for Financial Aid:** The application process for financial aid is viewed by underrepresented enrollees as both complex and cumbersome. And as a general rule, having unmet financial need is a significant barrier to students' enrollment and persistence in college. Research has shown that the low take-up rate of the Pell Grant and Helping Outstanding Pupils Educationally (HOPE) and Lifetime Learning tax credit programs is likely due to the complexity of the application process. One possible approach for ameliorating this perceived obstacle includes local tax return preparation businesses (such as Single Stop USA) partnering with community college financial offices to jointly host group advising sessions during the evening hours when students can receive guidance. This model provides access to low-income and first-generation students who often lack college and financial knowledge of the benefits of a wide variety of government community services and programs.

- **Assign a Financial Aid Mentor for Each Underrepresented Student:** The fast-paced environment of the Financial Aid Office is not perceived as a friendly environment by underrepresented student populations, who may become easily frustrated or are emotionally insecure. Their initial objective of pursuing all avenues of potential funding quickly shifts to a "get in, get out fast" mind-set as they wait to speak with their financial adviser. And because some of them have low self-esteem, they feel a sense of embarrassment by having to "ask" for money, not to mention being required to reveal their low levels of income (or types of income, such as child support and disability income) to college officials, who are perceived as authority figures. One feasible method for putting the student at ease is to establish a partnership between select college centers and the college's Financial Aid Office so as to enable students to receive a significant portion of their financial counseling from the same people who help them enroll and provide advising services.
- **Continue Expanding Pell Grants for Low-Income Students:** There is both anecdotal evidence and limited research that suggests that Latino students are more reluctant than other ethnic and racial populations to become heavily indebted as a result of college loans. It might be easily supposed that other minority and impoverished students with children may have a similar mind-set in that regard, particularly if they already have a long list of fixed debt obligations (mortgage payments, auto loans, etc.). Students with this mind-set rarely envision their college experience happening on a full-time basis. Thus, they take one or two classes per semester, believing their only possible way to obtain a college education is to take five or six years of their lives to accomplish what a full-time student often finishes in two years. But there is ample research that reveals that the longer the

college experience is drawn out without attainment of a credential, the more likely the college experience will end with a transcript dropout. And more community college students are eligible for the Pell Grant than receive it. Given that the Pell Grant covers less than the total cost of education—which includes tuition and fees, books and supplies, transportation, and other allowed expenses depending on the student's circumstance—the maximum award may not be enough to cover the student costs.

- **Incorporate Mandatory Financial Training Workshops and Financial Literacy Programs as Part of a "First-Year" Seminar Series:** Colleges can work with faculty and outside agencies to host a "First-Year" seminar series during which students participate in a sequence of mandatory financial literacy workshops highlighting the role of budgeting, cost analysis, and household finances. The workshops— evening seminars specifically designed for underrepresented student populations in their first year of college—should include activities dealing with analyzing financial literacy profiles, gaining access to applications for scholarships and additional monies, and learning how to effectively balance a budget through interactive and hands-on lessons. Such programs will help to enable students to plot more efficient academic routes in between peer support cohort models and mandatory counseling.

- **Increase Participation in Federal Work-Study Programs:** There are numerous federal and state programs for which low-income students at community colleges are eligible, including workforce development, human resource and income-maintenance support, postsecondary and adult education, and career and technical education. Given the many minority students who are low income, this alignment could improve their financial engagement in community college. In the last 10 years, there has been a decrease in community college students participating in federal work-study. The rules that govern these programs limit their efficient administration and implementation. Furthermore, the onus is usually on the students to discover the programs, and they are required to apply separately for each one in order to receive support. Aligning the administration and funding for at least some of these programs, and simplifying the application for students, can help ensure that students and trainees complete programs and progress toward earning postsecondary credentials.

The Friendship Factor

It is important to create an institution that creates "meaningful collisions" among [all students]. Students must be encouraged to take part in service-learning so they can be mentored by African Americans. They need to attend classes taught by Hispanic Americans, tutor poor White Americans, and raise funds with Native Americans. . . . They also need to be taught to break bread regularly with students who are not American. . . . For community colleges, one of the best ways to impart those skills is by bringing diverse students into close proximity with each other.

—Lee Lambert, Pima Community College District (p. 170, this volume)

The fundamental objective of the Friendship Factor is to promote the imagery of a caring institution—a college wherein all employees, from its president down through the ranks to the custodial staff, are collectively concerned about the academic prowess of their student body. And in order to optimize that image, there must be open channels of communication between students of the college's staff and faculty.

Positive connections on campus are critical to the well-being and happiness of underserved students. For many minority and underrepresented students, the act of engagement on campus may serve as a challenge when outside demands require the student's attention to be placed elsewhere, especially in light of the fact that the community college is a student "commuter culture," when compared to the campus living at traditional colleges and universities.

The lack of continued engagement with college life for minority students will create some challenges. Thus, colleges must create ways for students to connect with each other both in and outside the classroom environment. Effective retention programs involve students to help recruit one another to be a part of such groups. As such, the key for opening the door to the Friendship Factor is for colleges to proactively strive to create a sharing, cooperative partnership—a team environment that celebrates development and growth not only for the students but also for the college itself and its personnel. The following strategies are useful in promoting an interactive environment of this kind:

- **Initiate Positive First Encounters:** Several weeks before college classes commence, it behooves college personnel to begin tracking the number of first-time enrollees on campus by compiling an accurate and complete listing of their names, residential addresses, e-mail addresses, and cell phone (or home telephone) numbers. Before the first week of classes, colleges ought to consider sending out a written letter or e-mail to each freshman student, personally welcoming them to the campus, congratulating them on their decision to advance their educations by enrolling in college, and inviting them to participate in a special orientation session with college administrators and faculty. It is important that each of these enrollees be given printed information regarding any special college services or specialized programs that may be available for their use. Since this is their first contact, follow up with a personalized telephone call (or e-mail) confirming their participation. In these meetings, allow students to sit down with faculty, advisers, and former students who have been successful in their studies, so as to familiarize them with the college's campus.

- **Establish Academic Advisers as "Life Coaches":** The function of academic advisers within the community college system should be reanalyzed for the purpose of redesigning adviser responsibilities and roles. It is recommended for colleges to consider revamping their current advising structure to train their advisers to serve as "life coaches" rather than introducing students to a random encounter with an advising specialist who may be quick, to the point, and scattered. Life coaches are specifically trained as specialists to work with their assigned student so as to provide structured, detailed, and consistent academic, career, and life-planning support from the onset of the student's college experience to post-graduation follow-up. Life coach advisers provide meaningful academic and career guidance for their minority and impoverished students and have a solid understanding of the cultures and values of these select students so as to provide proper course placement. In our current system of advising, the lack of clearly defined, explicit pathways to transfer and degree completion beyond the community college is creating confusion, wasted credits, and misalignment of goals for many community college students, especially minority students and impoverished students who are first-generation.
- **Establish Learning Communities for Cohorts of Students:** Learning communities are powerful contributors to student success. Community college faculty members report that students who participate in a cohort model come to trust each other, listen effectively, and work collaboratively across cultures. Within this model, students participate in courses that are linked and clustered together during a school term around an interdisciplinary theme and enroll as a common cohort of students. Dedicated counselors work with the learning communities and work collaboratively with instructional faculty to assess each student's progress and challenges. Faculty members are assigned to students to encourage close connections and promote a pedagogy of self-reflection and personal narrative in

the classroom. Such a structure will help both faculty and counselors to engage minority students to bond with one another and create lasting friendships throughout their college experience.

- **Assign Each Student a Staff Mentor:** Campus mentoring programs are crucial to providing the necessary support for underrepresented students. In order to establish such programs, colleges must recruit staff mentors who are willing to volunteer for 30 minutes per week over the course of a semester. Such mentors are selected from a list of employees on campus who match up to the career goals of the student. For example, a student interested in the nursing field would be assigned a faculty member from the nursing department. Campus mentors are advised to sign a contract with their students and meet once a week providing advising assistance, friendship, and guidance on college resources and activities. Typically, mentors are given a mentoring packet and invited to participate in a mentor luncheon with their newly assigned student at the beginning of each semester. Mentoring relationships can take place over one semester, one full year, or beyond. It is important to expose minority and impoverished students to faculty and staff who will help them find meaning in their college experience and enhance their ability to adapt successfully as they transition from college to career.

The Faculty Factor

Positive messages from faculty and staff are "I expect an 'A' from you next time"; "I believe you can continue on to a professional school after graduating from college"; "When you complete your associate degree from this community college, you need to transfer to a four-year college"; and "Do not give up; I believe you can be successful with some tutorial support."

—Kenneth Atwater, President, Hillsborough Community College, and
Joan B. Holmes, Assistant to the President, Hillsborough Community College
(p. 49, this volume)

As the foundation of any college institution, faculty employees have a direct and profound impact on their student groups in the classroom. Research has shown that students who interact frequently with faculty members are more likely than any other students to express satisfaction with all aspects of their institutional experience, including student friendships, variety of courses, intellectual environment, and even the administration of the institution. The role of faculty in promoting a climate of student success is founded on the attitudes and interactions portrayed in the classroom. Positive encounters produce positive results. When faculty members demonstrate high levels of trust in their students, students will learn quickly and learn with enthusiasm.

Conversely, negative encounters produce negative results. In certain circumstances, when students achieve poorly, some faculty have been known to blame the victim, believing the student to be responsible for their lack of success. The cultural disconnect that exists for many minority students on community college campuses affects not only their interaction with faculty, but also the way they access services such as student organizations or utilize campus facilities. The following recommendations may be considered when training faculty to avoid an educational racism mind-set:

- **Mandate Interactive Faculty Development Seminars:** Provide faculty (both full-time and part-time) an effective professional development opportunity annually, with a proposed two- or three-day summer institute that facilitates faculty development and offers training in culturally responsive teaching, as well as methods for teaching integrated learning communities with a focus on developmental to college-level courses. The workshop series should include the sharing of best practices related to the teaching and design of learning communities, minority populations, poverty mind-set, cohort learning, and other interdisciplinary learning models. Faculty and counselors can work in a one-on-one engagement format with college administrators to discuss and review the college's education mission, as well as discuss educational racism practices. Additional outside speakers may be brought in to engage best practice learning and present the latest research on various topics. The key to such a model is to promote interactive discussion and creative thought among faculty, staff, and administration with the goal of aligning academic affairs and student affairs toward a common and unified purpose.

- **Embrace a Culturally Relevant Curriculum:** Educators can help in minimizing stereotypes by promoting literacy and discussions on history from minority and impoverished students' points of view. Faculty are encouraged to reflect upon the critical components to helping students achieve in the classroom by affirming (a) respect for the diversity of minority and impoverished communities; (b) curriculum that recognizes the importance of cultural traditions and histories; (c) assignments that connect course readings to students' personal, familial, and community experiences; and, (d) use of the Friendship Factor to build peer support networks inside and outside of the classroom. Ultimately, forming personal, meaningful relationships with students can serve as a source of motivation and encouragement that can help minority and at-risk students persist through graduation.

- **Tap Into Students' "Multiple Intelligences":** According to Howard Gardner, author of the multiple intelligences theory, there are nine multiple intelligences that encompass the adult learner (Gardner, 2006). These intelligences—musical, bodily-kinesthetic, spatial, existential, naturalist, linguistic, mathematical-logistical, intrapersonal, and interpersonal—must all be taken into account before teachers instruct and assign tasks to adult learners of varying backgrounds. Recommendations include (a) allowing the student to express himself or herself in a myriad of ways when completing assignments or presenting new information to others, rather than only via the "paper and pencil" approach; (b) assessing student learning gains, by recognizing the individual potential of each student; and (c) allowing students to exercise their talents by participating in internship opportunities within the community, which may lead to potential future employment prospects.

- **Understand Student Needs and Cultural Differences:** It is critical that faculty demonstrate an understanding of the many cultural differences that exist among their student groups and honor these differences. The goal is to reach out to all students with care and create a learning environment where trust, respect, fairness *(i.e. doing what is right for individual students based on individual needs)*, and flexibility take precedence in the classroom. Students of varying backgrounds may enter the college environment with different expectations as to how they are to act, behave, and perform in the classroom. For this reason, it is recommended that instructors from the onset of the course convey their clear and reasonable expectations in both written and verbal form as to what they desire from their students. Instructors must be reminded that many of their students may be living in a daily mode of survival and will fail to carry out the instructor's requests. For example, students may skip class, arrive late, or fail to turn in homework assignments because of outside stressors. In these instances, it is recommended that instructors report the student's behavior to campus support personnel and then work to provide an outlet for those who fall short of navigating the myriad mandates of college life.

The Freedom-to-Learn-From-Failure Factor

We strive to assist students living in poverty with creating a new outlook on life—an outlook that removes fear and replaces it with hope, belief in oneself, and a focus on the future.

—Russell Lowery-Hart, President, Amarillo College, and and Cara Crowle, Chief of Staff, Amarillo College (p. 258, this volume)

Teddy Roosevelt once said, "Show me a man who has never made a mistake, and I'll show you a man who has never done anything." Indeed, who among America's most notable entrepreneurs never experienced a single failure while they were building their small businesses into corporate empires? Practitioners with years of classroom instruction similarly have observed students who failed tests miserably rebound from their failures to subsequently perform very well during their course-work examinations. But sometimes failure in the classroom is attributable more to one's mind-set regarding how to deal with a failing grade on a test than to innate intelligence or diligence in doing one's homework.

The fundamental objective of the Freedom-to-Learn-From-Failure Factor is to communicate the notion that everyone is subject to failure and that failure can be turned into either a negative or a positive experience—as well as a temporary or a permanent thing—depending on how one handles it. For many, failure may be a common theme experienced throughout life, and, as such, it conjures up negative and demeaning self-perceptions. Hence, it is critically important for minority and at-risk students to perceive "failure" as a learning tool rather than an ignoble thing. The Freedom-to-Learn-From-Failure Factor is designed to encourage students who have been "knocked down," whether academically or emotionally, to stand again and turn that particular negative event into a positive learning experience. Following are a few suggested methods whereby college personnel can help a student develop a positive mind-set:

- **Promote the Concept of Risk-Taking:** Taking risks of some type is an everyday occurrence for nearly everyone. People confronted with risk-taking decisions react in one of two ways: some approach the decision by saying, "What do I have to lose if I take this risk?" whereas others say, "What do I have to gain by taking this risk?" Within select programs on campus and in the classroom environment, faculty and staff must hold high standards of excellence for all their students conveying the notion that true learning takes place in an environment of risk-taking where mistakes are bound to occur. Rather than experiencing a sense of loss and dejection from a risk-taking venture that failed, students must "seize the day," so to speak, and view that circumstance as an opportunity to gain another layer of wisdom. It is especially important for college faculty to constructively critique the academic performance of their students in a caring, positive manner, that is, pointing out deficiencies in need of improvement as helpful "coaches," not as uncaring "critics." In so doing, college educators will create an environment of risk-taking and provide the freedom for students to learn from their failures, not be crippled by them.

- **Establish Academic Advisement and Early Alert Systems:** When a minority or impoverished student struggles academically in any given class, the issuance of a "mid-term warning" by the instructor of that class comes, as a general rule, too late for the student to salvage a high grade. More often than not, students tend to wait until the last minute to pull out of a class in an attempt to avert a pending "F" on their accumulated GPA or, worse yet, stop attending class altogether and simply walk away. Thus, that student drops out of college before the final examination is given, believing there is no hope to get a grade better than a "D." Early warning systems are developed on the premise that intervention within the first month of enrollment is critical to coaching the student back on track after a failure. Some of the more notable telltale indicators that a student needs an early warning include irregular attendance or non-attendance; recurrent lack of preparedness for class participation; poor quality of written assignments; poor performance on quizzes and chapter tests; and expressions of mild anxiety or lack of confidence in completing college-level work. If a student does not register for an upcoming term, it is recommended that college personnel send a letter, informing the student that he or she is missed. Students, along with staff members, will be hired to assist with this program and will follow up with a telephone call, asking if the student will be reenrolling the following semester.

- **Establish Peer Mentoring and Peer Tutoring Programs:** The purpose of the peer mentoring/tutoring programs is to connect newly enrolled students with other successful students (e.g., second-year student enrollees) who have completed at least one year of their college experience. Such partnerships allow the freshmen students to learn from the prior year's cohort, who successfully persisted through their own sets of frustrations and hardships during their first year as students. By connecting the two cohorts, the preceding year's cohort of completers—peer mentors—serves as a living example of the "If I did it, you can do it, too!" archetype. Needless to say, all student mentors and tutors selected for the prior year's cohort must have not only demonstrable academic prowess but also a willingness to undergo mandatory training sessions through the auspices of trained counselors. As part of their tutoring/mentoring duties, peer mentors will assist their matched peers by forming study groups, providing assistance with campus resources, and checking in via phone or in person at least once a week.

The Functional Factor

If lives are reinvented in this atmosphere, then surely the institution itself has set the precedent.

—Eduardo J. Padrón, President, Miami Dade College (p. 95, this voume)

Whenever frustrated students on the brink of dropping out of college ask themselves the question "education for what?" the institution must have a retention rationale to assist those students in finding answers to their self-imposed query. Certainly a part of that rationale must include the notion of functionalism, that is, the practice of adapting method, form, and materials, primarily in regard to the purpose at hand. For example, the function of a student is to "study." Therefore, the Functional Factor is squarely founded on the premise that students must not only have a stake in their own learning experience but also serve as a functional component of the college's purpose. Thus, the goal of the Functional Factor is to engage students both on and off campus by providing opportunities for service, leadership, committee roles, and in-class teaching opportunities via a constructivist, hands-on approach. Some ways in which this task can be accomplished include the following:

- **Host an Orientation Week:** Hosting an orientation week for all first-time enrolled students just one week prior to the beginning of the first semester is an excellent way to engage students as functional members of the campus. The orientation week will host a variety of activities arranged for specific days. During this week students will review their program's purpose, the role of the student, services the college offers, and class schedules. While a "Faculty Meet and Greet" event may not strike either full-time or part-time staff as particularly worthy of their time, their attendance creates a positive image of a "caring" college in the minds of minority and impoverished students that pays big dividends later on in respect to boosting the college's persistence rates.

Additional activities for the week can include a campus tour and an induction ceremony for all first-time enrolled students. It is recommended that family members be invited as guests of the enrollees and that gifts of college promotional items be given to the incoming class to welcome them to the orientation gathering. Orientation is to be mandatory and may be offered as a 1-credit course.

- **Offer "Soft Skills" and "Life Skills" Courses:** The goal of this particular act of intervention is to require students to take a first-year course or attend select seminars focused on soft skills learning as part of their first-year experience. Course topics include providing students with tips on note-taking, test-taking, communication, leadership, time management, decision-making, and stress management skills. Of greatest importance, the courses are designed to prepare students to navigate the college system in regard to expected conduct, faculty expectations, and communication expectations. Students who enter with documented deficiencies in mathematics and writing may enroll in a section that meets two days per week and provides a more intense focus on study skills, test-taking, and time management. In order for these courses to be thought of as productive, students must be given opportunity to interact and "teach" on the topic. A purely lecture-driven format is often non-engaging and irrelevant to the students' lives.

- **Create Opportunities for Minority and Underrepresented Students to Serve the College:** In order to advocate for leadership opportunities, colleges must appoint minority students to task forces and committees that explore reasons why students drop out of college so that they can make recommendations to administrators as to how dropouts can be brought back to the college. This specific objective will utilize the student government, as well as members of the Student Life Department, to recruit the minority and underrepresented populations to serve on campus and be involved with student life activities. Other examples of service include participation in leadership conferences, town hall meetings, on-campus internship opportunities, and volunteerism connected to the Office of Civic Engagement, where students earn civic engagement credits for participating in community activities. Colleges can use the power of student leadership and invite former graduates who have transitioned successfully through the postsecondary process to visit community programs, training facilities, Job Corps sites, and even prisons to share the value of moving forward in obtaining further credentials.

The Fondness Factor

Throughout campus, significant buildings, meeting rooms, and outdoor areas are named for prominent Native American donors or are adorned with the artwork of noted local artists. The distinct and determined use of artwork, cultural activities, and Welcome Week events demonstrates to students from their very first days on campus that SSC values their cultures.

—James Utterback, President, Seminole State College (p. 145, this volume)

The goal of the Fondness Factor is, figuratively speaking, to make the students fall in love with your college by celebrating the successes of individual students and by giving evidence of your appreciation and love for them. Create opportunities for students that encourage an atmosphere of excitement, engagement, and involvement in the campus experience. When students love their campus and are engaged, it is assumed that the campus faculty and staff are having fun as well. When everyone is having fun, the campus environment takes on an exciting new life of its own. Creating an engaging environment involves not only community college faculty but also the administration, staff, counseling personnel, financial aid, and admissions office.

- **Portray an Image of Excellence:** Communicate to the minority and impoverished student that he or she is being welcomed into a leading organization that truly cares about the welfare of its members—an organization always there to lift up any individual who stumbles and falls. The college environment must be promoted in such a way that students feel it a privilege to be a part of the organization. By the very nature of the staff and faculty represented, colleges should treat their students as royalty and foundational to the success of the college. In order for this to take place, the administration, faculty, and staff must view themselves as capable leaders and their institution as an incredible place to be, work, and thrive.
- **Foster School Connections With Concrete Symbols:** Making students feel welcome and connected on campus is an important aspect of cultural sensitivity. The college must give its minority and underrepresented students some kind of physical evidence that bears witness to their positive relationship with the college (e.g., lapel pins, necklaces, t-shirts, etc.). A caring relationship is often evidenced by some kind of outward sign or symbol, such as an engagement ring. As members of an honored organization, students are to be given promotional items as evidence of their positive relationship with the college. For example, articles such as college t-shirts, school-based

key chains, hats, bumper stickers, padfolios, book bags, and other institutional apparel display evidence that the student is officially a valued member of the school.

- **Celebrate Student Success and Culture:** A climate of celebration must be adopted on community college campuses to affirm student achievements and recognition of cultural awareness. Through establishment of various college-wide awards, graduation, and celebration ceremonies throughout the year, students will derive a sense of motivation and well-being. It is recommended for colleges to hold outside and on-campus functions to which students are welcome to bring their family and friends in order to incorporate them into the college atmosphere. Holding cohort dinners to celebrate various events at which students are honored and listen to motivational speakers and other successful students, is critically important for many students. If students feel relaxed in a comforting atmosphere where family and friends affirm their college experience, that feeling will linger when they come back to class, making them more comfortable on campus. For example, Seminole State College in Oklahoma welcomes several tribes on campus to hold events for their members. These have included college fairs, job fairs, graduation ceremonies, festivals, and celebrations. Through such interactions, students are able to experience a sense of pride as members of the campus environment while forging new friendships.

When properly implemented, each of these factors can powerfully and significantly improve the persistence and retention rates for both students of color and students living in poverty. Furthermore, these factors also work exceedingly well in overcoming educational racism practices in the college classroom.

References

Coley, R., & Baker, B. (2013). *Poverty and education: Finding the way forward.* Princeton, NJ: Educational Testing Center, Research on Human Capital and Education. Retrieved from https://www.ets.org/s/research/pdf/poverty_and_education_report.pdf

Gardner, H. (2006). *Multiple intelligences: New horizons in theory and practice.* New York, NY: Basic Books.

ABOUT THE CONTRIBUTORS

Kenneth Atwater, PhD, serves as president of Hillsborough Community College (HCC) in Tampa, Florida, and is the former chairman of the board of directors at the American Association of Community Colleges (AACC) in Washington, DC. Founded in 1968 as part of a 28-member community college system, HCC is currently the seventh largest community college in the state of Florida, serving more than 46,000 students each year at its five campuses and three centers. HCC has an annual budget of over $220 million and employs more than 2,500. HCC offers more than 160 academic programs, including 18 associate in arts tracks and over 150 workforce programs. In addition to his work as president, Atwater is actively engaged as the chairman of the AACC Commission on Diversity, Inclusion, and Equity and is a member of the Presidents' Round Table of African American CEOs. Atwater is a graduate of the prestigious Executive Leadership Institute of the League for Innovation in the Community College and is also a graduate of the Institute for Leadership Effectiveness, University of Tennessee-Knoxville.

Glennda M. Bivens, PhD, earned her doctorate in education with an emphasis on community college leadership while working full-time as a community and economic development field specialist with Iowa State University Extension and Outreach. Her research focuses on the retention and persistence of Black women attending community colleges, the post-transfer experiences of Black women in higher education, and higher education access and equity. Her scholarship has been published in New Directions for Community Colleges and Reclaiming Children and Youth. Committed to using research to facilitate social change, she is also a contributor to the Business Record and Community Matters, community publications that are distributed throughout the state of Iowa. Bivens is a recipient of the President's Volunteer Service Award, ACPA Commission for Social Justice Educator's Award, and the Martin Luther King Jr. Advancing One Community Award.

Walter G. Bumphus, PhD, is president and CEO of the American Association of Community Colleges. From 2007 to 2011 Bumphus served as a professor in the Community College Leadership Program and as chair of the Department of Educational Administration at the University of Texas at Austin. He also held the A. M. Aikin Regents Endowed Chair in Junior and Community College Education Leadership. He previously served as president of the Louisiana Community and Technical College System (LCTCS) from 2001 to 2007. LCTCS later conferred upon him the title of president emeritus of the Louisiana Community and Technical College System. From November 2000 to September 2001 he was chancellor of Baton Rouge Community College (BRCC). Prior to joining BRCC, Bumphus worked in the corporate world serving as president of the higher education division of Voyager Expanded Learning. Six years prior, he served as president of Brookhaven College in Dallas County Community College District. Bumphus holds a BA in speech communications and an MA in guidance and counseling from Murray State University, and a PhD in higher education administration from the Community College Leadership Program at The University of Texas at Austin. In 1992, Bumphus was recognized as a distinguished graduate from both Murray State University and The University of Texas at Austin. Bumphus holds the distinction of being one of the few leaders in the field of education to receive the ACCT Marie Y. Martin CEO of the Year Award, to chair the AACC board of directors, and to receive the AACC Leadership Award.

Edward Bush, PhD, has over 19 years of experience in higher education, and he currently serves as the president of Cosumnes River College in Sacramento, California. His research has focused on African American male achievement in California community colleges. Bush is a published author with articles appearing in *Black Issues in Higher Education, Community College Week, Educational Horizons,* and the *Community College Journal.* He is also the coauthor of *The Plan: A Guide for Women Raising African American Boys from Conception to College* (Third World Press, 2013); in addition, he is the coauthor of the article "Introducing African American Male Theory (AAMT)" (*Journal of African Americans,* 2013). Bush is a founding member of the African American Male Education Network and Development (AMEND). He received his bachelor of arts degree in political science from the University of California, Riverside; his master's degree in public administration from California State University, San Bernardino; and his doctorate in urban educational leadership at Claremont Graduate University.

Cara Crowley, MA, serves as the chief of staff for Amarillo College in Amarillo, Texas, where she has worked for 10 years. She provides leadership, guidance, and support to Amarillo College's president, presidential initiatives, and the Offices of Institutional Research and Grants Development and Compliance. As part of Amarillo College's No Excuses University initiative, Cara served as the cochair of the Poverty Committee and cochair of the Course Redesign Committee until 2014. Since 2003, Cara has served as adjunct faculty in the History department. She has a master's degree in American history and a master's degree in business administration, both from West Texas A&M University. In 2014, she received the Top 20 Under Age 40 award from the Amarillo Chamber of Commerce for outstanding service to Amarillo College and the Amarillo community.

Maria Harper-Marinick, PhD, is chancellor of the Maricopa Community College District, one of the largest community college systems in the nation. She oversees operations for the system, which serves 200,000 students and nearly 10,000 faculty and staff members across 10 colleges, a corporate college, two skills centers, and several satellite campuses as well as business/industry, technical, and customized training institutes. In addition, Harper-Marinick sets the vision for the higher educational institution's strategic plan; guides policy development; and oversees initiatives and outcomes related to workforce, economic and community development, civic and global engagement, and increasing student success. Harper-Marinick serves on national and local boards and advisory committees, including the Arizona Minority Education Policy Analysis Center, chair; National Community College Hispanic Council, president-elect; Western Alliance of Community College Academic Leaders, chair-elect; American Association for Community Colleges' Commission on Diversity, Inclusion, and Equity; American College and University President's Climate Commitment-Academic Committee; Latino Advisory Committee and CTE Advisory Committee for the Morrison Institute; and the League for Innovation in the Community College, to name a few. Harper-Marinick came to Arizona in 1982 as a Fulbright Scholar. She holds a PhD in educational technology and an MA in instructional media from Arizona State University and is a licentiate in school administration and pedagogy from Universidad Nacional Pedro Henriquez Urena in the Dominican Republic.

Joan B. Holmes, EdD, is the special assistant to the president for equity, diversity, and special programs at Hillsborough Community College since 2009. Before this position, Holmes served as assistant dean of the Graduate School at the University of South Florida (USF) for diversity and student services. During her 23-year tenure at USF, she established expertise in creating and directing student retention and scholar programs for disadvantaged and underrepresented students at the undergraduate and graduate levels. She authored 11 federal grants focused on disadvantaged and minority college student populations. Nine (82%) were funded and valued at over $10 million. She has been an adjunct professor at USF in Africana studies since 2004. She has received numerous awards for creating and implementing successful programs that produced high retention and completion rates of underrepresented student populations. She earned her doctorate of education degree from Ball State University in educational leadership and curriculum in 1985.

G. Edward Hughes, PhD, became the founding president and chief executive officer of Gateway Community and Technical College on December 1, 2001. Under Hughes' leadership, Gateway has transformed into a comprehensive two-year college with emphasis on workforce development and training, transfer education, and adult education and services. He is known as an innovative leader and educator and community collaborator. With him at the helm, Gateway received regional accreditation by the Commission on Colleges of the Southern Association of Colleges and Universities, effective January 2008. The college also has seen dramatic growth and was the seventh fastest growing two-year college in its category in the United States in 2005– 2006. Prior to coming to Gateway, Hughes became one of the youngest college presidents in America in 1985 when he assumed the presidency of Hazard Community College at age 34. His 16-year leadership there is viewed as transformational and included regional, state, and national recognition for programs and services. He is currently the senior public college or university president in Kentucky. A lifelong educator, Hughes has served as a teacher, program coordinator, and academic and student affairs administrator in community and technical colleges in Arkansas, Illinois, and Tennessee. Before he came to Kentucky, he served as dean of academic and student affairs at North Country Community College in Saranac Lake, New York. Hughes holds a PhD in higher education from Southern Illinois University in Carbondale. He earned a master of arts degree in psychology from Middle Tennessee State University and a bachelor of arts degree in psychology from Catawba College, Salisbury, North Carolina.

Lee Lambert, JD, has been chancellor of Pima Community College in Tuscon, Arizona, since July 1, 2013, and has been named as one of the top five community college presidents in the nation. A U.S. Army veteran, Lambert was born in Seoul, South Korea; grew up on three continents; and graduated from high school in the Olympia, Washington, area. He currently serves on the Board of Directors of the American Association of Community Colleges

(AACC), and in 2013–2014 he served on AACC's executive committee. He is a former chair of AACC's Committee on Program Initiatives and Workforce Training. He has served as board chair of the National Coalition of Certification Centers and, in July 2014, received the group's Founders Award for Vision and Leadership. In April 2014, Lambert was named to the Executive Committee of the Arizona Manufacturing Partnership. He also is a founding member of the Manufacturing Institute Education Council and a member of the Founders Circle and Board of Directors of Tucson Regional Economic Development (TREO). Before coming to PCC, Lambert was president of Shoreline Community College in Shoreline, Washington, outside Seattle, serving from June 2006 to June 2013. He received the Pacific Region 2009 Chief Executive Officer Award from the Association of Community College Trustees. He contributes to and serves on the editorial board of *The Source* online magazine. He is a member of the Washington State Bar Association and has taught courses on law, civil rights and social justice, and employment law at Evergreen State College.

Cynthia Lindquist, PhD, whose Dakota name is Star Horse Woman, serves as the president of Cankdeska Cikana Community College in North Dakota and is the current chair of the American Indian Higher Education Consortium (AIHEC) Board of Directors in Alexandria, Virginia. AIHEC is the member organization for the 37 tribal colleges and universities in the United States, and one located in Canada. Lindquist earned her bachelor's degree in Indian studies and English at the University of North Dakota in 1981 and a master's degree in public administration (Indian health systems emphasis) at the University of South Dakota in 1988. As a Bush Foundation Leadership Fellow, she earned a doctorate in educational leadership at the University of North Dakota in 2006. In October 2003, she began responsibilities as president of Cankdeska Cikana (Little Hoop) Community College, which serves the Spirit Lake Dakota community, her home reservation. Lindquist is an adjunct faculty member in community medicine and rural health at the UND School of Medicine and Health Sciences. She is a founding member of the National Indian Women's Health Resource Center, a nonprofit advocacy organization. Lindquist served as member of the Council of Public Representatives (COPR), an advisory council to the director of the National Institutes of Health (NIH), and is a former executive director of the North Dakota Indian Affairs Commission. She currently serves on the Board of Trustees for the American Indian College Fund, which is the scholarship fund-raising organization for tribal colleges and universities. She served for six years on the Board of Trustees for the Higher Learning Commission, North Central Association of Colleges and Schools.

Angela Long, EdD, serves as coeditor of the Innovative Ideas for Community Colleges book series, published through Stylus Publishing. In addition to this role, she works as a consultant on nontraditional student retention issues in higher education, with specific emphasis on community college research. In 2014, she coedited a groundbreaking publication titled *America's Forgotten Student Population: Creating a Path to College Success for GED Completers* (Stylus, 2015), along with Christopher M. Mullin, executive vice chancellor of the Division of Florida Colleges. She is the author of the Five Factors theory for increasing nontraditional student retention and speaks nationally on this topic. She has participated in three White House summit meetings on educational excellence for Hispanics and has shared her findings before participants at the Achieving the Dream national conference; Florida Association of Community Colleges, U.S. Department of Education; the White House Summit Meeting on Educational Excellence for Hispanics in Miami, Florida; the Consortium for Student Retention and Data Exchange; the American Association of Community Colleges; and the Florida Council of Student Affairs, to name a few. In 2011, she worked with student leaders to found the Pathways to Persistence Scholars program at Santa Fe College (ranked the number one community college in the nation in 2015) in Gainesville, Florida. She holds a doctorate of education degree in community college leadership from Oregon State University, a master of education in school counseling and consultation from Northwest Christian University, and a bachelor of arts in elementary education from Northwest Christian University. She has experience teaching and working in the K–college setting and was the first to publish a national document titled "*Community College Attrition of GED Certificate Holders and Regular High School Graduates: A Comparative Study Using National BPS Data.*"

Russell Lowery-Hart, PhD, currently serves as president for Amarillo College in Amarillo, Texas, recently named a Leader College for Achieving the Dream. His leadership is focused on improving student success through systemic and cultural change. In his career, he created several institution-wide initiatives targeting a systemic approach to poverty, a common reader program, international travel programs for first-year students, curricular reform, instructional improvement, advising and academic orientation expansions, first-year seminars, service-learning across the curriculum, and partnership development across campus "silos." He served as the chair for the Executive Committee for the Amarillo "No Limits/No Excuses" Partners for Postsecondary Success Gates grant—a two-organization collaborative focused on education certificate and degree completion leading to living wage employment. As president and founding member of Panhandle Twenty/20, Lowery-Hart facilitated a community-wide, year long study on education attainment that was the foundation for a profound transformation within the city of Amarillo. He is a P–16 Regional Advisor for the Texas Higher Education Coordinating Board, and he also served as the chair for the Texas Higher Education Coordinating Board Undergraduate Education Advisory Committee, charged with evaluating and redesigning the state of Texas general education requirements. He currently serves on the LEAP Texas board of directors with the goal to build on the LEAP principles in assessment and instruction statewide. Lowery-Hart previously served as vice president of academic affairs for Amarillo College. He was named the National Council of Instructional Administrators Academic Leader of the Year for 2014. He received his PhD in gender and diversity in communication from Ohio University in 1996. He received his MA in communication studies from Texas Tech in 1993 and his BS in speech from West Texas State University in 1991.

Jamillah Moore, PhD, serves as the vice chancellor for educational services and planning for the San Mateo County Community College District in San Mateo, California, which includes San Mateo, Skyline, and Canada Colleges. Moore is the author of *Race and College Admissions: A Case for Affirmative Action* (McFarland & Company, 2015). Before serving as chancellor for the Ventura Community College District, she served as president of Los Angeles City College, senior vice chancellor for governmental and external relations for the California Community College Chancellor's Office, and interim superintendent/president of Compton Community College. At the national level, she is active in the American Association of Community Colleges and in the Society for Media Psychology and Technology of the American Psychological Association. Moore's accomplishments, skills, educational background, and training reflect a commitment to the philosophy and mission of community colleges and higher education. Her career, at every level, has been seminal in advocating for workforce development, achieving upward mobility through success in career and technical programs, and "putting America back to work." She is frequently consulted by news media on social issues related to diversity and equity, accreditation, career and technical education, and the international role of community colleges in global higher education. She earned her doctorate in international and multicultural education from the University of San Francisco, a master's degree in intercultural communication and public policy, and a bachelor of arts degree in communication from California State University Sacramento.

Christopher M. Mullin, PhD, serves as the executive vice chancellor of the Division of Florida Colleges, Florida Department of Education. In this role he oversees all operations related to academics, student affairs, financial policy, budgeting, and analytics for a system of 28 colleges that serves over 800,000 students. Previously he served as the assistant vice chancellor for policy and research at the State University System of Florida Board of Governors, where he provided leadership and direction in regard to academic and student affairs policies and programs, strategic planning, research, analysis, and special projects in support of the Board of Governors' constitutional responsibilities. Before joining the Board of Governors, Mullin served as the program director for policy analysis of the American Association of Community Colleges (AACC) in Washington, DC. In this capacity, his chief responsibility was to provide analysis and supporting data with an emphasis on federal student financial assistance, accountability, institutional performance, college costs, and related institutional policies. Additionally, he responded to immediate needs for the analysis of federal legislative, regulatory, and related policies while also playing a central role in shaping AACC's long-term federal policy agenda. Mullin worked for the Illinois Education Research Council, an entity statutorily charged with providing policy research for the state's P–20 Council, before joining AACC in 2009. He has taught at the early childhood, elementary, middle, and high school levels as well as at three universities. Among other publications he is the coauthor of *Community College Finance: A Guide for Institutional Leaders* and *Higher Education Finance Research* (Wiley, 2015). Mullin earned a bachelor of arts degree from the University of Florida in 1999; a master of education degree from Teachers College, Columbia University; in 2005, and a doctorate of philosophy in higher education administration from the University of Florida in 2008.

Brian Murphy, PhD, is the president of De Anza College in Cupertino, California. In 2011, he was instrumental in the development of the Democracy Commitment, a national project aimed at ensuring that every community college student has an education in democratic practice. Before becoming president of De Anza in 2004, Murphy served as the director of external affairs at San Francisco State University (SFSU), senior advisor to the California State University's chancellor with special responsibility for strategic planning, and the founding executive director of SFSU's Urban Institute. Murphy previously served as the chief consultant to the California State Legislature's review of the Master Plan for Higher Education and was the principal consultant for the legislature's community college reform process in the late 1980s. He also served as research director for Caribbean research at the Data Center in Oakland, California, and was a founding member of Faculty for Human Rights in El Salvador and Central America.

Eduardo J. Padrón, PhD, president of Miami Dade College in Florida, is widely recognized as one of the top educational leaders in the world, and he is often invited to participate in educational policy forums in the United States and abroad. In 1993, President Bill Clinton recognized him as one of America's foremost educators. President George W. Bush nominated him to the National Institute for Literacy Advisory Board and the National Economic Summit. More recently, he represented the United States at UNESCO's World Conference on Higher Education at the invitation of the Obama administration, and President Obama appointed him chairman of the White House Commission on Educational Excellence for Hispanic Americans. During his career, he has been selected to serve on posts of national prominence by six American presidents. Internationally, Padrón's accomplishments have been recognized by numerous nations and organizations including, among others, the Republic of France, which named him Commandeur in the Ordre des Palmes Académiques; the Republic of Argentina, which awarded him the Order of San Martin; and Spain's King Juan Carlos I, who bestowed upon him the Order of Queen Isabella. Padrón's work at Miami Dade College has been hailed as a model of innovation in higher education. He is credited with engineering a culture of success that has produced impressive results in student access, retention, graduation, and overall achievement. Miami Dade College enrolls and graduates more minorities, including Hispanics and African Americans, than any other institution in the United States. He currently chairs the board of the Business–Higher Education Forum and serves on the boards of the Council on Foreign Relations; RC 2020; White House Fellows Selection Panel (Chair); the International Association of University Presidents; and Achieving the Dream. Padrón's accomplishments at Miami Dade College have been acknowledged by the national media, including the *New York Times*, the *Washington Post*, NBC Nightly News, *Time*, the *Wall Street Journal*, CNN, and *The Chronicle of Higher Education*.

Deborah A. Santiago, MA, is the cofounder, chief operating officer, and vice president for policy at Excelencia in Education in Washington, DC. For more than 20 years, she has led research and policy efforts from the community to national and federal levels to improve educational opportunities and success for all students. She cofounded Excelencia in Education to inform policy and practice to accelerate Latino student success in higher education. Her current work focuses on federal and state policy, financial aid, Hispanic-serving institutions (HSIs), and effective institutional practices for student success in higher education. She has been cited in numerous publications for her work, including *The Economist*, the *New York Times*, the *Washington Post*, AP, and *The Chronicle of Higher Education*. She serves on the board of the National Student Clearinghouse and the advisory boards of thedream.us and Univision's Education Campaign.

Wei Song, PhD, is director of data management and research at Achieving the Dream, a national reform network dedicated to community college student success and completion. She oversees data collection and reporting for the network and the publication of data reports and research briefs. She was director of research projects at Council of Independent Colleges (CIC), overseeing CIC's three assessment consortia and institutional benchmarking services. Before that she worked for American Council on Education's GED Testing Service for five years, first as a research associate and then as assistant director for data management and research. She holds a PhD in public administration and an MA in international development from American University.

Robert Teranishi, PhD, is professor of social science and comparative education, the Morgan and Helen Chu Endowed Chair in Asian American Studies, and codirector for the Institute for Immigration, Globalization, and Education at the University of California, Los Angeles. He is also a senior fellow with the Steinhardt Institute for Higher Education Policy at New York University and principal investigator for the National Commission on Asian American and Pacific Islander Research in Education. In 2015, he was appointed by President Barack Obama to serve as a member of the board for the Institute for Education Sciences. He has also served as a strategic planning and restructuring consultant for the Ford Foundation. Teranishi has been ranked among the most influential academics in the field of education by *Education Weekly* and was named one of the nation's top "up-and-coming" leaders by *Diverse Issues in Higher Education*. He received his BA in sociology from the University of California, Santa Cruz and his MA and PhD in higher education and organizational change from the University of California, Los Angeles.

Rowena M. Tomaneng, MA, has been associate vice president of instruction at De Anza College in Cupertino, California, since 2010. A key focus of her teaching and administrative leadership is the fostering of a teaching and learning community that integrates critical pedagogy, multicultural education, and community and civic engagement. She received her BA in

English from the University of California, Irvine and her MA in English from the University of California, Santa Barbara. She is currently pursuing a doctorate in international multicultural education at the University of San Francisco. She began her career at De Anza in 1996 as a faculty member in English, intercultural studies, and women's studies. She served as the English Department chair from 2003 to 2007, founding codirector for the Institute of Community and Civic Engagement (now the Vasconcellos Institute for Democracy in Action) from 2006 to 2008, and Interim Dean of the Language Arts Division from 2008 to 2010. Currently, she serves as the college's grants administrator for state and federal grants related to student success and student equity, including Asian American and Native American Pacific Islander–serving institutions (AANAPISIs), the Basic Skills Initiative, and the Student Equity Initiative.

James Utterback, PhD, has served as president of Seminole State College in Oklahoma since 1997. Previously, he served as dean of student services at Dodge City Community College in Kansas (1990–1997). His family is from Oklahoma, where he is a member of the Choctaw Nation. Utterback was named the Seminole Citizen of the Year in 2004 and has authored or coauthored multiple publications, including "Gender and Ethnic Issues in the Development of Intimacy Among College Students" (*NASPA Journal*, 1995) and "Closing the Door: A Critical Review of Forced Academic Placement" (*Journal of College Reading and Learning*, 1992, republished 1998). He is the past chair of the Oklahoma State Regents for Higher Education Council of Presidents, past chair of the Oklahoma State Regents for Higher Education Council of Two-Year Presidents, member of Jasmine Moran Children's Museum Advisory Board, past chair of the Oklahoma Educational Television Authority Board of Directors, and past president of the Seminole Chamber of Commerce. Utterback served on the Board of Directors of the American Association of Community Colleges (AACC). His service to AACC has included serving on the Board Committee on Community College Advancement, the Commission on Diversity, Equity, and Inclusion, and the Commission on Global Education, and he was cochair of the Commission on Economic and Workforce Development. Utterback holds a PhD in college student personnel administration from the University of Northern Colorado, Greeley, and an MS in applied psychology as well as a BS in psychology from Southwestern Oklahoma State University.

J. Luke Wood, PhD, is associate professor of community college leadership and the director of the Doctoral Program Concentration in Community College Leadership at San Diego State University (SDSU). He is codirector of the Minority Male Community College Collaborative (M2C3), a national project of the Interwork Institute at SDSU that partners with community colleges across the United States to enhance access, achievement, and success among minority male community college students. He is also coeditor of the *Journal of Applied Research in the Community College*, chair-elect for the Council on Ethnic Participation (CEP) for the Association for the Study of Higher Education (ASHE), and director of the Center for African American Research and Policy (CAARP). He has authored over 80 publications, including five coauthored books, five edited books, and 40 peer-reviewed journal articles. His scholarship and professional practice have been lauded through awards and honors, including the Council for the Study of the Community College Barbara K. Townsend Emerging Scholar Award; the National Association for Student Personnel Administrator's Newly Published Research Award from the Knowledge Community on Men and Masculinities; the ASHE Council on Ethnic Participation Mildred Garcia Award for Exemplary Scholarship; the ASU Alumni Association Outstanding Graduate Award; and the *Sacramento Observer's* Top 30 Under 30 Award, to name a few. Wood received his PhD (2010) in educational leadership and policy studies with an emphasis in higher education from Arizona State University. He also holds a master's degree in higher education leadership with a concentration in student affairs and a bachelor's degree in Black history and politics from California State University Sacramento.

student success promoted by, 256
TCU lack of, 134–35
faculty and peer mentoring, 255
Black student retention for, 52–53
Faculty Factor, 255
federal loans, 19
Latino students for, 71
financial aid
for Latino students, 75, 86, 88, 98
for Native American students, 120, 138
for nontraditional students
integration, 250
first-generation college goers
Amarillo College at, 224
for Black students, 16
for Latino students, 69
validation for, 23
first-time-in-college students
Black, 43
Latino, 82, 93
Fleming, Jacqueline, 45, 49
Florida State Equity, 43
Focus 2 Career, 102
Fondness Factor, 262–63
Forum for Education and Democracy, 28
Four Pillars of Academic Achievement, for Black students, 46–52, 53
academic achievement culture of, 47–49
adequate resources of, 52
ethnic/cultural differences understood in, 49–51
new environments and opportunities of, 51
Fourteenth Amendment, 2
Free Application Federal Student Aid, 99
Freedom-to-Learn-From-Failure Factor, 258
early alert assistance and warning systems of, 259
"failure" learning tool as, 258

peer mentoring and tutoring
programs of, 259
Friendship Factor, 253, 256
full-time student enrollment, 41, 65
Functional Factor
life skills courses for, 261
minority opportunities for, 261
Orientation Week of, 260

Galdeno Calderon, E., 64
Gans, Herbert, 206
Gardner, Howard, 257
Gardner, John W., 91
Gasman, M., 52
GEAR UP, 123, 145
gender
disparities, Black students and, 17–18
of students, 177
generational poverty, 202, 221
oral communication style of, 222
Georgetown Center on Education and the Workforce, 94
Glenn, F. S., 21
graduation
for Black students, 16–17, 19, 21–22, 29
Caucasian students in poverty and risks for, 193
of Latino students, 81
of Native American students, 116, 131, 137, 141
by race/ethnicity of, 117
of White students, 29
Grutter v. Bollinger, 147
Guam Community College, 161
Guillory, R., 121

HACER. See Hispanic Access to College Education Resources
Haney, Enoch Kelly, 144
Harpel, R. L., 35
Harper, Shaun, 54
Harper, S. R., 49, 52

leadership of, 131
locations of, 130
mainstream outreach for, 138
Pell Grants use by, 132
qualifiers for, 129–30
retention rate for, 136–37
strengthening career paths
 importance of, 138
student demographics of, 131
Tribally Controlled College or
 University Assistance Act of 1978,
 129
TRIO program, 123
Truman, Harry, 79
Truman Commission on Higher
 Education, 79, 80, 85
 community college popularized by,
 4–5
Tubman, Harriet, 165
Turn Around Schools, 216
21st Century Commission on the
 Future of Community Colleges,
 4, 245
 attainment gap concerns of, 5
 remedies of, 5–6
two-year institutions, 16–17

under-achievement, of Black students,
 30, 32
unemployment rates, 122
United Nations, xv, 139
United Way of Amarillo and Canyon,
 216
University of California, 75
University of Florida, 92

University of Miami Cuban Heritage
 Collection, 91
University of South Florida, 92
University of Texas, 75
urban colleges, 13, 41–42
Utterback, Jim, 262

validation, ethnically diverse
 backgrounds for, 22–23

Walkingstick, Ben, 144–45
Walkingstick, Bonnie, 144–45
War on Poverty, 200
War on the Poor (Gans), 206
Washington, Booker T., 153
Whites, 45
 middle-class, 241
 as minority by 2050, xvii
 as 90% in 1950s, xv
 as percentage of U.S. population, xvi
White students, 29, 81, 198
Whitt, E., 35
Why Are All the Black Kids Sitting
 Together in the Cafeteria?
 (Tatum), 45
Williams, Damon, 54
Wolfson Campus, 95
Wolverton, M., 121
Wood, J. L., 21–22
Wood, Luke, 54
work-study programs, 76

Ybor City community college, 41–42
Yosso, T., 22
Yousafzai, Malala, 200

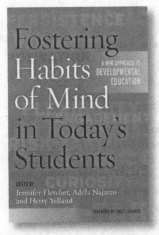

Fostering Habits of Mind in Today's Students
A New Approach to Developmental Education

Edited by Jennifer Fletcher, Adela Najarro, and Hetty Yelland

Foreword by Emily Lardner

"Innovative, engaging, and cheerful, this highly readable book invokes the spirit of Mina Shaughnessy in its positive regard for developmental writers. The authors make a powerful case against a 'deficit-based' view of developmental instruction in favor of a long view that values each learner's unique gifts, intellectual capacity, and potential for growth. The theoretically grounded and effectively scaffolded chapters are loaded with class tested assignments for teaching the 'habits of mind' needed for college and job success. A collaborative effort of 15 veteran teachers of developmental English and math, this must-read book will help any teacher create a transformative classroom that promotes engagement, curiosity, motivation, risk-taking, self-efficacy, and persistence."—*John C. Bean, author of* Engaging Ideas: The Professor's Guide to Writing, Critical Thinking, and Active Learning in the Classroom *and Professor of English (Emeritus), Seattle University.*

Co-published in association with **NISOD**

Sty/us

22883 Quicksilver Drive
Sterling, VA 20166-2102

Subscribe to our e-mail alerts: www.Styluspub.com

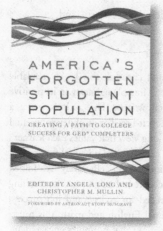

America's Forgotten Student Population
Creating a Path to College Success for GED® Completers

Edited by Angela Long and Christopher M. Mullin

Foreword by Story Musgrave

"Using a wealth of data and perspectives from stakeholders who range from researchers and administrators to students, this book seeks to sensitize those in charge of America's higher education enterprise to the uniqueness of a vulnerable student population that, with a little recalibration, could better integrate into the world of higher education. The value *America's Forgotten Student Population* brings is that it shows that ideas on how to better serve the GED population, while not necessarily inexpensive, are actionable and worthwhile. And it points out, in dollars and cents, just how costly the consequences of inaction can be."—*Diverse Issues in Higher Education.*

"*America's Forgotten Student Population* shines a spotlight on the many difficult challenges that GED recipients face when they pursue post-secondary education. But fortunately, for the thousands of GED recipients in the United States, this book highlights steps that colleges, schools, and communities can take to provide GED recipients with the kinds of information, support, and advice that can propel them to success in higher education and careers. This book makes clear that we should no longer consider GED recipients second to high school graduates; rather, with the right kind of assistance and support they can be just as successful."—*Betsy Brand*, *Executive Director, America Youth Policy Forum.*

This is the first book to remedy the dearth of data on this forgotten population; to present original research on these students, describing their characteristics and motivations; and to provide proven models for identifying, retaining and graduating this undercounted and underestimated cohort. It addresses the issue of the pipeline from GED centers to postsecondary education, and includes first-person narratives that offer vivid insights into GED earners' resilience and needs. It constitutes a comprehensive resource for college administrators and for educational policymakers and researchers, offering both broad policy recommendations and tested ideas and models that can be implemented at the state and institutional level.